FAILED
DIPLOMACY

FAILED DIPLOMACY

The Tragic Story of How North Korea Got the Bomb

Charles L. Pritchard

BROOKINGS INSTITUTION PRESS
Washington, D.C.

ABOUT BROOKINGS

The Brookings Institution is a private nonprofit organization devoted to research, education, and publication on important issues of domestic and foreign policy. Its principal purpose is to bring the highest quality independent research and analysis to bear on current and emerging policy problems. Interpretations or conclusions in Brookings publications should be understood to be solely those of the authors.

Copyright © 2007

THE BROOKINGS INSTITUTION

1775 Massachusetts Avenue, N.W., Washington, D.C. 20036
www.brookings.edu

Library of Congress Cataloging-in-Publication data

Pritchard, Charles L.
  Failed diplomacy : the tragic story of how North Korea got the bomb / Charles L. Pritchard.
      p.   cm.
  Includes bibliographical references and index.
  ISBN-13: 978-0-8157-7200-2 (cloth : alk. paper)
  ISBN-10: 0-8157-7200-9 (cloth : alk. paper)
  1. Nuclear nonproliferation—Korea (North) 2. Nuclear weapons—Korea (North)
  3. United States—Foreign relations—Korea (North) 4. Korea (North)—Foreign rela-
tions—United States. I. Title.
  JZ5675.P75 2007
  355.02'17095193—dc22   2007006949

1 3 5 7 9 8 6 4 2

Printed on acid-free paper

Typeset in Minion

Composition by Pete Lindeman, OSP Inc.
Arlington, Virginia

Printed by R.R. Donnelley
Harrisonburg, Virginia

To my wife,

Jean,

who always thought I had a story to tell
and encouraged me to write this book

Contents

Preface

This book combines my personal, first-hand account of the development and implementation of U.S. policy toward North Korea during the first term of President George W. Bush; my analysis of events as they unfolded after I resigned as special envoy for negotiations with North Korea at the end of August 2003; and my recommendations for developing a permanent organization that can serve as a forum for security dialogue in Northeast Asia.

I find it somewhat amusing that I have been described both as being hard-nosed toward North Korea during the Clinton administration and as being a dove during the Bush administration. Perhaps a few words on my background are warranted. Driven by the example of my father (twenty-nine years of service in the U.S. Army) and my father-in-law (thirty years' combined service in both the British and the U.S. Army), I began my twenty-eight-year Army career in 1972. Early on I spent five years with the 101st Airborne Division, followed by two tours of duty in Japan totaling nine years. My last assignment in Tokyo was as the U.S. Army attaché, a job once held by Black Jack Pershing. My Asia experience led me to the Office of the Secretary of Defense, where I worked on Japanese issues, and eventually to the National Security Council, where I served five years as director of Asian affairs and finally as special assistant to the president for national security affairs and senior director for Asia. When President Bush took office, I was asked to replace Ambassador Charles Kartman as the special envoy for North Korea at the State Department. I also was U.S. representative to the Korean Peninsula Energy Development Organization (KEDO). In practical terms, I reported initially to the assistant secretary of state for East Asia and Pacific affairs.

As a practitioner of foreign policy rather than a scholar or historian by training, I do not attempt to present opposing views on issues in which I was personally involved. It is my hope that my account adds a new perspective to the overall understanding of how U.S. policy toward North Korea was conceived and initially managed under President Bush. Even though the six-party process continued—in theory—as this book went to press, the practical outcome is clear to me: the six-party talks failed. Nonetheless, the book is intended to provide insight into the process, in the belief that we have something to learn from missed opportunities and failed diplomacy. For example, regardless of the outcome, the near continuous consultations that arose from the six-party process lead to the natural conclusion that the time is right for formal regional cooperation in Northeast Asia.

Readers will quickly come to the realization that I find fault with both the Bush administration's North Korea policy and the manner in which it has attempted to deal with serious issues surrounding North Korea. If, at times, it seems as though my criticism of the manner in which these issues have been handled implies empathy or support for the North Korean regime, nothing could be further from the truth. Pejorative descriptions of the regime and its leadership are, for the most part, on target. I have no doubt that President Bush truly believes that Kim Jong-il is evil incarnate and that what is happening to the people of North Korea is a humanitarian tragedy. Believing it is fine. Speaking publicly about it in a gratuitous manner that sets back the prospects of controlling the potential proliferation of fissile material and technology, which may have a serious impact on the security of the United States, is altogether another matter.

Throughout the book, I use the term "hardliners" to describe a group of individuals in the administration who generally believe that North Korea is evil and should cease to exist but who have not thought through either the practical or the policy consequences of their views. This group issues policy prescriptions characterized by such slogans as "We don't reward bad behavior," "We don't negotiate with evil, we destroy it," "North Korea has never kept an agreement," and "We tried bilateral talks once and they failed." When a rationale cannot be fully articulated, the need for "moral clarity" is invoked to end the discussion. In general, the hardliners oppose any kind of engagement strategy that would result in the continuation of the North Korean regime. When faced with apparent short-term decisions to engage North Korea, they work behind the scenes to undermine meaningful diplomacy. In chapter 3 I list several of the senior members of the group. They are by no means the only ones, but by virtue of their seniority they have exerted the most influence.

I often have been asked about the role that Secretary of State Colin Powell played in North Korea policy development and, more specifically, why he did not intervene to "put the hardliners in their place" when they were working so feverishly to undermine many of his initiatives. I believe that Powell made a good-faith attempt to craft a workable U.S. policy that would both succeed and elicit the support of our key ally South Korea. What Powell was not was the North Korea policy coordinator. His responsibilities as secretary of state were enormous. I liken Powell to a "plate spinner," who has to keep a series of plates spinning on poles simultaneously. As one plate begins to slow down and wobble, he rushes over and does enough to keep it going as he makes his way to the next wobbling plate. North Korea policy was just one of Powell's many "plates." As he turned his attention to other areas of the world, the hardliners went to work trying to convince the senior people in the administration that Powell had the North Korea plate turning in the wrong direction. A more practical explanation has been offered by Powell's former chief of staff, Larry Wilkerson (see chapter 3). In an address to the New America Foundation on October 19, 2005, Wilkerson described a cabal of two, Vice President Cheney and Secretary of Defense Rumsfeld, that made decisions in secret, contradicting the formal decisions in which Powell participated. In short, Powell was not an insider. He had to pick and choose the circumstances and the timing of his interventions on North Korea policy, and in the end, his actions were neither sufficient nor successful.

While I gave more than 500 interviews in my two and half years at the Brookings Institution and have written and spoken publicly about North Korea, the Bush administration, and the six-party talks, much of what I have included in this book has not been made public before now. Most of the text was written while I was a visiting scholar at the Brookings Institution. Some materials that I used in previous conference papers have been reworked for this book. As with my public comments, I take full responsibility for the accuracy (and hopefully few shortcomings) of the recollections that I have recorded in this volume.

I gratefully acknowledge the invaluable contributions made by my Brookings colleagues Ambassador James Goodby, nonresident senior fellow, Center for Northeast Asian Policy Studies; Michael O'Hanlon, senior fellow, Foreign

Policy Studies; and Carlos Pascual, vice president, Foreign Policy Studies, in reviewing my initial draft manuscript. Brookings Press likewise did a marvelous job of shepherding the manuscript along to its final form. In that regard, I especially would like to thank Eileen Hughes for her diligence and grace during the editing process. And a special thanks to my part-time typist, Pewter.

1

Prelude to Crisis

> The DPRK is fully ready to cope with whatever stand to be taken by the new U.S. administration towards it. The DPRK appreciates the progress so far made in the bilateral ties through negotiations with U.S. politicians of reason but has no idea of pinning any hope on those forces displeased with this process. If the U.S. brandishes a sword at us, we will counter it with a sword and if it shows good faith, we will reciprocate it.
> —*Spokesman, North Korean Foreign Ministry, January 25, 2001*

North Korea's view of the world order underwent a radical revision on January 20, 2001, with the inauguration of George W. Bush as president of the United States. Chances are, however, that Pyongyang would have had a significant shock had any Republican succeeded President Bill Clinton. Understanding the dynamics of political change in a democracy is not the strong suit of the North Koreans, and the changes that occur when one political party replaces another—or in this case, when the Democrats handed over the keys to the White House to the Republicans—fully mystified Pyongyang.

From the point of view of the Democratic People's Republic of Korea (DPRK), it had overcome a rocky start with the Clinton administration—one that included the real possibility of war breaking out on the Korean Peninsula over North Korea's nuclear weapons program in 1993–94—to reach a point at the end of the administration where it appeared possible that Clinton would travel to Pyongyang to meet with North Korea's leader, Kim Jong-il. That potential summit between Clinton and Kim had been made possible by a series of high-level meetings held in late 2000. First, South Korea's president, Kim Dae-jung, made a historic trip to Pyongyang to meet with Kim Jong-il. Second, Kim Jong-il sent his number two, Vice Marshal Jo Myong-nok, to Washington to meet with Clinton and to invite Clinton to travel to Pyongyang to meet with Kim and resolve "all U.S. security concerns." And finally, in late October 2000, Secretary of State Madeleine Albright traveled to Pyongyang and met with Kim Jong-il to assess the merits of a possible Clinton-Kim summit. The North Korean attitude toward the Bush administration, however, is summed up best in a paper written by Li Gun, DPRK director general for American affairs:

> During the Clinton administration, as the result of DPRK-US negotiations to resolve the nuclear question, U.S. policy toward North Korea showed signs of moving away from pure hostility to partial engagement. For a time there was even a glimmer of hope for the eventual solution to the nuclear question, in light of the freezing of graphite-moderated reactor facilities and spent fuel rods and the supply of heavy oil and light-water reactors. But with the Bush administration putting an end to bilateral political dialogue, its "axis of evil" pronouncement, and defining North Korea as a target of preemptive nuclear strike, the nuclear question has come back to the starting point.[1]

The presidential campaign of 2000 did not focus much on North Korea, but there certainly were indicators that a new Bush administration's approach to foreign policy would be different—that is to say, it would declare Clinton's policies a failure and work to distance itself from the underlying principles associated with those policies. An example of that approach is found in an article by Condoleezza Rice, Governor Bush's foreign policy adviser during the 2000 presidential campaign:

> The regime of Kim Jong Il is so opaque that it is difficult to know its motivations, other than that they are malign. But North Korea also lives outside of the international system. Like East Germany, North Korea is the evil twin of a successful regime just across its border. It must fear its eventual demise from the sheer power and pull of South Korea. Pyongyang, too, has little to gain and everything to lose from engagement in the international economy. The development of WMD thus provides the destructive way out for Kim Jong Il.
>
> President Kim Dae Jung of South Korea is attempting to find a peaceful resolution with the north through engagement. Any U.S. policy toward the north should depend heavily on coordination with Seoul and Tokyo. In that context, the 1994 framework agreement that attempted to bribe North Korea into forsaking nuclear weapons cannot easily be set aside. Still, there is a trap inherent in this approach: sooner or later Pyongyang will threaten to test a missile one too many times, and

the United States will not respond with further benefits. Then what will Kim Jong Il do? The possibility for miscalculation is very high.

One thing is clear: the United States must approach regimes like North Korea resolutely and decisively. The Clinton administration has failed here, sometimes threatening to use force and then backing down, as it often has with Iraq. These regimes are living on borrowed time, so there need be no sense of panic about them. Rather, the first line of defense should be a clear and classical statement of deterrence—if they do acquire WMD, their weapons will be unusable because any attempt to use them will bring national obliteration. Second, we should accelerate efforts to defend against these weapons. This is the most important reason to deploy national and theater missile defenses as soon as possible, to focus attention on U.S. homeland defenses against chemical and biological agents, and to expand intelligence capabilities against terrorism of all kinds.[2]

In an interview after the election in December 2000, Peter Rodman, who would become assistant secretary of defense during the first term of President Bush, said that the Republican position was much more skeptical of North Korea and that the incoming Bush administration had "very different policy views" on North Korea "that ought to inhibit the outgoing administration from dramatic initiatives," such as embarking on a presidential trip to North Korea.[3]

When South Korean president Kim Dae-jung visited Washington to meet with President Bush in early March 2001, Secretary of State Colin Powell announced that the administration was prepared to pick up where Clinton had left off in negotiating with North Korea. The following day, Powell retracted his statement (see chapter 5), jokingly saying that he had gotten ahead of his skis and that the administration's policy would be guided by an ongoing policy review.

What most upset Republicans about the Clinton legacy on North Korea was the Agreed Framework of October 1994, which was designed to freeze North Korea's nuclear program and allow for monitoring of its facilities by the International Atomic Energy Agency (IAEA). Eventually the facilities were to be dismantled and thousands of spent fuel rods shipped out of North Korea. In exchange, the United States was to organize an international consortium, the Korean Peninsula Energy Development Organization (KEDO), which would build two proliferation-resistant light-water reactors (LWRs) over a period of approximately ten years. The United States also would take responsibility for providing 500,000 metric tons of heavy fuel oil each year until the first LWR was completed. In addition, the United States and North Korea pledged to reduce trade and investment barriers (U.S. economic sanctions had been imposed on North Korea as a result of the Korean War) and to open liaison offices in each other's capital. Most Republicans believed the agreement rewarded the DPRK's "bad behavior" with a nuclear reactor that could give Pyongyang access to fissile material.

The Clinton administration had gone through its own growing pains in dealing with North Korea and developing a policy that it was comfortable with. By the end of the Clinton administration, U.S. policy toward North Korea was marked by close coordination with Seoul and Tokyo, a continued freeze on Pyongyang's nuclear program accompanied by IAEA monitoring, and direct dialogue with Pyongyang that allowed the United States to pursue its missile concerns as well as potential violations of the Agreed Framework.

The First North Korea Policy Review

On June 6, 2001, the Bush White House announced the conclusions of the administration's North Korea policy review. The original intention was to review them with Han Song-soo, the foreign minister of the Republic of Korea (ROK), when he arrived in Washington on June 6, take his comments into consideration, and produce a final, coordinated version. The symbolism of taking a coordinated position on North Korea was important, especially following the disastrous and, from South Korea's point of view, humiliating summit meeting between President Bush and President Kim Dae-jung in March 2001.

Kim, a Nobel Peace Prize winner recognized by the Nobel committee for his extensive efforts to engage North Korea, had expected to have a meaningful dialogue with Bush to convince him of the wisdom of continuing the engagement effort. However, he had been publicly rebuffed by Bush, a novice with no knowledge of the issues involved. The South Koreans took particular offense at Bush's public reference to Kim as "this man." Rather than cement the bilateral relationship, as Kim sought to do, Bush had questioned the value of South Korea's approach to North Korea.

Unfortunately, someone leaked the results of the administration's policy review to the news media, and rather than wait to consult with Foreign Minister Han Song-soo, the White House scrambled to make the announcement itself, trying to ensure that the appropriate "spin" accompanied the story.

At the time I was special envoy for negotiations with the DPRK and the U.S. representative to KEDO. In an effort to ensure that the South Koreans knew about the results before the story broke, I quickly summoned Yu Myung-hwan, the South Korean deputy chief of mission (the number two at South Korea's embassy in Washington), to the State Department before he went to Andrews Air Force Base to meet the foreign minister, who was at that moment en route from New York. I hurriedly summarized the results of the review and shared the statement that the White House intended to make public shortly. As a result, he was able to brief Foreign Minister Han Song-soo at the airport as the White House announcement was made. A casualty of this rush to get the announcement on the air was, of course, the consultative process that the government normally engages in with a close U.S. ally.

If faced with the prospect of the news media "breaking" a story that is bound to include opposing views and analysis of a process or policy, the White House would inevitably choose to tell the story in its own words first. The White House wanted to minimize any suggestion that the policymaking process had been contentious. Getting its version on the record first allowed it go through a complete news cycle without having to answer questions about someone else's assertion that the administration was split on its policy views on North Korea. In this case, some of the first stories reporting the White House announcement contained suggestions that the hard-liners at the Pentagon and the National Security Council (NSC) were pitted against more moderate officials at the State Department.[4] And as is the case a lot of the time, the reporters were right.

To make sure that the correct message got out, NSC staff developed the following background points to be used when the press was briefed on the North Korea policy announcement:

—We have conducted a major review of our policy toward North Korea over the past three months. We have taken a comprehensive look at our objectives and our options.

—We have consulted closely with our South Korean and Japanese allies, whose views have played an important role in our policy deliberations. Preserving strong alliances with South Korea and Japan is a top priority for us as we go forward.

—We also have carefully considered the approach of the previous administration. Some of the elements of its approach were useful and important, and we have incorporated them into our thinking.

—We have decided to pursue the following course:

We are ready to enter serious discussions with the DPRK in a straightforward fashion as to how we can address issues of concern to our South Korean and Asian allies and to the United States.

We have in mind a comprehensive approach on which we make progress on all fronts simultaneously. North Korea's steps would involve real progress toward North-South reconciliation and peace on the Korean peninsula. If North Korea responds affirmatively, our steps would involve expanding our efforts to help the North Korean people, easing economic sanctions, and other political steps.

—Our discussions will include such matters as the following:

Improved implementation of the Agreed Framework relating to North Korea's nuclear activities and IAEA compliance;

An effectively verifiable ban on missile exports and constraints on indigenous missile programs; and

Adoption of a less threatening conventional military posture.

—We are serious about changing the nature of our relationship with North Korea. Our goal is to offer Kim Jong-il the opportunity to demonstrate his seriousness about his desire for an improved relationship.

—Let me describe a few of our guiding principles.

First of all, as President Bush has made clear, we strongly support President Kim's reconciliation efforts with North Korea. Ultimately, solving the fundamental security problems on the Peninsula requires North-South rapprochement.

In fact, a key element of our approach will be to encourage North-South reconciliation; we do not want to distract or divert North Korea from making progress with the South.

Secondly, as we have said before, we want to change the basis on which we interact with North Korea. We will not be driven into dialogue with North Korea through threats or provocations, and we will not reward bad behavior. But we will respond positively to positive steps by North Korea.

Thirdly, the Administration is skeptical about the intentions and sincerity of the DPRK regime. That is why any agreements we may pursue must be effectively verifiable.

Finally, our priority is in the curtailing of DPRK activities that threaten us, our allies, and regional stability—in East Asia and other regions.[5]

Many of the same principles were incorporated into proposals made by the United States during the June 2004 third round of six-party talks, which included the United States, the Republic of Korea, China, Japan, Russia, and the DPRK.

Seeking Bilateral Discussions with Pyongyang

In the week following the president's June 6 announcement of the policy review conclusions, I transmitted to my North Korean counterpart, Vice Minister Kim Gye-gwan, the administration's interest in meeting for bilateral talks. I arranged to host a lunch in New York on June 13 for Ambassador Li Hyong-chol, North Korea's permanent representative to the United Nations, in order to have Li convey a letter from me to Kim Gye-gwan advising him of the results of the administration's policy review and offering to meet to begin a dialogue. Having already had too many fights with the hard-line elements at the White House, I waited until the last moment before inviting a National Security Council staffer to accompany me. I also waited until we were in a taxi from the airport headed to Manhattan before showing her my letter to Kim; I did not want predictable objections and wordsmithing to delay a simple letter. In the letter I set no preconditions, and I deferred to Vice Minister Kim on selecting a date and venue.[6] Several people later suggested that I should have proposed a date and location for the initial meeting, forcing Kim to accept the proposal or counter with a specific date of his own. My intention at the time was to convey orally through Li that I understood that Kim was a vice minister, senior in rank and experience to me, and that I would adjust my schedule to fit his.

Kim Gye-gwan did not have an opportunity to assess my offer or to appreciate my deference to his seniority. Once the announcement of the policy review had been prematurely made public, Pyongyang began working on its own public response to the White House announcement before my letter to Kim arrived. On June 17, the Korean Central News Agency (KCNA), the government news agency, carried the Foreign Ministry's reaction:

> Even while proposing to resume the negotiations without preconditions, the U.S. side unilaterally decided on the agenda of the negotiations and publicly presented it even before the two sides sit face to face. The agenda concerns our so-called nuclear, missile, and conventional forces, and we cannot construe otherwise than an attempt for the United States to achieve the goal of disarming us through negotiations.

For dialogue between sovereign states to be held on a fair and equal basis is a basic requirement recognized internationally. This is proven by the fact the past DPRK-U.S. dialogue brought about results that were in the interests of the two sides and beneficial to improving the bilateral relations.

In this respect, we cannot but assess that the U.S. administration's recent proposal to resume dialogue, in nature, is unilateral and precon-ditioned and, in intent, hostile.[7]

What Pyongyang had done in its instant analysis of the conclusions of the president's North Korea policy review was consistent with past North Korean negotiating behavior and should have been seen as nothing more. Pyongyang inevitably sought to devalue U.S. proposals while affecting diplomatic hurt over the perceived slights that it had suffered. That tactic serves to put the "offending" party on the defensive and requires it to come hat in hand, apol-ogizing for the egregious error it has committed, and then to revise its proposal to fit the offended party's expectations. In this case, Pyongyang's gripe with the United States was not on a matter of substance but of procedure, because the administration had publicly announced the results of its policy review with-out first notifying Pyongyang. Not having a strong hand to play, Pyongyang reverted to the equivalent of a scam artist's claim of a whiplash injury in a minor fender bender—or in political terms, "hostile intent." There is no satis-factory way for a country to prove that it does not have any hostile intent unless Pyongyang declares itself satisfied.

The concern expressed by Pyongyang over U.S. hostile intent is an ongoing issue; it did not originate with the Bush administration. To alleviate those con-cerns, a U.S.-DPRK joint communiqué was issued during the October 9–12, 2000, visit to Washington of Kim Jong-il's special envoy, Vice Marshal Jo Myong-nok, the first vice chairman of the National Defense Commission and someone who was considered at the time to be the number-two official in the DPRK. The communiqué directly addressed the issue of hostile intent:

> Recognizing that improving ties is a natural goal in relations among states and that better relations would benefit both nations in the twenty-first century while helping ensure peace and security on the Korean Peninsula and in the Asia-Pacific region, the U.S. and the DPRK sides stated that they are prepared to undertake a new direction in their rela-tions. As a crucial first step, the two stated that neither government would have hostile intent toward the other and confirmed the commit-

ment of both governments to make every effort in the future to build a new relationship free of past enmity."[8]

Communiqués such as this are highly regarded by the North Koreans. They tend to cite them as the rationale for cooperating with the United States, or, if they are displeased by the course of events, they hold them up as evidence of a broken promise. In this particular case, Pyongyang agreed to the communiqué because it prized the implication of an improved relationship with the United States. Later, Pyongyang would refer to it as evidence that the Bush administration was moving away from the positive position that the two governments had once agreed on.

The Role of Rhetoric

Five years into the Bush presidency, Pyongyang continued to express concerns about U.S. hostile policy. In response, Washington was unable to move beyond what the president had articulated in Seoul in February 2002—that the United States did not intend to attack or invade the DPRK. Glenn Kessler of the *Washington Post* wrote an article on the subject in February 2005:

> "This year, the president made a clear statement that he had no hostile intent toward North Korea," Powell said on CBS's *Face the Nation*. "And he said that in South Korea earlier this year." On Fox News, Powell quoted Bush as saying, "I have no hostile intent toward the North."
>
> Actually, Bush had said no such thing. Speaking to reporters in Seoul one month after the "axis of evil" speech, Bush again said that North Korea's government was evil and that he would not "change my opinion on the man, on Kim Jong Il, until he frees his people."
>
> But Bush added: "We have no intention of invading North Korea. South Korea has no intention of attacking North Korea, nor does America."
>
> Experts say this language does not impress the North Koreans, especially after they were labeled part of an "axis of evil."
>
> Powell's language on "no hostile intent" was picked up by the State Department spokesman, Richard A. Boucher, when he briefed the news media in the weeks after Powell's television appearance. But the language disturbed hard-liners in the administration, who believed that North Korea had clearly demonstrated a hostile policy toward the United States— and that the phrase limited the administration's options in using

economic and other weapons to pressure Pyongyang. They began to press for its elimination from the administration's talking points.

Defense Secretary Donald H. Rumsfeld raised the issue with Rice, who was then national security adviser, an official familiar with the conversation said. Rice agreed that the language should be dropped, and that only Bush's earlier comment about not attacking and invading be used."[9]

On July 26, 2001, in testimony before the Subcommittee on East Asia and the Pacific of the House of Representatives' Committee on International Relations, I noted that the administration's approach was to seek serious (bilateral) discussions on a broad agenda that included issues related to missiles, nuclear and conventional forces, and humanitarian concerns. I noted that while North Korea had not offered a direct answer to the administration's offer of talks, they had not rejected it either. I told the subcommittee that the North had complained that we were trying to dictate the agenda and that we had left out issues that they deemed important. I emphasized that we were working through what we referred to as the "New York channel."[10]

In describing our policy, I told the subcommittee that we did not want to get bogged down in procedural matters; rather, we hoped to discuss issues of mutual concern and to offer North Korea the opportunity to demonstrate the seriousness of its stated desire for improved relations with the United States.[11] At the conclusion of the hearing, chairman Jim Leach asked how the United States communicated with North Korea. I repeated that we used a communications channel dubbed the New York channel, which had been used primarily by the State Department's director of Korean affairs and North Korea's deputy permanent representative to its UN mission in New York. The channel was used as necessary to conduct the day-to-day business of coordinating meetings and travel—in short, to handle the logistics associated with interactions between U.S. and North Korean officials. I had not yet gotten the North Koreans to designate the channel an officially sanctioned method of communication between me (as special envoy for negotiations with North Korea) and the DPRK's ambassador to the United Nations. That would come later. Chairman Leach expressed disappointment that the working-level New York channel was the only means of communication, stressing his belief that the issues outstanding between our two countries were too important not to have multiple channels of communication. He was, of course, correct.

I took Leach's admonition seriously and determined to find another, more senior level of communication with North Korea. The departure of North

Korea's permanent UN representative, Ambassador Li Hyong-chol, presented the opportunity that I was looking for. I arranged to host a farewell lunch for him on Friday, November 16, 2001, at Jimmy Sung's Restaurant near the DPRK mission. Over lunch, Ambassador Li and I agreed that it would be useful to establish a regular channel of dialogue at our level, and he promised that he would recommend doing so when he returned to Pyongyang.

Ambassador Li was true to his word. I received information that his replacement, Ambassador Pak Gil-yon, who had served as North Korea's UN ambassador before Li, had been permitted to meet with me periodically. For the awkward first meeting, face and protocol came into play. I initially suggested that I host a lunch for Pak Gil-yon, but his deputy, Li Gun, refused, saying that the first meeting should be on neutral ground. In the past, we often had met our North Korean counterparts either at the U.S. mission across from the UN General Assembly or at a local restaurant. For this first meeting, the North Koreans insisted that we reserve a conference room at the United Nations. While doable, it required us to go through the U.S. mission at the United Nations to make the reservation and to get each of the Washington-based participants a temporary ID card to gain entry into the UN.

The only room available was a conference room in the basement, which was much too large for the number of people involved. It had a series of tables arranged in an open square format that put Ambassador Pak and a couple of his staff on one side, separated by about ten feet from the American delegation. The meeting went well, and after our positive first encounter, it became obvious to both of us that the formality of using a large UN conference room was unnecessary. We established a basis for regular meetings in the future. I had expected Pak, a former vice minister and former UN ambassador, to be somewhat cool toward me because of his seniority and status, but that was not the case. He even said that in the future, meeting for lunch would not be a problem. One interesting point that Pak made at the meeting was that while it was the policy of the DPRK to resolve issues of concern peacefully through negotiations, the provocative statements that Pyongyang had heard coming from Washington had led the North Korean military to believe that the statements demanded a strong reaction and to oppose any response to offers to talk.

For the most part, our future meetings were held at the DPRK's UN mission—an arrangement that was far more practical for conducting the business of the day. While it may have seemed somewhat redundant given the New York channel between the DPRK deputy permanent representative and the State Department's director for Korean affairs, it was in fact a significant development. It elevated the level of the conversation from a discussion of routine, day-to-day business to a discussion of policy and created an opportunity for relaying senior-level communications from or through the secretary of state without having to go through undue layers of staff.

We spent the next several months attempting to convince Pyongyang to agree to a bilateral meeting with us. It was not an easy task. Pyongyang had not yet come to terms with the change in U.S. administrations and seemingly wanted a blanket commitment from the new Bush administration to pick up where the Clinton administration had left off. It was hard for Pyongyang to realize that it had waited too long before seriously engaging Washington at a sufficiently senior level at the end of the Clinton administration and that it had lost the opportunity for a presidential visit before Bill Clinton left office. During the transition from Clinton to Bush, the incoming administration made public, pejorative references to Kim Jong-il by name—something that officials in Pyongyang were unused to and that left them at a loss as to how to react. Pyongyang, in turn, reacted with an equal amount of rhetoric aimed at the new administration.[12]

In preparing to participate in his first Asia-Pacific Economic Cooperation (APEC) summit in Shanghai, President Bush conducted a roundtable interview at the White House with a group of Asian newspaper editors on October 16, 2001. The editors brought up the topic of the stalled talks between North and South Korea and a recently cancelled exchange of Korean families separated during the Korean War, and they asked the president whether he had any message for Kim Jong-il. President Bush replied:

> I've got a message to Kim Jong-il: fulfill your end of the bargain; you said you would meet—meet. No one in the United States is stopping him from doing this. This is a decision he made. He can blame it on who he wants, but he ought to fulfill his end of the agreement.[13]
>
> And, secondly, I want to remind your readers that we offered to meet with Kim Jong-il. In June of this year we said we'll be glad to send a representative to meet with you to discuss a variety of issues. And, yet, he chooses not to meet with us, either. He won't meet with you; he won't meet with us—which kind of leads me to believe that perhaps he doesn't want to meet.
>
> So he can blame it on who he wants, but it's up to him to make that decision.
>
> Secondly, I think that he needs to earn the trust of the world. I think he needs to take pressure off of South Korea and off of the DMZ. I think he needs to say—send a signal, clearest message, that he's for peace, not

war. And he can do that very easily by removing conventional forces back. That's very simple to do. I know he needs to stop spreading weapons of mass destruction around the world. And I look forward to—my government looks forward to explaining that to him, in no uncertain terms.

By the way, I fully understand how this issue affects the other nations of the Far East, as well. And so we want to have discussions with Kim Jong-il. We've made the offer to have discussions with Kim Jong-il. But he refuses to talk. And I'm always—which makes me wonder why? Why would he not want to talk? What is it about this man who refuses to—not only to talk with us, but to fulfill an agreement he made with your government?

Later in the same interview, President Bush said:

Listen, I am interested in—again, I repeat something I said before: I want our government to help starving people. On the other hand, I don't want to send aid to a government that doesn't help its people. It's one thing to help the people, it's another thing to send the aid and then the government doesn't help the people.

And so I must tell you that I've been disappointed in Kim Jong-il not rising to the occasion, being so suspicious, so secretive. I believe he must lead his nation into the modern era—starting with making sure his people are fed and well-treated, and working with his neighbor. He ought to assume the responsibility of a good leader, and do that.[14]

That interview earned Bush three days of sarcastic responses from Pyongyang. A Foreign Ministry spokesman initially responded by saying:

Shortly ago U.S. President Bush once again indiscreetly pulled up the DPRK. At a news conference held prior to the APEC summit he told the lie that the DPRK does not respond to the DPRK-U.S. dialogue though Washington stands for it. He went the length of speaking ill of its supreme leadership, saying it is too doubtful and shrouded in secrecy and it refuses to keep the promise and he is a person quite not understandable. Ignoring his past behavior, he argued that the DPRK is so suspicious and that it should do what it has committed itself to do. This is as ridiculous as the pot calling the kettle black.

A thaw was brought to the frozen DPRK-U.S. relations with much efforts. But they got refrozen and the bilateral dialogue came to a rupture entirely due to Bush and his administration with deep-rooted conception of hostility towards the DPRK. In the last period of the Clinton administration, the two countries became brisk in dialogue and published even a joint communiqué that promised an end to the hostile relations between them. However, the new U.S. administration broke all those agreements as soon as it took office. The Bush administration proposed last June to "resume" the suspended dialogue with the DPRK. This proposal, too, is, in essence, a brigandish demand intended to unilaterally disarm the DPRK.

We consider the resumption of the DPRK-U.S. dialogue to be a matter that may be discussed only when the Bush administration takes at least the same position as taken by the Clinton administration in its last period.[15]

Three days later, KCNA carried a commentary attributed to the government newspaper *Minju Chosun*:

His remarks prove that he does not know any elementary etiquette and has no common sense as a statesman, not to speak of a head of state. The "resumption" of the bilateral dialogue proposed by the Bush administration in June is, in essence, a product of a sinister purpose to shift the responsibility for the rupture of dialogue onto the DPRK, not for the resumption of dialogue.

The Bush administration should make a sincere apology to the Korean people for Bush's reckless remarks and adopt at least the same stand as taken by the preceding administration in its last period. Only then will an atmosphere for unbiased DPRK-U.S. dialogue be created."[16]

On the same day, KCNA carried a similar story, attributed to the newspaper *Rodong Shinmun*:

Indeed, Bush is an incompetent and rude president who is senseless and ignorant as he does not know even elementary diplomatic etiquette and lacks diplomatic ability. It is natural that things cannot go well in the U.S. as long as such a person administers state politics as its top leader. Bush should have looked back on his unreasonable attitude and dishonest behaviour against the DPRK since he took office and repented of them. Yet, he asserted that the DPRK is doubtful and should implement its commitments.

This is a height of folly."[17]

In early November, discussing the visit of a European Union delegation to North Korea that had occurred when the KCNA reports quoted above came out, a senior EU official told me that the North Koreans had "hinted" that they were on the verge of entering into talks with the United States before President Bush's comments to the Asian editors on October 16. But, according to the North Koreans, it became impossible to do so without losing face. In the EU-DPRK talks, the Europeans also learned that Pyongyang was concerned about the U.S. focus on terrorism. The North Koreans confirmed to them that they would sign another UN convention on terrorism (regarding financing) and would adhere to the other conventions on terrorism not yet signed. In their conversation on terrorism, the North Koreans told the EU that they thought they had had a deal with the Clinton administration regarding cooperation on antiterrorism efforts, and they expressed a certain nostalgia for the Clinton period. As if to answer President Bush's charge of failing to live up to their agreement for a second summit, the North Koreans quoted Kim Jong-il's message to Kim Dae-jung of a year earlier, in which he said that a second summit would take place but that the "conditions" were not good.

The issue of loss of face was confirmed to a former American official who was also in Pyongyang around the same time as the European delegation but who had met with different officials from the Ministry of Foreign Affairs. The DPRK Foreign Ministry, like its counterparts around the world, is divided among regional and functional categories headed by vice ministers. In the meeting with American affairs specialists, the American official heard the North Koreans suggest that the Foreign Ministry's statement had been "very carefully" crafted, looking for an opening to save face.

That carefully crafted statement by the Foreign Ministry was not all that well received. Telling the Bush administration—whose early North Korea policy has been described as the "ABC (Anything But Clinton) policy"—that North Korea "consider[ed] the resumption of the DPRK-U.S. dialogue to be a matter that may be discussed only when the Bush administration takes at least the same position as taken by the Clinton administration in its last period" was like waving a red flag in front of an angry bull. Not only did the Bush team resent the suggestion, they were determined not to accede to any demands from Pyongyang if doing so might leave them open to comparison with the Clinton administration.

Five years into the Bush presidency, the administration and Pyongyang continued to trade personalized attacks. In an April 28, 2005, press conference, President Bush seemed to go out of his way to seek an opportunity to attack Kim Jong-il. While his comments did not break any new ground, they were seen as undermining assistant secretary of state Chris Hill, his newly appointed negotiator in the six-party talks, who was at that moment in Asia on his first official trip as the assistant secretary of state for East Asian and Pacific affairs in an effort to gain support for the six-party process. Bush was most likely directing his comments to his domestic U.S. audience rather than making any attempt to send a diplomatic signal to foreign capitals:

Bush: Let me talk about North Korea, if you don't mind. Is that your question?

Question: Go right ahead.

(Laughter)

Bush: I'm surprised you didn't ask it. Look, Kim Jong Il is a dangerous person. He's a man who starves his people. He's got huge concentration camps. And, as David accurately noted, there is concern about his capacity to deliver a nuclear weapon. We don't know if he can or not, but I think it's best, when you're dealing with a tyrant like Kim Jong Il, to assume he can. That's why I've decided that the best way to deal with this diplomatically is to bring more leverage to the situation by including other countries.

It used to be that it was just America dealing with North Korea. And when Kim Jong Il would make a move that would scare people, everybody would say, America, go fix it. I felt it didn't work. In other words, the bilateral approach didn't work. The man said he was going to do something and he didn't do it, for starters.

So I felt a better approach would be to include the people in the neighborhood into a consortium to deal with him. And it's particularly important to have China involved. China's got a lot of influence in North Korea. We went down to Crawford with Jiang Zemin, and it was there that Jiang Zemin and I issued a statement saying that we would work for a nuclear weapons–free Korean Peninsula. And so, when Kim Jong Il announced the other day about his nuclear intentions and weapons, it certainly caught the attention of the Chinese, because they had laid out a policy that was contradicted by Kim Jong Il.[18]

Within two weeks Pyongyang responded in the *Rodong Shinmun*, "It is a wise decision for our republic not to expect any settlement of the nuclear issue or any improvement in its relations with the United States during Bush's term of office. Bush is the world's worst fascist dictator, a first-class warmaniac and Hitler, Junior, who is jerking his hands stained with blood of innocent people."[19] In response to a May 12, 2005, CNN interview with Secretary of State

Condoleezza Rice in which she indicated that it was Pyongyang that violated the 1994 Agreed Framework, the Korean Central News Agency said, "All the remarks of Rice prove that she is either a woman ignorant of the DPRK-U.S. history or a brazenfaced liar. We cannot but be confused by such incoherent remarks made by the Secretary of State of the superpower. Call a spade a spade."[20] Rice was referring to Pyongyang's clandestine highly enriched uranium (HEU) program, which was a violation of both the spirit and letter of the Agreed Framework. Since Pyongyang denied any involvement in HEU, it viewed the U.S. action to halt shipments of heavy fuel oil as a violation of the Agreed Framework that had precipitated the nuclear crisis.

There was an attempt early in the first term of the Bush administration to get beyond the ever-increasing intensity and ugliness of rhetoric coming out of Washington and Pyongyang. In February 2001, while I was still on the staff of the National Security Council, I was invited to a dinner hosted by Young C. Kim, a professor emeritus at George Washington University. Kim had helped arrange a visit to Washington and the World Bank for a North Korean delegation, and the members of the delegation were to attend the dinner. One of the members was Han Song-ryol, who was a senior researcher at the time but who had been the minister-counselor at North Korea's UN mission in New York, in charge of interaction with U.S. government officials. I took the opportunity, with NSC approval, to attend the dinner and have a quiet conversation with Han. My message was simple: Pyongyang needed to understand the democratic process at work in the United States and to realize that the transition from one administration to another of the same political party, let alone of different parties, always resulted in policy reviews and perhaps new methods of carrying out policy objectives. The review of the U.S. policy toward North Korea currently under way was a natural part of the American democratic process. I cautioned Han that the unnecessary and harsh rhetoric coming out of Pyongyang would cast a pall on the U.S. review process, and I recommended that he urge restraint on the part of Pyongyang. Han cited the rhetoric coming out of Washington as the primary reason for Pyongyang's response.

The personalization of attacks and frequency of rhetoric traded between Washington and Pyongyang continued unabated. In his 2002 State of the Union speech, the president spoke directly of the threat posed by North Korea:

> Our second goal is to prevent regimes that sponsor terror from threatening America or our friends and allies with weapons of mass destruction. Some of these regimes have been pretty quiet since September 11, but we know their true nature. North Korea is a regime

arming with missiles and weapons of mass destruction, while starving its citizens. . . . States like these, and their terrorist allies, constitute an axis of evil, arming to threaten the peace of the world. By seeking weapons of mass destruction, these regimes pose a grave and growing danger. They could provide these arms to terrorists, giving them the means to match their hatred. They could attack our allies or attempt to blackmail the United States. . . . We'll be deliberate, yet time is not on our side. I will not wait on events while dangers gather. I will not stand by as peril draws closer and closer. The United States of America will not permit the world's most dangerous regimes to threaten us with the world's most destructive weapons.[21]

To me, the reaction by North Korea was predictable. In New York, the DPRK deputy permanent representative to the United Nations told me that Pyongyang had come to the conclusion that the United States was not interested in dialogue but instead was preparing for war—that the State of the Union address was tantamount to a declaration of war. Pyongyang had made the decision that there would be no overtures toward the United States. He complained that every time Pyongyang took steps, something would occur "out of the blue" and Pyongyang would be labeled in some pejorative way. He went on to say that it would not matter what the president said during his trip to Seoul; Pyongyang had made up its mind not to respond to our offer to talk. The North Korean news agency carried similar remarks:

> U.S. President Bush in a "state of the union address" before the Congress on January 30 cited the DPRK and some other nations as "an axis of evil" and "states threatening the world peace." And he blustered that the U.S. will not permit them to do so and operations should be carried on as planned. This reveals the U.S. reckless intention to seize the DPRK by force of arms after designating it as the second target of "anti-terrorism war."
>
> His outburst is little short of a declaration of war against the DPRK, and this may once again bring the military situation on the Korean peninsula to the brink of war His remarks clearly show that the U.S.-proposed "resumption of dialogue" with the DPRK is intended not for the improvement of the bilateral relations but for the realization of the U.S. aggressive military strategy.[22]

The reaction in South Korea was equally unwelcoming. By the time the president arrived in Seoul for his first visit in mid-February, it became necessary to publicly defuse the rising tension that the apparent differences in the ROK and the U.S. policy approaches to North Korea had created. I was not invited to be part of the official delegation, but I did persuade James A. Kelly, then the assistant secretary of state for East Asian and Pacific affairs, that the physical presence of the president's special envoy for negotiations with the DPRK at the president's public remarks at Mount Dora would send a positive, reinforcing signal to our South Korean allies that the administration was serious in wanting a negotiated rather than a military solution to our mutual concerns regarding North Korea. I traveled separately to Seoul, arriving at Mount Dora in transportation set up for "other" invited guests. Dora Station was the newly built "last" railroad station along the rail line designed to connect the two Koreas through the demilitarized zone (DMZ) dividing them. The South Koreans had completed their portion of the rail project pending work in the DMZ to de-mine the area, prepare the railroad bed, and pave the adjacent road, while little had been accomplished on the North Korean side.

Before traveling to Dora Station, in response to a question about his State of the Union speech, the president had said: "We're peaceful people. We have no intention of invading North Korea. South Korea has no intention of attacking North Korea, nor does America."[23] That appears to have been the first of many times that the president would declare that the United States had no intention of invading North Korea.

Pyongyang's response to the president's attempt to defuse tension came two days later in the form of a statement from the Foreign Ministry:

> During his trip to Asia from February 17 to 22, Bush made clearer the U.S. intention to violate the sovereignty of the DPRK, openly interfere in its internal affairs and stifle it by force. Engaging himself in mud slinging at the DPRK, he talked about "change" of its system and, furthermore, outrageously slandered the supreme headquarters during his current trip. The facts prove that his description of the DPRK as a member of "axis of evil" came not from such issues as weapons or "relationship with terrorism" but, in essence, from his personified denial to the supreme headquarters and political system of the DPRK, as estimated by the world public. . . . We are not willing to have contact with his clan which is trying to change by force of arms the system chosen by the Korean people. Useless is such dialogue advocated by the U.S. to find a pretext for invasion, not admitting the DPRK system.[24]

Getting to Yes

We spent the next several months attempting to convince Pyongyang that the president was sincere in his desire to have direct, serious talks. One of the keys to getting Pyongyang to agree to meet with us to begin the discussions that the president envisioned was getting a White House representative to accompany me when I met periodically with North Korea's ambassador to the UN. Having served on the National Security Council staff for almost five years, I knew from my own experience that the North Koreans viewed a White House presence as an indication of presidential approval of the message. The North Koreans were already assuming that while a message that I delivered might be the official U.S. government position and even one supported by the secretary of state, it did not represent the views of the president. In short, Pyongyang believed that there were two distinct camps within the administration—a moderate one headed by Secretary of State Powell and a more hard-line one composed of virtually everyone else in the administration.

After the president's trip to Seoul and the negative reaction by Pyongyang to the president's message, Secretary Powell wanted me to meet with Ambassador Pak in New York to make sure Pyongyang knew that he was fully engaged in our North Korea policy and to emphasize certain other points that had been part of the president's message at Dora Station but apparently had been misunderstood by Pyongyang. After consulting with Steve Hadley, the deputy national security adviser, Michael Green, who was director for Asian affairs for the NSC, was able to get authorization to accompany me to New York to meet with Ambassador Pak in March 2002. I had originally attempted to have an NSC representative with me at all my meetings with the North Koreans, much as my predecessor, Ambassador Charles Kartman, had done, but early White House aversion to the idea precluded that. It was only in the aftermath of the president's trip to Korea that Mike Green was allowed to go, and, even then, I sensed that it was more to keep an eye on what I might say to the North Koreans. The basic objectives of my message were developed before I went to New York, but no specific talking points or script had been prepared. When Mike Green and I linked up at the U.S. mission to the UN, he was concerned that I did not intend to use specific language. I probably reacted a bit too harshly to his suggestions, telling him that I fully understood the objective points and had no intention of reading prepared language.

One of the most amazing turns of events that occurred during the first term of the Bush administration was the reversal of roles among American diplomats and their Asian counterparts. In the past, even seasoned Asian diplomats had relied heavily on prepared scripts while their American peers took advantage of broad authority and comfortably wove unscripted responses and probed for unforeseen possibilities in exercising American leadership, as they were expected to do. From the beginning of the Bush administration, the lack of trust and consensus on North Korean policy resulted in the practice of scripts being written and scrupulously followed by relatively senior officials. As a result, Asian diplomats abandoned their scripts and, in the face of Americans following such restrictive scripts, picked up the leadership mantle.

The meeting with Pak and Green went well. It was important for Pyongyang to see through the presence of Mike Green the symbolic endorsement by the White House of what I was saying, even if the North Koreans fully understood that I had been delivering the White House message all along. As a result, Ambassador Pak Gil-yon finally indicated in early April 2002 that Pyongyang was ready to meet. When I reported Pak's response, I was told not to reply — that the White House was reconsidering its options. We had been working since June 2001 to get Pyongyang to agree to a meeting and when it finally did, we pulled back. This reversal of course came as a surprise to me, and I assumed that it was also a surprise to Secretary Powell, who had been pushing hard for a meeting "anytime, anyplace, and without preconditions."

PART I
The Role of Rhetoric: Getting to Yes

2

Confrontation over Highly Enriched Uranium

> We are a part of the axis of evil and you are a gentleman. This is our relationship. We cannot discuss matters like gentlemen. If we disarm ourselves because of U.S. pressure, then we will become like Yugoslavia or Afghanistan's Taliban, to be beaten to death.
>
> —*First Vice Minister Kang Sok-ju, North Korean Ministry of Foreign Affairs, October 4, 2002*

As it turned out, the White House had pulled back from engaging in talks with Pyongyang because it was about to undertake a second review of its North Korea policy. This time the review was directed by the president, who said, through Condoleezza Rice, his national security adviser, that he had a "gut feeling" that the government should not get bogged down in protracted negotiations. He decided instead on an approach designed to address all of his concerns faster. He was prepared to offer more in exchange for the North taking bold steps in each of the areas outlined in the original policy review statement of June 6, 2001; accordingly, the new approach was dubbed the Bold Approach.

The process of coming up with an actual policy framework along the lines that the president had sketched took only a matter of weeks, but it was a difficult process nonetheless. When those of us charged with writing North Korea policy—primarily State Department staff—asked for more specific guidance, none was forthcoming. "Think creatively; we'll know it when we see it," was all we were told. We went through several iterations before arriving at an acceptable option. While the president instinctively knew that he would have to offer Pyongyang something meaningful in exchange for the substantial changes he had in mind, the details of what "meaningful" meant were left to the staff to decide. What was not understood, then or now, is why, after excoriating Kim Jong-il, the president opted for such a positive move, which would, in theory, ensure the survival of the North Korean regime.

25

While a new policy option was being developed, a search was being conducted among senior members of the administration for a presidential envoy to deliver the Bold Approach message to the most senior North Korean recipient possible, to underscore the seriousness of the president's intentions. The idea was to have an envoy of sufficient stature gain a meeting with Kim Jong-il. In originally accepting the proposal to meet with me (as the administration's special envoy for negotiations with the DPRK), Pyongyang had indicated that Vice Minister Kim Gye-gwan would be my main interlocutor and that I would also have a meeting with First Vice Minister Kang Sok-ju, the most senior Foreign Ministry official and the one closest to Kim Jong-il. Kim Jong-il does not normally meet with foreign visitors below the rank of head of state, and deviations from protocol are rare. In the case of the United States, an exception had been granted for the October 2000 meeting with former secretary of state Madeleine Albright.

Accordingly, the thrust of one State Department memo that I wrote was that anyone below the secretary of state did not have a chance of meeting with Kim Jong-il. In that memo, I added that, realistically, only the secretaries of state and defense, the national security adviser, or the vice president could expect to meet with the North Korean leader—assuming that the goal of resolving our concerns through diplomacy remained the same. Shortly after the memo went to the secretary of state, James A. Kelly, the assistant secretary of state for East Asia and Pacific affairs, chortled that someone had actually recommended that the vice president be considered for the envoy position. I reminded him that he had signed the memo that listed the vice president as a possibility.

When no cabinet member or deputy secretary was forthcoming, Jim Kelly was chosen for the mission. It has been suggested to me that the lesson here is that, without an obvious opportunity for political gain, politicians will not endanger their careers. In that respect, Kelly is to be admired for accepting the assignment.

Preparing to Brief Pyongyang on the Bold Approach

In late June 2002, with the new Bold Approach policy and a presidential envoy in hand, I again engaged Ambassador Pak to propose a trip by Kelly to Pyongyang on July 10. We had always had problems getting a timely response from Pyongyang to our requests and correspondence, and this time was no exception. A routine official trip to Pyongyang was anything but routine. Under the terms of the armistice ending the Korean War, the demilitarized zone was established to divide North and South Korea. Pyongyang controlled access into and transit over or through its territory and required any flight on military aircraft (which is what we used for official business to North Korea) to originate in Japan, fly north into international airspace, and, just before reaching Russian airspace, turn south into DPRK airspace, ultimately landing at Pyongyang. Occasionally, the North Koreans would remind us that taking this circuitous route, which required three hours or more, was for our own good, since they could not guarantee the safety of military aircraft flying from South Korea into North Korea—and over the anti-aircraft guns along the DMZ.

When I requested the July 10 meeting, I reminded Ambassador Pak that it was essential that we be notified of the decision in a timely manner because the Fourth of July, a U.S. national holiday, was approaching and we did not want to make the pilots work through the holiday to plan the mission and get the visas that they would need for the trip. In addition, I preferred not to travel from Washington to Asia until after July 4, because most of the key personnel in the U.S. embassies would then be at their desks.

Before the North Koreans could confirm the details of the trip, two events occurred. One was an unfortunate incident in which a DPRK naval vessel sank an ROK patrol boat in the West Sea and several South Korean sailors were killed. It was also about this same time that the U.S. intelligence community put together a new assessment of the DPRK's covert highly enriched uranium (HEU) program.[1] There are basically two methods of creating nuclear weapons. When the United States negotiated the Agreed Framework in 1994, North Korea had only one plutonium-based program, but the language of the agreement captured in spirit and letter any potential program involving the other method of creating a nuclear weapon, which requires the use of enriched uranium.

An earlier, 1992 agreement between the ROK and the DPRK that forbade either side from possessing uranium-based facilities had been cited in the Agreed Framework, even though the agreement was never implemented. These two events turned out to be both the reason and the rationale for canceling the trip to Pyongyang.

Highly Enriched Uranium

Because I am still bound by oath and by law not to reveal classified material, I cannot discuss the information on HEU that I had access to while in government. However, it is important for me to assign a level of credibility to that information since there has been a great deal of second-guessing of its validity in light of what the American public has learned about how the Bush administration dealt with intelligence in the run-up to the war in Iraq.

I find the best way to explain my own views on the veracity of the HEU intelligence at the time is to briefly note that I began my twenty-eight-year career in the U.S. Army as a military intelligence officer. I am very familiar with the intelligence collection and analysis process used by the U.S. intelligence community, and I have had a number of intelligence-related jobs. The next-best credential to lay before the reader is that I continued to express deep skepticism when, in the summer of 1998, the Defense Intelligence Agency (DIA) was busy trying to convince (with mixed results) the rest of the U.S. intelligence community that certain activities being observed at Kumchang-ri, North Korea, could mean only that Pyongyang was engaged in replicating underground its nuclear weapons complex at Yongbyon, which had been frozen. Ultimately, through tough negotiations, the United States gained access to Kumchang-ri on multiple occasions and found that DIA was absolutely wrong: there was no nuclear activity at Kumchang-ri.

In contrast, I was convinced that the information that I had access to in late June 2002 clearly demonstrated that North Korea had embarked on a program to create nuclear weapons by using highly enriched uranium. More important than my own analysis was the fact that the intelligence community was unanimous in its view that North Korea had already obtained a certain level of equipment and expertise and had embarked on a program that, if left unchecked, would result in a uranium-based nuclear weapons program. In time, additional information was discovered and made public, reinforcing my initial assessment of the veracity of the intelligence community's estimate. Mitchell Reiss and Robert Gallucci wrote:

> Although there is a great deal of information in the public domain about North Korea's enrichment activities, two points are particularly worth noting. First, as the news media have reported, Abdul Qadeer Khan (who ran a black-market nuclear supply ring from Pakistan) has confessed to providing North Korea with centrifuge prototypes and blueprints, which enabled Pyongyang to begin its centrifuge enrichment program. North Korea's decision, apparently reached in 2000, to begin acquiring materials in larger quantities for a uranium-enrichment facility with several thousand centrifuges suggests that its R&D-level enrichment endeavors have been successful. Likewise, its procurement of equipment suitable for use in uranium hexafluoride feed and withdrawal systems also points to planning for a uranium-enrichment facility. Pyongyang has yet to

address these points and denies the existence of uranium-enrichment activities of any kind.

Second, in April 2003, French, German, and Egyptian authorities intercepted a 22-ton shipment of high-strength aluminum tubes acquired for North Korea by a German firm. In November of that year, a representative from Urenco, the European uranium-enrichment consortium, testified in a German court that the dimensions of those tubes—which were intercepted en route to North Korea—matched the technical requirements for vacuum casings for a Urenco centrifuge. A German newspaper reported that North Korea had attempted to circumvent German, and presumably Chinese, export controls by claiming that the tubes were intended for a Chinese company, Shenyang Aircraft Corporation. It is particularly noteworthy that the specifications for the German aluminum tubes are essentially identical to those used by a Malaysian company in manufacturing outer centrifuge casings for Libya's formerly clandestine gas-centrifuge uranium-enrichment program. Details on those tubes were publicized in the February 2004 press release issued by the Malaysian Inspector-General of Police.[2]

When we discovered that Pyongyang had begun in earnest a program designed to give it a nuclear weapons capability denied by the Agreed Framework, it became obvious that we could not proceed to Pyongyang and lay out the Bold Approach concept, which the North Koreans understood to be a possible roadmap to normalization of relations with Washington. On July 1 we withdrew our request for a meeting, citing the inappropriateness of meeting with the DPRK in the wake of the West Sea incident, which left several South Koreans dead. It was the right action to take simply because of the West Sea incident, but it must be noted, to give the reader a sense of how bizarre the relationship between the United States and South Korea was, that it was Seoul that urged us to ignore the naval clash and proceed with our proposed July 10 meeting in Pyongyang. We cautioned our South Korean counterparts that their fellow citizens would soon demand more than business as usual in dealing with Pyongyang. The anticipated public outcry came when President Kim Dae-jung was in Japan attending a World Cup opening ceremony and the funerals of the sailors were aired live on South Korean television. To be clear, we had not yet informed Seoul of our most recent concerns or shared any information about Pyongyang's HEU program.

Pyongyang reacted in typical fashion to claims by South Korea and the United States that it had deliberately ambushed the ROK patrol boats:

The South Korean Army chief is claiming that the North side should take "responsibility" and make "apology," pulling up the DPRK over the incident. This is the height of impudence.

With no false propaganda can the South Korean military authorities evade the responsibility for their criminal acts. They should, first of all, admit the illegality of the so-called "northern boundary line." The media should clearly distinguish between lies and truth and stop acting a waiting maid in the base plot-breeding operation.[3]

The postponed trip to Pyongyang was one that the DPRK Foreign Ministry had wanted to occur, and the ministry was looking for a way out of this unexpected problem. After several months of verbal sparring between the United States and the DPRK, the prospect again arose of a visit by a presidential envoy to discuss an approach that might lead to normalization. It was a welcome development, and the timing of the prospective trip could not have been better. In July, Pyongyang introduced an economic reform package that looked as if it were going to gradually allow market-oriented forces to coexist with its command economy. At the time, no one believed that the reforms, which permitted prices and exchange rates to float, were any more than an attempt by Pyongyang to institutionalize "coping mechanisms"—workers' attempts to circumvent regulations in an effort to survive, such as by underreporting crops and selling the "surplus" on the black market, whose operations were out of control. Few believed that the reforms were significant or would last. However, Pyongyang hoped to improve its relations with the United States, with an eye toward gaining eventual U.S. support for DPRK access to international financial institutions (IFIs) that could support its economic reforms. The Bold Approach meeting was a necessary first step.

Getting Back on Track

In an early July 2002 telephone call to the DPRK's UN mission in New York, I suggested that Pyongyang take the initiative to resolve the West Sea incident as quickly as possible. While Pyongyang was not prepared to repeat a public apology such as the one that it had issued in December 1996 over a submarine incursion into ROK territorial waters, it did convey to Seoul its regret over the loss of life in the West Sea incident, paving the way for future contact with the United States.[4] In late July, Pyongyang indicated a willingness to accept a rescheduled U.S. visit. Days later, Secretary of State Colin Powell had a "chance meeting" with his DPRK counterpart, Foreign Minister Paek Nam-sun. In reality, nothing had been left to chance.

The secretary had expressed his desire to meet with Paek on the margins of the ASEAN Regional Forum (ARF) meeting being held in Brunei in late July. Since there was still an internal argument on the wisdom of reengaging the North, we believed that a meeting between the two would go a long way toward resolving the argument in favor of engagement. To ensure that the "chance" encounter would actually occur, I arranged for Ed Dong, director for Korean affairs at the State Department, to travel to Brunei and assist in making whatever arrangements were necessary. In a separate call to the North Korean UN mission, I talked to Ambassador Li Gun, the DPRK's deputy permanent representative, to see whether he and I could work on the timing and venue of an encounter. Because Foreign Minister Paek had already begun his trip from Pyongyang, Li Gun had difficulty making the connection on his end; I had to put Li and Ed Dong in direct contact to work out the final details. In the end, clear coordination did not prevail, and only by sheer luck did Paek show up at the right location. Ed Dong and the secretary's party took over and steered Paek into a brief meeting with Secretary Powell. Powell had made the decision to meet with Paek on his own, without prior coordination with the White House. Following press reports of the meeting, there were howls of indignation from the hard-line group within the administration, which objected to any bilateral contact with North Korea. The secretary subsequently downplayed the significance of the meeting.

The next piece of the puzzle to be put in place before we could reschedule the Kelly trip to Pyongyang was getting approval for me to attend a concrete-pouring "ceremony" to be held by the Korean Peninsula Energy Development Organization (KEDO) in Kumho, North Korea, to commemorate a visible milestone in the construction of one of the light-water reactors (LWRs). In my capacity as the U.S. representative to KEDO, I had a leadership role to play in managing the Agreed Framework's provision of heavy fuel oil to North Korea and development of two light-water reactors, both part of the bargain freezing the DPRK's nuclear facilities and program at Yongbyon. Given the new information about the HEU program, there was understandable reluctance to have me participate in an event that was being described as a ceremony and that was continuing to implement our end of the Agreed Framework when most officials in the U.S. administration believed that Pyongyang was in clear violation of its agreement. However, if we did not let our friends and allies (and fellow KEDO board members) know about our HEU discovery, we risked creating animosity among our friends and suspicions on the part of North Korea by not participating in an event in which we were expected to play a leading role. While the internal debate swirled about the advisability of my participating, I drafted a speech to give should I be allowed to participate.[5]

Since time was running out, I began to try to extract a decision about my participation from Secretary Powell. I finally got Tom Hubbard, the U.S. ambassador to Seoul, to raise the issue from an alliance management perspective. Our South Korean allies were very uncomfortable that no decision had been made, and they were embarrassed at the prospect of the U.S. KEDO board member boycotting an event that was being organized for the most part by the South Korean contractor at the LWR site. In the end, I received Powell's permission to participate in the event, one hour before I was scheduled to leave my home for the airport. Again, the decision to allow me to attend was made by Powell, without consultation with the White House. While I was en route to Seoul, the Department of Defense (DOD) proposed significant changes to my speech that I found utterly unacceptable. To avoid a showdown over the clearance process, I called John Rood, a staffer in the NSC counterproliferation directorate, who had made several suggestions for changes that I believed that I could accept. We reworked the changes over the phone to our mutual satisfaction and agreed that the NSC changes trumped the suggestions by DOD.

In the speech that I delivered at the event on August 7, 2002, I said, "When we agreed to the terms of the Agreed Framework, we did so with the full expectation that all aspects of our concerns over North Korea's nuclear program would be resolved finally and completely. As administration officials have stated many times, the United States will continue to abide by the terms of this accord so long as North Korea does the same; we expect the DPRK to abide by the fact and spirit of the agreement."[6] This portion of the speech was written solely with the HEU revelation in mind. Reports of my speech and participation were reported in a straightforward manner and were generally well received in Washington. Later I was told that Secretary Powell expressed relief that the right tone had been achieved and that any second-guessing of his decision to permit my participation had dissipated.

Confrontation over HEU

By September 2002, the United States was ready to meet with the DPRK, but the subject had changed radically. Instead of delivering the Bold Approach message, the United States was preparing to confront the DPRK over its HEU program—but not without some objections. Secretary of Defense Rumsfeld sent a memo to the White House objecting to sending anyone to meet with the

North Koreans; however, he noted, if there were going to be a meeting, either Bob Joseph, the senior director for counterproliferation at the National Security Council, or John Bolton, under secretary of state, would be the preferred (and trusted) envoy. Rumsfeld believed that the Agreed Framework was suspended and that we should cut off shipment of the heavy fuel oil that we were continuing to supply to North Korea. He advocated informing Congress and our allies of the intelligence about the North Korean HEU program and then telling the North Koreans what they needed to do to resolve the situation.

Once it had been decided to inform the North Koreans directly of our knowledge of the HEU program, I traveled to New York City to see Ambassador Pak. In seeking a new date for the postponed Kelly trip of July 10, I requested a number of things, including direct flights from Seoul to Pyongyang by U.S. military aircraft and entry through the DMZ by vehicle for a small number in the U.S. delegation who could not be accommodated in the small aircraft that we were using. The primary purpose of these ancillary requests, which were not significant enough to jeopardize the overall undertaking, was to require coordination between the North Korean People's Army (KPA) and the U.S. military. The requests had nothing to do with our primary mission, but little had been accomplished on that front since the departure of Air Force Major General Michael Hayden, the deputy chief of staff for the UN Command/U.S. Forces Korea.[7] I judged the occasion to be the best opportunity to create conditions that required coordination and made it possible to employ confidence-building measures. The worst that could happen would be for Pyongyang to deny the additional requests, forcing me to requisition a second military aircraft.

I reminded Ambassador Pak of the previously withdrawn request for a July meeting and the need for a prompt reply from Pyongyang. With uncharacteristic speed, Pyongyang approved all aspects of our request within seventeen hours. Pyongyang had approved the overland travel through the DMZ and, more important, it had approved a direct flight by a U.S. military aircraft from South Korea to Pyongyang. The actual flight plan would take us over water around the DMZ, but no one in the U.S. delegation minded not flying over North Korean anti-aircraft emplacements. The speed with which Pyongyang approved the request (and all the add-ons) was testimony to how much it valued the opportunity to develop a relationship with the United States and the Bush administration.[8]

En route to Pyongyang we stopped in Tokyo and Seoul to brief our counterparts on the basic message that we intended to convey to Pyongyang regarding our knowledge of its HEU program. Needless to say, our Japanese and South Korean colleagues were most anxious to get a full briefing on our return.

The Meeting

Soonan Airport at Pyongyang has one of the longest and most desolate runways in the world, or so it seems. We flew from Osan Airbase in South Korea aboard an Air Force C-21, a twin turbofan engine aircraft—the military version of the Lear Jet 35A business jet. It has a crew of two and can carry eight passengers; a more comfortable load is six passengers. I had already committed two in our delegation of eight to travel across the DMZ by car. The North Korean air traffic controllers required us to touch down at the far end of the runway and taxi the remainder of the way to the terminal, about two miles away. A traveler is immediately struck by the lack of activity, in addition to the size of the airfield. Regular service to Beijing, for example, is scheduled only twice a week, on Tuesdays and Saturdays.

We were met at the airport by a Mr. Song, the director of American affairs at the DPRK Foreign Ministry. He guided us to a lounge, where our first conversation focused on a miscommunication that had occurred while we were en route. In working out the details for the agenda, we had originally agreed to reciprocate a dinner that the North Koreans would host after the first day of talks. However, when the hard-line element within the administration saw the agenda, they focused on the proposed reciprocal dinner and declared it absolutely inappropriate—failing to take into account that we had not signaled in advance to Pyongyang our true intention, which was to raise the HEU issue. The final decision resulted in U.S. refusal to reciprocate the dinner and to allow Kelly to engage in a toast at the dinner hosted by North Korea. The rationale, meager as it was, was that we could commit to only one dinner if the trip was to be low-key rather than celebratory in nature.

Sitting in the terminal lounge, our host began by saying that he was disappointed that Mr. Kelly could not attend the dinner that Vice Minister Kim Gye-gwan was hosting in our honor that evening. He told us that North Korea's mission at the UN in New York had been informed by the Korea Desk at the State Department that because the United States wanted the trip to be "low-key," Mr. Kelly could not participate in the dinner and there would be no reciprocal dinner. Rather than begin our trip on a substantive note, we had to unravel the convoluted message that had been passed while we were traveling to Pyongyang. It was a bad caricature of a party game gone wrong. While still not understanding why Pyongyang was stuck with hosting (and paying for) a dinner without a reciprocal dinner by the United States, the North Koreans were relieved that Kelly would attend the Kim Gye-gwan dinner. The reciprocal dinner fiasco should have been a warning signal to Pyongyang that the intentions of the U.S. delegation may not have been as advertised—that is, to discuss the Bold Approach, which might lead to the beginning of normalization of relations.

Perhaps Pyongyang was a little nervous after learning that Kelly would not be allowed to attend the dinner and that the reciprocal dinner had been cancelled. A presidential envoy normally could expect to stay in one of the several guest houses that were available to the Foreign Ministry, but instead we were taken to the Koryo Hotel to check in along with regular tourists. Our first meeting came in the afternoon of October 3, 2002. Our intention was to have a relatively short discussion with Kim Gye-gwan, one of seven vice ministers in charge of regional and functional issues for the Foreign Ministry. Kim had been part of the original North Korean delegation that had negotiated the 1994 Agreed Framework; subsequently he was promoted to the position of vice minister in charge of North American affairs. The following morning, October 4, we would have a more expansive meeting with Kim before ultimately seeing First Vice Minister Kang Sok-ju, the policy right-hand man to North Korean leader Kim Jong-il.

In our first meeting with Kim Gye-gwan, he invited Kelly to begin, saying that he wanted to hear about the current U.S. policy toward the DPRK in order to understand the true intention of the United States with regard to dialogue. He said that he wanted to analyze where the relationship was at this stage. For his part, Kelly read from his prepared script. Having been in countless hours of negotiations with Kim Gye-gwan as the deputy of Ambassador Charles Kartman, the former special envoy, I focused on Kim's facial expressions to see whether I could discern any hint of surprise as Kelly introduced the subject of HEU. I could not, but I also believed that most likely he was uninformed about the HEU program. The basic message that Kelly conveyed to Kim was that the president had been prepared to have serious discussions about transforming the U.S.-DPRK relationship that would benefit the North Korean people while addressing U.S. concerns. But because we now had irrefutable evidence that North Korea had embarked on a covert program to produce nuclear weapons through uranium enrichment, it was impossible to have the intended dialogue. Kelly offered no evidence to Kim. The initial presentation, which also covered our concerns about the Agreed Framework, terrorism, conventional forces, missiles, and humanitarian and human rights issues, lasted a little less than an hour.

Kim Gye-gwan thanked Kelly for making the presentation and for undertaking the trip. He then called for a break. I assumed that the conference room in the Foreign Ministry building, just off Kim Il-sung Square, was bugged and our conversation recorded, but when I saw Kim hustling down the hall I knew that he was going to report in person to Kang Sok-ju. When we reconvened after the break, Kim's response was short and predictable. He said that Kelly's charge of a covert nuclear weapons program was another fabrication, just like the false charge concerning Kumchang-ri in 1998.[9] Kim contended that the charge had been made up by those in the U.S. government who were unhappy with the new relationship between the United States and the DPRK. Similarly, Kim claimed, the suspicions that Kelly brought up now were being circulated by forces that were intent on putting the brakes on the positive developments between the DPRK and its neighboring countries. Once he got that out of the way, he returned to the talking points that he would have delivered had we simply shown up to talk about the Bold Approach policy without mentioning HEU.

That evening Vice Minister Kim hosted a lavish dinner that included fruit, raw salmon, vegetables, fried pigeon, roast pork, lobster and steamed fish, rice cakes, quail egg consommé, rainbow trout, pine nut porridge, *sinsollo*, mushroom and pheasant meatballs, cold noodles, and tea. It is little wonder, given the effort and expense involved, that the North Koreans appeared offended that the United States had withdrawn its offer to host a reciprocal dinner. (Almost four years later, when Representative Tom Lantos visited Pyongyang, he was handed an agenda that had a question mark next to a proposed reciprocal dinner to be hosted by him. His guide told him that the question mark was there because they were not certain whether he would reciprocate the dinner to be hosted by the North Koreans.[10]) As Kim offered a toast, I wondered whether Kelly would simply refuse to raise his glass or ask Kim whether he had actually heard any of the presentation earlier in the day in which the United States accused North Korea of cheating on the 1994 Agreed Framework. To his credit, Kelly responded to the toast in a professional manner. I could imagine the consternation in Washington as one of his "political minders" reported his transgression on their return.

After a few drinks, Kim quipped aloud, "If we could only exclude the DOD and JCS [Joint Chiefs of Staff] representatives, we could get down to business." I thought that the DOD representative on the trip, Mary Tighe, who took the comment quite seriously, was about to come unglued.

The following morning we met again with Vice Minister Kim in the same conference room. The original intent was to expand upon the initial presentation that was given the day before, giving more detail and explaining what might have happened had we not been confronted with the HEU revelation. The script prepared for Kelly was practically identical in language to the previous day's, with a few new sentences added in select paragraphs. Using a previous script as a starting point and drawing on one's own background and experience to enhance the points made is one thing; rereading the exact script is quite another. Kelly chose to read the script without variation. I am sure that the North Koreans were perplexed as to what new information they were supposed to have gleaned from the presentation.

At the conclusion of Kelly's presentation, Kim said that he had listened attentively and his tentative conclusion from the previous day had been confirmed. He said that the United States did not have a real desire to move forward to resolve the issues and that the United States was attempting to disarm North Korea and change its system by means of force, coercion, and pressure. Kim warned that now that it was clear that the United States intended to carry out a policy of "strangulation," Pyongyang had no choice but to counter with an ultra-hard-line response of its own. Kim reviewed the DPRK's conventional forces posture and its missile program but refused to talk about uranium enrichment, saying that the question was not worthy of a response. Kim ended the meeting by noting that Kelly had clarified the position of the Bush administration and told North Korea what it should do in response. Kim continued, saying in reference to the ultra-hard-line response mentioned above, "We will take this path, and it will not be so good for you. I have nothing more to say."

Following a semi-surreal protocol meeting with the president of the Supreme People's Assembly, at which nothing of substance was discussed, we met with First Vice Minister Kang Sok-ju. Kang began the fifty-five minute meeting with a monologue in which he declared that he had been briefed thoroughly by Vice Minister Kim Gye-gwan. As a result, Kang said, he had met throughout the night, "until dawn," with representatives from the concerned agencies, including the military and military arms production agencies. The position of the party and the North Korean government was that the 1994 Agreed Framework had been completely destroyed by the United States. His justification was the U.S. designation of North Korea as a member of the axis of evil, the preemptive strike policy, and the inclusion of North Korea among potential targets for a nuclear attack. Kang said that as a result, the DPRK had decided to reinforce its "Military First" policy by modernizing the military to the maximum extent possible. Ambassador Li Gun later reiterated this argument, first citing the language of the Agreed Framework and then complaining about the threat of preemption by the United States:

As per Article III of the Agreed Framework the U.S. is neither to use nuclear weapons against us nor threaten us with nuclear weapons.

Since assuming office the Bush administration has mentioned with respect to its newly formed national security strategy the right to take preemptive strike against security threats and has included our Republic among that target. Moreover, the U.S. has publicly stated that the use of nuclear weapons would not be excluded from the options available to such preemptive strikes.[11]

Much has been made, after the fact, of the actual language of Kang's admission of the HEU program. While there was no precise, irrefutable statement—a smoking gun—many factors led all eight members of the U.S. delegation to reach the conclusion that Kang had effectively and defiantly admitted to having an HEU program. Kang acknowledged that we said that his country had begun a uranium enrichment program for the production of nuclear weapons. Immediately following that statement, he declared that the DPRK was in fact prepared to manufacture even more developed weapons; he then said that the DPRK needed to be on equal footing with the United States if it was to discuss the issue of denuclearization. We understood him to mean that Pyongyang was prepared to manufacture weapons that were even more developed than uranium-based nuclear weapons, whether they turned out to be biological or chemical weapons, plutonium-based nuclear weapons (which we suspected the North already had the capability to produce), or something else.

Kang sarcastically added: "We are a part of the axis of evil and you are a gentleman. This is our relationship. We cannot discuss matters like gentlemen. If we disarm ourselves because of U.S. pressure, then we will become like Yugoslavia or Afghanistan's Taliban, to be beaten to death." He continued by saying that he expected the United States to make the HEU information publicly known and to take measures to apply pressure against the DPRK. Kang declared, pointedly: "We are going to announce this issue publicly. We have sufficient grounds and conditions to justify our position."

When Kelly prodded Kang specifically about our HEU accusation, Kang said that he understood that the United States had evidence regarding the DPRK's uranium enrichment activities and believed that the DPRK should be subject to IAEA inspections. Kang repeated that the United States had said that North Korea was manufacturing nuclear weapons, then added, "But what about the U.S.? The U.S. is also making nuclear weapons. You say that you are going to attack us with nuclear weapons; we have to do the same." That exchange sounded very much like an admission. But his next pronouncement made Kelly and me feel fairly sure that Kang was explicitly acknowledging the DPRK's uranium program: he said that for the DPRK to engage in dialogue with the United States, it needed leverage—either from uranium enrichment or nuclear weapons. He stated his understanding that if Pyongyang halted uranium enrichment, then the United States would give it "everything." Kang countered that understanding with a DPRK proposal: that the United States should recognize North Korea's system of government; conclude a peace agreement with a nonaggression commitment; and not interfere with North Korea's economic development. Once that was accomplished, the United States and the DPRK could discuss U.S. concerns about uranium enrichment on an equal footing.

In the final exchange between Kelly and Kang, Kelly indicated that the news that we were hearing from Kang was most unwelcome. Kang, for his part, made a final reference to uranium, saying that the United States was pushing the DPRK into a position where it was necessary to counter the "physical declaration of war" by the United States. "In addition to uranium enrichment," he asserted, "all sorts of other things are ready to be produced"; whether the "other things" were nuclear, chemical, or biological weapons was not specified. While we believed that it was possible for Pyongyang to admit to the HEU program in light of Kim Jong-il's admission a month earlier to Japanese prime minister Junichiro Koizumi of North Korea's abduction of Japanese citizens, we had no instructions on how to respond other than to report back to Washington as quickly as possible.

A combination of factors led the U.S. delegation to unanimously agree that Kang had, in effect, defiantly acknowledged the DPRK uranium enrichment program. Moreover, Kang had the same opportunity to respond as Kim Gyegwan had responded: through denial. But Kang, after an all-night meeting with key party and government officials, chose to convey to us that the DPRK did have a uranium enrichment program. Of the delegation of eight, five of us did not speak Korean and fully appreciated that our initial reaction to Kang's comments was in fact a reaction to the quality of the North Korean translation. We had earlier been offered assistance from Jim Hoare, the British chargé d'affaires in Pyongyang. Because of the gravity of the situation and the need to communicate the results of the meeting with Kang, we called Hoare and asked to use his secure communications facilities at the British Embassy. Shortly after we returned to the Koryo Hotel, Hoare arrived with two British Land Rovers flying the Union Jack. We all crammed into the vehicles and were taken to the British Embassy.

We isolated our Korean linguists, one of whom was the interpreter used by the president of the United States, with instructions to recreate First Vice Minister Kang's remarks from what they remembered him saying or from notes that they took from his presentation in Korean instead of from what they heard the North Korean interpreter say in English. The three were able to reach a consensus and create a document that accurately reflected Kang's remarks. We asked Hoare to send a cable from Kelly to Secretary Powell along with the recreated remarks by Kang. The plan was for Hoare to send the cable to the British Embassy in Washington and have it hand-delivered directly to Powell.

We later found out that once the cable got into the British system, it was widely disseminated within British circles and, contrary to our original instructions, hand-delivered to the Pentagon before it ultimately made its way to Powell. While we were attempting to limit access to the information until Powell had an opportunity to brief the president, the British and the Department of Defense were rapidly spreading the information, without Kelly's knowledge. We got our first indication that the cable, intended for Powell's eyes only, was more widely available when we returned to Osan Airbase from Pyongyang and were met by an Air Force major whose comments made it clear that he had read the cable. That was a sharp contrast to how the information was being closely held within the State Department. Thomas Hubbard, the ambassador to Seoul, had not yet seen the cable, nor had he been briefed by Washington. He was not at all pleased that an Air Force major knew of the events that had taken place in Pyongyang before he did.

It was important that we debrief the South Koreans on what we had done and discovered during our trip, but we had a minor problem to overcome: protocol. We needed to get the information to the key people quickly and decided that it would best be done in a single briefing; otherwise we risked having to choose which audience to brief first. We worked out a compromise in which the briefing would be given at the foreign minister's official residence and Lim Dong-won, the national security adviser, would be present. In Tokyo, we managed to execute the same kind of maneuver, having the briefing in U.S. Ambassador Thomas Foley's official residence with the Japanese foreign minister and chief cabinet secretary present.

Actions Following the HEU Admission

One of the first reactions that emerged as senior members of the administration began to discuss the "Kang admission" was a call to end heavy fuel oil (HFO) shipments immediately. DOD officials wanted to turn back a shipment of oil that was in international waters en route to North Korea and had to be reminded that the HFO, while purchased primarily through U.S. contributions to KEDO, was in fact the property of KEDO and that any attempt to divert or terminate the shipment required the agreement of KEDO's executive board.

Stopping that particular shipment before it reached North Korean waters was not practical, but the administration continued to focus on KEDO, as the supplier of heavy fuel oil under the terms of the 1994 Agreed Framework, to apply pressure on North Korea. Specifically, KEDO had been created to carry out U.S. obligations under the terms of the Agreed Framework. For its part, the DPRK had agreed to freeze and ultimately dismantle its nuclear program. The DPRK facilities subject to the freeze included an operational five-megawatt electric experimental graphite-moderated reactor, a reprocessing facility, and a fifty-megawatt electric reactor under construction, all at the Yongbyon Nuclear Research Center, as well as a 200-megawatt electric reactor under construction at Taechon.

In return for the DPRK agreeing to freeze and ultimately dismantle its nuclear program, the United States agreed, as mentioned, to finance and construct in the DPRK two light-water reactors of the South Korean standard nuclear power plant model and to provide the DPRK with an alternative source of energy in the form of 500,000 metric tons of heavy fuel oil each year for heating and electricity production until the first of the reactors was completed. In addition, the United States agreed to conduct its construction activities in a manner that met or exceeded international standards of nuclear safety and environmental protection and to provide for implementation of those and any other measures deemed necessary to accomplish the objectives of the Agreed Framework.

To support those goals, KEDO was established on March 9, 1995, when Japan, the Republic of Korea, and the United States expressed their common desire to implement the key provisions of the Agreed Framework and signed the Agreement on the Establishment of the Korean Peninsula Energy Development Organization.[12] The European Union later joined as a member of the KEDO executive board.

Unable to affect the October HFO shipment, the administration sought to convince its allies and fellow KEDO board members that it did not make sense to continue to provide North Korea with heavy fuel oil. The first step was to convince Japanese and South Korean government representatives at a Trilateral Coordination and Oversight Group (TCOG) meeting in Tokyo November 8–9, 2002, that the appropriate first step was to cut off HFO as soon as possible. The United States pushed for suspension of oil deliveries beginning in November. In the end, the Japanese and South Koreans agreed in principle to support the U.S. proposal but proposed ceasing delivery in December since the November shipment was already under contract and the oil was in transit to North Korea. While both Tokyo and Seoul clearly understood the political and security argument, by then the financial investment in KEDO was considerable and neither government wanted KEDO's action to precipitate a wider crisis.

The financial arrangements governing the light-water reactor project were complex. The basic Agreed Framework was a bilateral U.S.-DPRK understanding, but the United States never intended to fund the LWR project. The United States was able to enlist the support of Seoul to fund 70 percent of the LWR costs while Tokyo agreed to a set figure, the yen equivalent of $1 billion. The combination of the two commitments left the estimated $4.65 billion program perpetually underfunded by 8 percent. For its part, the United States undertook to organize funding for the annual 500,000 metric tons of HFO. The United States paid the entire amount in some years but sought contributions from other nations as the price of oil increased. From 1995 through 2002, the United States provided approximately $350 million for the HFO purchases.

On November 14, 2002, the KEDO executive board met in New York City to discuss suspension of HFO shipments to North Korea beginning with the December shipment and eventually agreed to the proposal. Even though the TCOG had reached a political agreement, it took a full day of talks for KEDO board members, who except for me had not participated in the Tokyo meeting, to agree on the final language for a statement. The difficulty in crafting the statement arose from continuing "kibitzing" from John Rood, the National Security Council counterproliferation staffer mentioned earlier, requiring exceedingly tough language. With little interceding on my behalf by the State Department, I finally refused to take any more calls from the counterproliferation staff, instead requiring the regional directorate, NSC Asian affairs, to act as the clearinghouse for the required language. In addition to the calls from the NSC, I received one from North Korea's UN mission asking for the results of the board's deliberations. Finally, the KEDO executive board issued a statement after 7:00 p.m. that evening condemning North Korea's pursuit of a nuclear weapons program, calling it a challenge to all responsible states to prevent North Korea from acquiring nuclear weapons. The board also demanded that North Korea promptly eliminate its nuclear weapons program in a visible and verifiable manner.[13]

The following day the White House issued a statement welcoming KEDO's suspension of HFO shipments and calling for the elimination of Pyongyang's nuclear program. In contrast to the NSC counterproliferation staff's attempt to craft an extremely tough message to North Korea, the president's own statement, in which he declared that "the United States seeks friendship with the people of North Korea," was full of hope and promise.[14] The White House managed to get a tough statement and action from the KEDO board and to be seen nevertheless as compassionate toward the people of North Korea.

Pyongyang's first indication of how it would ultimately react came in a November 25, 2002, commentary in *Rodong Shinmun* designed in part to reject multilateralism and focus responsibility for resolving the nuclear crisis exclusively on the United States:

> The concerned signatories to the DPRK-U.S. Agreed Framework are not the KEDO but the United States and we. The United States is leading the KEDO. The aforementioned facts show the U.S. Government first having decided to suspend the heavy fuel oil provision to us, and then announcing the decision using the KEDO's name. The United States is trying to cover up their unilateral maneuvers with a so-called wrapping cloth of collective opinion."[15]

On December 12, 2002, Ambassador Pak Gil-yon, the DPRK permanent representative to the United Nations, sent me a letter informing the United States of the DPRK's decision in connection with KEDO's decision to suspend fuel oil shipments. Pak wrote, "The USA has completely broken the Agreed Framework by giving up unilaterally its HFO supply obligation after systematically violating the DPRK-USA Agreed Framework. We have already made clear who is to blame for it. The Government of the Democratic People's Republic of Korea has decided to take measures to fully lift the freeze on our nuclear facilities, which has been in effect on the premise of the 500,000MT of HFO supply per annum under the Agreed Framework and to normalize first the operation of the facilities necessary for power generation."[16]

Action came in late December, when Pyongyang announced the expulsion of IAEA monitors and the removal of the IAEA's monitoring devices at Yongbyon. On January 10, 2003, the DPRK announced its withdrawal from the Treaty on the Non-Proliferation of Nuclear Weapons (NPT) and began the process of restarting its plutonium-based nuclear activities at facilities at Yongbyon. In point of fact, North Korea had started the ninety-day withdrawal process from the NPT ten years earlier. It suspended its withdrawal after eighty-nine days and several hours, when it entered talks with the United States that led to the 1994 Agreed Framework. The January 10 announcement simply restarted the original withdrawal process. From Pyongyang's point of view, it had completed the ninety-day withdrawal notification process in a matter of hours on January 10.

The October confrontation in Pyongyang was the tipping point in relations with North Korea. Under the Clinton administration, which had a process in place to deal with serious breaches by North Korea, the situation had been contained. At the beginning of the Clinton administration, North Korea was estimated to have enough plutonium to make one or two nuclear weapons; at the end of the administration, that estimate had not changed. Now, nineteen months into the Bush administration, the situation had become unconstrained. North Korea had declared its intent to develop nuclear weapons, and there were no spoken or unspoken "red lines" to halt its progress.

To be clear, it was North Korea that started down the path toward uranium enrichment, violating the spirit of the Agreed Framework, and it is North Korea that bears responsibility for that decision. However much Pyongyang did not like or trust the Bush administration, it cannot blame its decision to break with the Agreed Framework on President Bush. On the other hand, it was inexcusable for the administration to sit idly by and allow Pyongyang to announce its forthcoming nuclear weapons program advancements and then watch as it implemented each of its announced steps. The Bush administration was significantly softer on North Korea than the Clinton administration had been. In 1993 President Clinton was prepared to go to war over the prospect of North Korea reprocessing spent fuel to extract plutonium. The Bush administration remained silent as North Korea reprocessed spent fuel and extracted plutonium twice—possibly obtaining enough for eight additional nuclear weapons.

3

Influencing the Bush Team

"Peace Talks" is a Democratic term. This is a Republican administration; we need to think of something different to use.

— *James A. Kelly, assistant secretary of state for*
East Asian and Pacific affairs, May 2001

During the first term of the Bush administration, the number of people in positions of responsibility who had even a modicum of experience regarding North Korea was extremely limited. That was one of the main reasons that I accepted the offer to become the special envoy for the four-party peace talks (see chapter 11 for a description of the four-party peace initiative) as well as the U.S. representative to the Korean Peninsula Energy Development Organization.

I was impressed that the new administration would find value in the experience of someone who had served in the Clinton administration dealing with North Korea. As a career Army officer with extensive experience in Japanese affairs, I had been asked by the Clinton administration to curtail an assignment as the Army attaché in Tokyo to join the Asian Affairs Directorate of the National Security Council in June 1996. I remained on active duty until July 2000, even as I served on the NSC staff. After my retirement, which technically lasted one day, I was rehired as a civilian in the same position. One of the things that I appreciated while serving as a professional public servant during almost five years at the White House was that no one asked me what my political affiliation was. When there were clearly partisan activities at the White House, I was not included. Even when I was promoted to special assistant to the president for national security affairs and senior director for Asian affairs, no one asked whether I was a Democrat or even whether I had voted for President Clinton.

I believed that the same spirit was the rule rather than the exception when I joined the Bush administration. However, when I was nominated by the Bush White House for the rank of ambassador to go along with my duties as special envoy and U.S. representative to KEDO, I was asked to list my political affiliation. I truthfully recorded that I was an independent. The White House certainly has the right to know basic political information about a nominee, but as a politically sheltered Army officer and career public servant, I was just beginning to be introduced to the real world of politics.

During my service in the Clinton administration, I was viewed as somewhat tough on the North Koreans, and I assumed that my reputation was what had made me acceptable to the Bush team. I departed the White House at the end of March 2001 and began my duties at the State Department in April. One of the first indications that there was an "us versus them" mentality came when a former subordinate on the NSC staff began a conversation with me shortly after my arrival at the State Department with "You guys at the State Department." How had I become a member of the "them" category within days of departing the White House? The preconceived notion that anyone working at the State Department was automatically soft on North Korea had, in short order, been instilled into some of the professional staffers by the political appointees of the new Bush administration. It was the conceptual prelude to what everyone would hear after September 11, 2001: "You are either with us, or you are against us."

I have mentioned that I was asked to replace Ambassador Charles Kartman as special envoy for the four-party peace talks, a position that was established following a joint U.S.–South Korean suggestion to hold four-party talks made in April 1996 by President Clinton and the ROK's president, Kim Young-sam. Those talks ultimately broke down, but the position of special envoy continued to be the official interface with North Korea for talks on a variety of issues. The position itself does not require Senate confirmation, but the rank of ambassador, which the White House had nominated me for to go along with it, does. Pending confirmation of my nomination, I had business cards made to reflect the special envoy position. When I gave one of my new cards to a former colleague at the White House, she asked, "Who authorized you to use that title?" I ignored the question but realized that something really was amiss when James A. Kelly, the assistant secretary of state for East Asian and Pacific affairs, walked into my office and asked the same question. He had been called by his counterpart at the White House after my former colleague apparently complained to her boss. He dismissed the fact that both he and the White House had previously agreed to the position and title and said, "'Peace talks' is a Democratic term. This is a Republican administration; we need to think of something different to use." I tossed the box of 500 business cards in the trash. In reality, the position needed a new title to reflect what the job was going to be, not because the old title included the phrase "peace talks"—and thus a Democratic connotation. The new title became special envoy for negotiations with the Democratic People's Republic of Korea.

The change in title required that the White House paperwork be amended before it could be transmitted to the Senate for consideration. As a result, although the White House announced my nomination on July 12, 2001, the paperwork was not sent to the Senate until October 23, 2001. Senate confirmation was given on November 15, 2001. An interesting footnote to the musical chairs involving titles is that when my successor was nominated, his title was changed to "special envoy for six-party talks" and my title was retroactively relabeled on the White House website eighteen months after I resigned to indicate that I also had been nominated as special envoy for six-party talks. One of the primary reasons that I resigned was that I was *not* the special envoy for six-party talks, just as my successor was not permitted to function as the special envoy in charge of negotiations. Joseph DeTrani was chosen to be my successor by Jim Kelly within weeks of my departure at the end of August 2003; however, the White House did not nominate DeTrani for the rank of ambassador until January 14, 2005. He was confirmed by the Senate on March 17, 2005, and resigned at the end of December 2005 to take an intelligence position elsewhere in the administration.

National Security Presidential Directive 1

The National Security Presidential Directive 1 (NSPD 1) establishes the organizational hierarchy of the National Security Council.[1] The NSC Principals Committee (PC) is the cabinet-level interagency forum for consideration of policy issues affecting national security. This is the same system that has been in place since 1989. Regular attendees are the secretary of state, the secretary of the treasury, the secretary of defense, the chief of staff to the president, and the assistant to the president for national security affairs, who serves as chair. Others are invited to attend depending on the topic to be discussed.

The NSC Deputies Committee (DC) serves as the senior sub-cabinet interagency forum for consideration of policy issues affecting national security. The DC can prescribe and review the work of the NSC interagency groups; it also helps ensure that issues brought before the Principals Committee or the NSC have been properly analyzed and prepared for decision.

Management of the development and implementation of national security policies by multiple agencies of the government is the responsibility of the NSC Policy Coordination Committees (PCCs), which also handle day-to-day interagency policy coordination. The committees provide policy analysis for consideration by the more senior committees, the DC and the PC. Each PCC includes representatives from the executive departments, offices, and agencies represented in the DC.

NSPD 1 established six regional PCCs, for Europe and Eurasia, the Western Hemisphere, East Asia, South Asia, the Near East and North Africa, and Africa. Each of the PCCs is chaired by an official of the rank of under secretary or assistant secretary, designated by the secretary of state. Each PCC also has an executive secretary from the staff of the NSC, designated by the national security adviser. The executive secretary assists the PCC chair in scheduling the meetings of the PCC, determining its agenda, recording the actions it takes and the tasks it assigns, and ensuring timely responses to the DC or PC. Each PCC chair, in consultation with the executive secretary, may invite representatives of other executive departments and agencies to attend meetings of the PCC.

NSPD 1 was the product of a few key people who worked on the Bush transition team. When President Bush took office on January 20, 2001, most of the key players on the team joined his administration. One was Robert Joseph, who became senior director for counterproliferation. His close relationship with Condoleezza Rice, the national security adviser, and Stephen Hadley, her deputy, as well as the work that he did during the transition and early in the administration made him one of the most influential people on the NSC staff. Although Bob Joseph had little experience on Asian issues, he staked out North Korea as his turf.

In past administrations, a collegial approach to North Korea among the NSC's counterproliferation (previously "nonproliferation") and Asian affairs sections ensured that a mostly unified approach to North Korea policy prevailed. As the regional office, NSC Asia would take the lead in policy development rather than the counterproliferation office, which is a functional entity. The larger context of relations with allies and others in the region—along with issues such as humanitarian concerns, counterfeiting, and security—dictates that NSC Asian affairs should take the lead, but that was not the case in the first term of the Bush administration, primarily because of the influence of Bob Joseph.

The Players

To understand Joseph's influence, one has to understand the relative lack of influence of the NSC senior director of Asian affairs throughout the first term, when Joseph was senior director of counterproliferation. The first senior director at the start of the Bush administration was a temporary holdover from the Clinton administration—me. I was followed by Torkel Patterson, a good friend, who was originally scheduled (in the grand scheme of personnel maneuvers) to go to the Department of Defense as deputy assistant secretary for East Asia and the Pacific region when Richard Armitage was the presumptive next deputy secretary of defense. That all changed when Armitage and Defense Secretary Rumsfeld had a parting of ways during the interview process. Patterson's consolation prize was a more senior position on the NSC staff. Although extremely well qualified and one of the best Japan hands I have ever known, he served less than a year before resigning for personal reasons.

After a brief and unsuccessful external search for a successor to Patterson beginning in January 2003, national security adviser Condoleezza Rice chose China expert James Moriarty from within the Asian affairs section to be senior director. In January 2004, Michael Green was promoted from within NSC Asia to replace Moriarty. Each of the NSC senior directors for Asian affairs certainly was well qualified, but none had the relationship with Hadley and Rice that Joseph had had; in some cases, they had worked on the NSC staff in positions junior to that of Joseph before becoming his nominal equal in rank. In December 2005, Green departed to join the Center for Strategic and International Studies (CSIS) and Georgetown University. Green's replacement was not named until September 1, 2006.

Although Joseph lacked North Korea experience, he was able to have himself named co-chair of the PCC dealing with North Korea. In practical terms, that meant that he controlled the direction of policy development on North Korea. With Joseph as co-chair, the PCC executive secretary, an NSC member, soon interpreted NSPD 1 as giving the PCC executive secretary a veto over the agenda and the invitees that the State Department's co-chair suggested. The NSC exercised that "right" on more than one occasion, without objection from the State Department.

According to NSPD 1, the East Asia PCC, whose chair was selected by the secretary of state, was responsible for conducting "policy analysis" of North Korean issues for consideration by the DC and PC. What evolved was very different. The NSC counterproliferation section under Joseph, not the State

Department, controlled the writing of policy papers, and NSC Asia attempted to moderate some of the extreme views and recommendations that resulted.

(Fast forward from early 2001 to June 2005. Condoleezza Rice became secretary of state and took Bob Joseph with her. Joseph succeeded John Bolton at the State Department as under secretary of state for arms control and international security. After being sworn in, he arrived at his new office on his first day on the job at 2:45 p.m. By 3:15 p.m., he had called a meeting on North Korea.[2])

Another significant change at the White House was the active involvement of the vice president and his staff in North Korea policy development and discussions. In a January 22, 2001, staff meeting, Steven Hadley, the deputy national security adviser, told senior NSC staff that they and the vice president's staff would be treated as one staff. He directed us to share information and papers with those in the vice president's office who worked on national security issues.

An informal network including Bob Joseph, at the NSC; Douglas Feith, under secretary of defense for policy; John Bolton, under secretary of state for arms control and international security; Eric Edelman of the vice president's office; and J.D. Crouch, assistant secretary for international security policy, formed early in the first term of the Bush administration to develop a common position regarding North Korea, both officially and behind the scenes. These men, with the exception of John Bolton, represented either the stated views or the sympathies of their bosses: the vice president, the president (through the national security adviser and her deputy), and the secretary of defense. Likewise, their staffs enthusiastically represented their views in working group meetings and in day-to-day contacts. Some of the most frustrating meetings that I have attended involved subordinates of Joseph, Edelman, Bolton, and Feith, who could present their boss's point of view but did not have the authority (or perhaps the capacity) to compromise. One of the most maddening rationales that they used to support their position—offered repeatedly by one of Joseph's subordinates, John Rood—was "moral clarity." When challenged on a particular point—or in anticipation of being challenged—Rood would invoke "moral clarity" as the reason that a particular view should become policy. While I applaud both morality and clarity, "moral clarity" is not an adequate excuse for failing to articulate why and how a particular point supports a particular change in policy. More specifically, rather than use the DC or PC process to recommend policy changes, which would have required senior-level discussion, these subordinates often used "moral clarity" as a rationale for introducing new policy in routine talking points or speeches. I considered it an easy way for less-senior officials to present their own points of view as U.S. government policy.

In an address at the New America Foundation on October 19, 2005, Larry Wilkerson, Secretary of State Colin Powell's chief of staff, presented a critical overview of the secretive nature of decisionmaking in the first term of the Bush administration.[3] He cited a cabal composed of Vice President Cheney and Secretary of Defense Rumsfeld, who made decisions in secret that on occasion contradicted the formal decisions arrived at during the process of formulating national security policy. Wilkerson said that he viewed Condoleezza Rice as an extremely weak figure and a failure in her role as balancer of the views and options coming from the various departments for consideration by the president. Wilkerson believes that Rice deliberately decided to side with the president and the decisions of the Cheney-Rumsfeld cabal to build a close relationship with the president. Wilkerson's point was that secret decisionmaking had led to the breakdown of the national security process envisioned in the 1947 National Security Act and greatly weakened the administration and the bureaucratic mechanisms charged with supporting and implementing national security–related decisions.

During the August 2005 Senate recess, the president, using his constitutional authority to make recess appointments (appointments that would require Senate confirmation if the Senate were in session), appointed John Bolton to be the permanent representative of the United States to the United Nations (U.S. ambassador to the UN); Eric Edelman to be the under secretary of defense for policy; and Peter Flory to be assistant secretary of defense for international security policy. Flory had been principal deputy assistant secretary of defense for international security policy. J. D. Crouch was separately appointed deputy national security adviser when Steve Hadley became national security adviser. Former Joseph subordinate John Rood was named senior director for counterproliferation, coming full circle to replace his old boss. Another junior member of the vice president's staff during the first term, Samantha Ravitch, eventually made her way back to the vice president's office in the second term as the senior Asia adviser. These individuals, who previously played a supporting role to the more senior hard-liners who opposed any kind of engagement with North Korea, were now being promoted to key roles in which they could influence North Korea policy in their own right.

Compounding this structural imbalance, which favored hard-liners who inserted themselves in the development of North Korea policy over those whose job it was to develop North Korea policy, was the general lack of knowledge about Korea or Asia within the administration. The one exception was the relatively strong Japan connection of several key people, including Armitage, the deputy secretary of state; Torkel Patterson, NSC Asia senior director; Michael Green, NSC Asia director; and James Kelly, assistant secretary of state. But when it came to Korea—and more specifically to North Korea—there were no experts in government.

The President's Inclination

The administration's lack of Korea experience became evident early, when President Bush made his first telephone call to President Kim Dae-jung of South Korea in February 2001. President Bush was reaching out to world leaders in a deliberate manner, giving priority to U.S. neighbors Canada and Mexico and then to our allied partners. South Korea came fairly early in that sequence. In preparation for the phone call, a short paper was prepared for the president to use in his conversation with President Kim that included proposed talking points about the strength of the alliance and the importance of working together on North Korea policy. The paper was sent to the president through the national security adviser. When President Kim began telling the president about the need to engage North Korea, the president put his hand over the mouthpiece of the telephone and said, "Who is this guy? I can't believe how naïve he is!"

At the conclusion of the call, which he made from the treaty room in his private residence in the White House, he gave Steve Hadley, an Air Force colonel from the situation room who had made sure that the telephone connections were properly made, and me a tour of several of the private rooms. At the end of the short tour we ran into the First Lady. The president began to introduce us, referring first to "Hadley" and "Telephone Boy." I quickly introduced myself for fear of the nickname that I might get tagged with. Later that evening I got a call asking me to write a more expansive paper explaining to the president "who this guy is." I returned to the White House around 11:00 p.m. and had a paper on the national security adviser's desk before she arrived the next morning. The paper explained Kim Dae-jung's background, his role in the political opposition during South Korea's military dictatorships, his imprisonment, and the thirty years he spent preparing to lead South Korea and later engage North Korea through his "Sunshine" policy. It did not change the president's views.

In the epilogue of his book *Bush at War*, Bob Woodward describes an interview he had with the president on August 20, 2002, during which the president volunteered his views on North Korea. That exchange took place after we had learned of the scope of North Korea's highly enriched uranium program, but that concern did not come out in the president's remarks:

> "Let me talk about North Korea." The President sat forward in his chair. I thought he might jump up he became so emotional as he spoke about the North Korean leader. "I loathe Kim Jong Il!" Bush shouted, waving his finger in the air. "I've got a visceral reaction to this guy, because he is starving his people. And I have seen intelligence of these prison camps— they're huge—that he uses to break up families, and to torture people. I am appalled at. . . ." "I'm not foolish," the president continued. "They tell me, we don't need to move too fast, because the financial burdens on people will be immense if we try to—if this guy were to topple. Who would take care of—I just don't buy that. Either you believe in freedom, and want to—and worry about the human condition, or you don't."[4]

The president's exchange with Woodward was telling. The basic "North Korea bad" philosophy that the president brought with him into his presidency had not changed. The president's underlying views of Saddam Hussein and Kim Jong-il were similar: they were failed leaders who had tortured their people. While the description is not inaccurate, it is an inadequate basis for formulating policy. More important was the language that the president used to suggest that his policy was to overthrow Kim. Recognizing that he was speaking on the record, the president stopped short of explicitly declaring regime change to be U.S. policy. In going as far as he did, he volunteered that he understood the arguments that had been presented to him about the enormous cost that South Korea would have to shoulder if North Korea were to collapse and that he rejected the argument. His overriding vision regarding foreign policy was the spread of freedom. That vision was more clearly articulated in his second-term inaugural address in January 2005.

During the course of the first policy review, a few basic tenets were established by the White House–influenced participants: policy was to reflect the ABC (Anything But Clinton) ethos; bad behavior was not to be rewarded; the Agreed Framework was agreed to be a bad deal. Part of the policy review discussion assessed incentives and disincentives to be used in talks with North Korea to encourage Pyongyang to agree to U.S. proposals. An NSC staffer vehemently made the case that since we lacked few real incentives, we should view anything that Pyongyang wanted from us as something to withhold in exchange for something that we wanted from Pyongyang. While there is not much wrong with the basic logic, the application was off the mark: the argument meant that because Pyongyang desired bilateral contact with Washington, we should avoid it. In any case, the actual application of the idea was spotty at best. The formal result of the policy review of June 6, 2001, called for serious discussions between the United States and North Korea.

In seeking a ban on bilateral contacts, hard-liners discouraged practical efforts that could have enhanced U.S. security (see example below). When terrorists struck the World Trade Center and the Pentagon on September 11, 2001, there was, for the most part, a universal outcry of revulsion at the act. On September 12, a spokesman for the DPRK Foreign Ministry responded to the event by saying: "Terrorists' large-scale attacks made on the U.S. by blowing themselves up in planes on Tuesday have caught the international community by great surprise. The very regretful and tragic incident reminds it once again of the gravity of terrorism. As a UN member the DPRK is opposed to all forms of terrorism and whatever support to it and this stance will remain unchanged."[5]

North Korea's inexcusable track record as a sponsor of terrorism, mainly directed toward South Korea, belies that statement. One of the more famous incidents occurred in 1983, when North Korean agents set off a bomb in Rangoon, Burma, meant to kill visiting South Korean president Chun Doo Hwan. Chun's car was delayed in traffic and he escaped injury, but among the twenty-one people killed was South Korea's foreign minister. Then, in 1987, North Korean agents detonated a bomb aboard a Korea Air Line (KAL) aircraft, killing all 115 passengers and crew aboard. However, for whatever reason, Pyongyang seems to have gotten out of the terrorism business and has maintained a relatively clean record since 1987, not counting an occasional military skirmish with South Korea or the unresolved abduction of Japanese citizens.

At the time of the September 11 attacks, I was aboard a KAL aircraft, returning from a visit to Beijing and Seoul. The plane was diverted to Minneapolis–St. Paul. The crew did not explain to the passengers why the plane had been diverted, but when I saw that there was no activity at the airport I knew that something serious had occurred and suspected that the entire air transportation system had been shut down. As we sat on the tarmac, I finally convinced a flight attendant to allow me to monitor a news program from her station and so learned what had happened. Ultimately it would take three days before the KAL flight was allowed to proceed to its Washington, D.C., destination.

Within a couple of days of getting back to work, I told assistant secretary Kelly that we should take advantage of Pyongyang's public remarks opposing terrorism to remind the North Koreans that they signed an agreement with the United States in October 2000 to cooperate on terrorism and that we then should engage them with the objective of determining whether they had any former contacts or current information that would be useful to us in responding to the September 11 attacks. Kelly thought it was a useful idea but wanted me to get interagency approval before acting. I assumed (incorrectly) that this was a "no brainer" and that the desire to go after the terrorists, whatever the route, would take precedence over other considerations regarding any particular views about North Korea. On September 19, I convened an interagency meeting that was attended by officials who normally participated in North Korea issues. Included in the group were representatives from the State Department's counterterrorism office as well as Department of Defense personnel. I was stunned when I was accused of "engineering" an excuse to have bilateral contact with North Korea. The intelligence and counterterrorism representatives seemed to take their cue from the accusation, saying that although they did not know for certain, they doubted that Pyongyang would have any useful information regarding terrorism. The bottom line was that I found unanimous opposition to opening a dialogue with North Korea concerning terrorism because of concern that it would somehow reward Pyongyang with bilateral talks.

After the meeting an Air Force colonel, the Joint Chiefs of Staff (JCS) representative at the meeting, followed me into my office. I told him that I expected him to go back and report to the chairman of the Joint Chiefs that he had voted not to pursue an avenue that might help in the fight against terrorism. He literally slunk out of my office, embarrassed by his decision to join those who had reacted negatively more out of rote rejection of the idea of engaging North Korea than of the utility of my suggestion. Failing to rationally explore all possible avenues that might be beneficial in tracking down terrorists can have significant consequences for the Defense Department, which is charged with prosecuting the global war on terrorism. In this case, it lost an opportunity to see what North Korea had to offer.

The point I would make is that while history is full of examples of rogue nations, despicable leaders, and generally repugnant actions by some governments, Republican and Democratic presidents alike have kept open as many options as possible for changing undesirable behavior or regimes. Take, for example, Ronald Reagan's description of the USSR as an evil empire. Despite his strong convictions and his strong language, he nonetheless met and maintained relations with Soviet leaders. North Korea is not the Soviet Union, but our relations with North Korea exemplify the consequences of refusing to deal realistically with an enemy. The Bush administration wrongly judged that North Korea has an overriding stake in joining the international community of nations and can be forced to alter its behavior without serious direct engagement by the United States.

Engagement with North Korea would have given the United States the opportunity to exert influence on Pyongyang on a regular basis. Admittedly, the players in the Bush administration's first term would have had to have been shown a snapshot of 2006 to fully understand that their rigid policy of refusing to engage North Korea over the next six years would fail miserably and that, as a *New York Times* editorial of September 2, 2006, pointed out, "unless something changes soon, by the end of President Bush's second term North Korea will have produced enough plutonium for 10 or more nuclear weapons while Iran's scientists will be close to mastering the skills needed to build their own. That's quite a legacy for a president sworn to keep the world's most dangerous weapons out of the hands of the world's most dangerous regimes."[6]

4

Establishing a
Multilateral Framework

The talks will not last the scheduled three days. The North will walk out.
—Jack Pritchard, to Larry Wilkerson, chief of staff to Secretary of State
Colin Powell, April 22, 2003

The original rationale for holding six-party talks was negative, not positive. In response to Pyongyang's demand that the United States and North Korea resolve the emerging crisis over uranium enrichment bilaterally, the United States opted to broaden the field of players but refused to deal directly with Pyongyang. Objectively, that was the right decision, but it was based more on a desire not to be seen as repeating the "failure" of the Clinton's administration's Agreed Framework. A multilateral framework that included serious bilateral discussions between the United States and North Korea as an essential component from the very beginning might have worked, but the U.S. objective in taking the multilateral approach was to avoid bilateral contact with Pyongyang.

On January 15, 2003, I was in Seoul for talks with my South Korean counterparts. Deputy secretary of state Richard Armitage had the U.S. embassy track me down because Secretary Powell wanted to transmit a message to the North Koreans. As it turned out, Powell said that it could wait until I returned to Washington and had a chance to talk with him. Armitage repeatedly admonished me not to tell anyone about the upcoming contact with North Korea, stressing that he did not want even members of the department's East Asia bureau to know. The secretary, he said, was "a little out front" on this.

When I reached Chicago on January 15 (U.S. time), I called a colleague on the Korea desk and learned that Armitage had given him a sealed envelope to give to me as soon as I arrived at the department. As I was driving up, Armitage called and instructed me to retrieve the envelope and then report to Secretary Powell. Once I had digested the contents of the envelope, I reported to Secretary Powell, bringing a colleague from the Korea desk with me. With Powell in his office was Marc Grossman, under secretary for political affairs; Grant Green, under secretary for management; and Craig Kelly, Powell's executive assistant. Powell wanted to know whether I had read the contents of the envelope and whether I had seen New Mexico governor Bill Richardson's report to Powell of his recent meetings with the North Korean deputy permanent representative to the United Nations. I had not. He retrieved a file from the floor and told me to make a copy for myself.

Following the meeting, I placed a call to Ambassador Pak Gil-yon. The conversation, which lasted twenty-eight minutes, took place in English. The secretary had asked me whether the North Koreans would keep the call confidential, and while I was inclined to believe that they would, at both the beginning and the end of the call I stressed to Ambassador Pak the importance of maintaining the confidentiality of the conversation. Pak readily agreed.

The main purpose of the call was to convey to Pyongyang that the dynamic in Washington had shifted. Secretary Powell was now in charge of North Korea policy; accordingly, with respect to that policy, Pyongyang should listen only to the president and the secretary of state. I also told Pak that we had heard from Governor Richardson, but I noted that in the future the channel of communications should be government to government rather than through Richardson. Pak said that he fully understood but that he was somewhat confused about contradictory White House and Department of State press statements following remarks by the president and the secretary of state. I stressed to Pak that Pyongyang should pay careful attention to what the president and secretary actually said and not to statements by other members of the administration.

Since I was given strict instructions not to create a record of the conversation in the department's computer system, I made a handwritten report to Powell. When I reported the conversation to him, there was no one else in his office, and afterward I stayed to convey to him my view that Pyongyang had, contrary to our earlier expectations, made a final decision to proceed to produce nuclear weapons—that they were not engaging in a game of brinkmanship for tactical advantage. The secretary looked at me and asked, "For what purpose?" I told him that a combination of factors was involved: the North Korean economy and, especially, our refusal to hold talks with them, combined with Pyongyang's concerns about our perceived hostile policy and remarks that led them to believe that regime survival was at stake. Pyongyang needed some level of assurance that the United States would not move politically or militarily to isolate and threaten the regime. In that regard, the North viewed its acquisition of more than a couple of nuclear weapons as a real deterrence—and deterrence was related to security, which was directly related to regime survival.

I also said that it did not mean that we could not influence their actions. If the North was successful in getting a security guarantee or nonaggression pact, from their point of view it would serve the same objective: security and regime survival. My point was that we should not expect to see a series of decisions separated by pauses before Pyongyang moved on to the next step; the North Koreans had already made the end-game decision, and we would watch it play out on their timetable unless U.S. diplomatic intervention changed their minds.

A week later the secretary directed me to call Ambassador Pak again, this time regarding a variety of issues. I was to tell Pak that the United States had not yet been briefed on Russia's "Package Resolution" to end the North Korean nuclear crisis and reassure the DPRK of its national sovereignty, which deputy foreign minister Alexander Losyukov had delivered to Pyongyang earlier in January. I also was to indicate that we had taken note of the DPRK discussion with the International Atomic Energy Agency (IAEA) in Vienna regarding putting off the next IAEA board of governors meeting. I told Pak that the United States believed that it was essential for the board to meet but that there would be no pressure to have the UN Security Council discuss sanctions against North Korea. And finally, I was to convey our desire for the DPRK to respond positively to a proposal to convene a multilateral meeting of the P5 plus 5 (meaning the five permanent members of the Security Council plus Japan, South Korea, North Korea, Australia, and the European Union) to discuss the nuclear issue. The idea of a multilateral approach originated in the complaint by many Republicans that the Clinton administration's Agreed Framework, bilaterally negotiated with North Korea, was fundamentally flawed because it excluded South Korea. The P5 plus 5 approach, on the other hand, seemed like overcompensation and an overly complicated approach.

In my call to Pak on January 22, 2003, he had said that he had no comment about any of the points but that he needed clarification of what the P5 plus 5 was. I explained Secretary Powell's proposal and noted that Pyongyang was likely to have heard of the proposal already through its contacts with Japan or South Korea. Pak also asked for a copy of remarks made by Powell that Monday at the United Nations and for the transcripts of comments of other U.S.

government officials, including under secretary John Bolton. I reminded Pak that Pyongyang was to pay attention only to the remarks of the president and the secretary of state; therefore, I said, I would not provide transcripts of other government officials' remarks. Pak again said that he understood and would report our conversation to Pyongyang.

Three days later, the North Korean mission in New York requested that I call Ambassador Pak. The conversation lasted four minutes. Pak said that he had been instructed to tell me that Pyongyang had stressed to the Russian special envoy, deputy foreign minister Losyukov, that the nuclear issue must be resolved directly between the United States and the DPRK and that the envoy had expressed a positive attitude toward that position, saying that he would "try to make a success of direct negotiations between the United States and North Korea." Pak's second statement was short and to the point: "Regarding the proposed P5 plus 5 multilateral talks," he said, "we are opposed to multilateral talks and will never attend P5 plus 5 talks."

On January 27, 2003, Secretary Powell had me make another call to Pak. This time I was told to have our embassy in Seoul pass the same information to the South Korean special envoy so that he could make the points to someone in a senior position in North Korea, perhaps even directly to Kim Jong-il. Neither the South Koreans nor Ambassador Pak was aware that we were passing the message through two different channels to double the chances that the full message would be received in Pyongyang. I had four points to make with Pak: first, that we had heard Pyongyang's objections to multilateral talks; second, that the North should understand that holding multilateral talks was not an attempt to isolate them but to involve others who could be helpful and, more important, that the talks presented an opportunity for direct U.S.-DPRK talks; third, that we hoped that Pyongyang would consider the sincerity of the proposal; and fourth, that the United States was open to alternative suggestions by the DPRK involving a multilateral forum. Pak's initial response was "As I told you on January 25, we will never participate in any kind of multilateral talks"; then he added, "I think that is the official position of my government." I reiterated the second point, that multilateral talks were not intended to isolate Pyongyang, and stressed the opportunity that they afforded for direct talks, within a multilateral forum.

On January 28, assistant secretary Jim Kelly told me that Wendy Sherman, a former Department of State counselor, had suggested to deputy secretary Armitage that the department give the North Koreans a courtesy heads-up on the content of the president's State of the Union address as it pertained to North Korea, regardless of whether the news was good or bad. Armitage thought it was a good idea. Kelly had been given a copy of a single page of the latest draft of the address, at the bottom of which was a single paragraph referencing North Korea. Kelly told me that Powell had made a few pen-and-ink edits and that in addition the president had excised the phrase "We have no intention of invading North Korea." To be accurate, the phrase, first used in February 2002 by President Bush in a question-and-answer session at the South Korean Blue House (South Korea's equivalent of the White House), had been used so often as to lack any special significance and would have seemed out of place in the rest of the paragraph. The final version of the State of the Union address had three short paragraphs:

> On the Korean Peninsula, an oppressive regime rules a people living in fear and starvation. Throughout the 1990s, the United States relied on a negotiated framework to keep North Korea from gaining nuclear weapons. We now know that that regime was deceiving the world, and developing those weapons all along. And today the North Korean regime is using its nuclear program to incite fear and seek concessions. America and the world will not be blackmailed.
>
> America is working with the countries of the region—South Korea, Japan, China, and Russia—to find a peaceful solution, and to show the North Korean government that nuclear weapons will bring only isolation, economic stagnation, and continued hardship. The North Korean regime will find respect in the world and revival for its people only when it turns away from its nuclear ambitions.
>
> Our nation and the world must learn the lessons of the Korean Peninsula and not allow an even greater threat to rise up in Iraq. A brutal dictator, with a history of reckless aggression, with ties to terrorism, with great potential wealth, will not be permitted to dominate a vital region and threaten the United States.[1]

On Kelly's instructions, David Straub, the director of Korean affairs, faxed the three paragraphs to Han Song-ryol, the DPRK's deputy representative to the United Nations, shortly before the speech was delivered.

Pyongyang periodically called for direct talks with the United States to resolve the emerging nuclear issue, but one of the best examples of those calls was a March 11, 2003, commentary in *Rodong Shinmun*:

> The world is expressing great concern at how the DPRK-U.S. relations are spreading to a grim state of crisis, and demands that both parties of the DPRK and the United States resolve the nuclear issue on the Korean

peninsula through direct talks. In essence, the multilateral talks, which the United States insists on, are intended to avoid its responsibility as the ringleader that has developed the nuclear issue of the Korean peninsula. Reality shows that only DPRK-U.S. direct negotiations are the most reasonable method in resolving the nuclear issue on the Korean peninsula.[2]

That may have been the closest thing to an official response to the president's State of the Union message.

During a stop in China en route to the inauguration of ROK president Roh Moo-hyun in February 2003, Secretary Powell suggested that Beijing would be well positioned to organize and host multilateral talks involving the United States, China, Japan, and North and South Korea. Powell developed the idea after hearing a proposal to have Tokyo convene a multiparty dialogue in Japan with the United States as an observer; while he found merit in the idea of convening multilateral talks in Asia, he knew that Beijing was a more appropriate host and that the United States would join only as a full participant. The Chinese did not respond directly to the secretary, but they did pursue the suggestion in early March when the former foreign minister, Vice Premier Qian Qichen, went to Pyongyang. When the North Koreans rejected the Chinese offer of five-party talks, Qian revised his suggestion on the spot, offering instead three-party talks involving only the United States, China, and North Korea. However, Pyongyang continued to request bilateral talks through the U.S.-DPRK New York channel. By the second week of April 2003, the back-and-forth in both the New York channel and the Beijing-Pyongyang channel had ended with an agreement to hold trilateral meetings in Beijing later that month.

Officially unknown to the United States at the time but suspected by many was the diplomatic sleight of hand that Beijing had engaged in to get all of the parties to the table. Beijing had quietly promised Pyongyang that if it participated in the talks, it would have an opportunity to have direct, bilateral discussions with the United States during the session. Meanwhile, Beijing was assuring Washington that the talks truly would be trilateral in every sense of the word, not simply a stratagem to get the DPRK and the United States to meet bilaterally.

Given the fact that Pyongyang and Washington were exchanging information through the New York channel, Beijing needed to take control of any conversations dealing with the trilateral talks to preserve its benign deception. Beijing asked Washington to make Beijing the official and only channel of U.S. communications with Pyongyang regarding the trilateral talks. That arrangement was more than satisfactory with Washington, and it marked the beginning of the end of the use of the New York channel for senior-level communications. Washington believed that the path to resolving the North Korean problem lay with the leverage that Beijing had over Pyongyang. That belief, coupled with the fact that the hard-line element within the administration remained uncomfortable with the direct contact that the New York channel represented, led to an easy decision to cede the leading role to Beijing. When Pyongyang sent comments or questions through its UN mission in New York, Washington replied through Beijing.

That arrangement served Beijing's purposes well. It brought the DPRK and United States together in Beijing in April 2003 for an initial round of talks aimed at resolving the emerging nuclear crisis. What Beijing had not bargained for was that the United States continued to use Beijing to avoid talking directly with Pyongyang on issues that were not related to the mechanism or logistics of multilateral talks. The process that led to trilateral talks soon became an impediment to meaningful diplomacy. In the end, what Beijing had hoped for did not occur.

Pyongyang notified Beijing on April 12 that it would accept trilateral talks as described by Beijing. Even though I had been instrumental in getting the North Koreans to agree to the talks through the contacts that Secretary Powell had me make via the New York channel, I was not told of the North Koreans' decision until a regular staff meeting held by assistant secretary James Kelly on April 14. In that meeting Kelly mentioned that in his conversations with Secretary Powell over the previous weekend, Powell had asked why the White House had problems with my being the head of the delegation to the trilateral talks; following that discussion, Kelly said, it was decided that Kelly would lead the delegation instead.

I set up a separate meeting with Kelly to go over the exact nature of the conversation. Apparently, when a cable came in on Saturday morning from Ambassador Sandy Randt in Beijing detailing the North Koreans' agreement to participate in the talks—which were to begin on April 23 with Li Gun, the DPRK's deputy director for American affairs, as its head of delegation—Powell met with Kelly and Richard Armitage. When Powell suggested that I, as special envoy for negotiations with the DPRK, would be the natural choice to lead the U.S. delegation, Armitage and Kelly expressed the view that the White House would object. It seemed that I was viewed as a Clinton holdover, and because I advocated direct dialogue with the DPRK, I was out of favor with the hard-line element that dominated the Bush administration and objected to talks with Pyongyang. Powell accepted Armitage and Kelly's explanation. Just that quickly, I had gone from being instrumental in the process, working closely with Powell to achieve multilateral talks, to being cast aside by my superiors without so much as a peep of an objection from Powell. Adding insult to injury was the fact that no one in the U.S. government had more experience dealing with Li Gun, the designated head of the North Korean delegation, than I did. The Kelly, Armitage, and Powell performance in this case was indicative of the relative weakness of their policy positions compared with those of others in the administration. They chose not to challenge the perception that the White House might object to my being named head of delegation—as my job description actually specified.

Kelly was to depart Washington on April 21 for Beijing, so preparation for the trilateral meeting had to occur the week of April 14–18. I prepared a memo for Kelly outlining the objectives, themes, and goals for the upcoming trilateral talks.[3] Because it would be impossible to achieve consensus on the approach and the objectives of the talks among the different agencies that had declared interests, I also developed a set of instructions that were meant to be given as a directive from the secretary of state to Kelly. Knowing that few would agree to direct, bilateral talks between the U.S. and North Korean delegations, I inserted a commonsense guideline that gave Kelly the authority to have an informal, pull-aside discussion with his North Korea counterpart if, in his judgment, it was warranted. The instructions directed Kelly to inform the rest of his delegation of the contents of any such discussion and report it to Washington.

I gave the completed instructions to Kelly with a game plan that called for him to clear the instructions with Powell and then call a meeting of his delegation to inform them of the directive. Kelly called the meeting, allowing all interested parties to send representatives on April 17; approximately twenty people showed up. However, rather than present them with a cleared set of instructions from Powell, Kelly went over each item to seek the approval of the group before passing the instructions on to the secretary for approval. As anticipated, many of the hard-liners objected to any contact with the North Koreans that could remotely be described as bilateral. The meeting broke up around noon, and by 4:00 p.m. a new set of instructions had been written by National Security Council staff and distributed with the signature of Stephen Hadley, the deputy national security adviser, over the signature block of Condoleezza Rice. The new instructions expressly prohibited Kelly from any bilateral contact with his North Korean counterpart. When I read the new instructions, I sent an e-mail to Larry Wilkerson, Powell's chief of staff, telling him "The talks will not last the scheduled three days. The North will walk out." The next day I submitted my resignation to Secretary Powell.[4]

When the three parties met in late April 2003 in Beijing, the DPRK head of delegation asked to meet bilaterally with the United States delegation, as Pyongyang had been led to believe that it would be able to do. The U.S. delegation, on strict instructions, refused to meet the North Koreans. On the basis of that refusal, the North Koreans ended their participation in the talks and told their Chinese hosts that they were returning to Pyongyang. At a dinner that evening, the North Korean head of delegation, Li Gun, cornered his American counterpart and said, "You have always thought that we had nuclear weapons; well, I am here to tell you that we do. And what we do with them is up to you," implying that Pyongyang would consider proliferating the weapons to a third party. At that time, although Pyongyang was in the middle of reprocessing spent fuel rods that would later yield an additional five to six nuclear weapons' worth of plutonium, North Korea was estimated to have only one or two nuclear weapons.

There were no meetings on the second day of the scheduled three sessions. On the third day, as the U.S. and North Korean delegations were preparing to depart, the Chinese insisted that each pay a farewell courtesy call on the foreign minister. While the North Korean delegation was in the meeting room with the foreign minister, the Chinese hosts maneuvered the American delegation to a waiting area immediately adjacent. When both delegations were properly positioned, the Chinese threw open the doors to the meeting room and ushered the Americans inside with the North Koreans for a final trilateral meeting. Although the "meeting" lasted only minutes, the Chinese were able to describe the overall event as having lasted three days. My prediction was right on the mark.

PART II
Origin of the Six-Party Talks

5

Washington and Seoul: A Falling Out

As I said previously, and especially in my confirmation hearings, we do plan to engage with North Korea to pick up where President Clinton and his administration left off. Some promising elements were left on the table and we will be examining those elements.
—*Secretary of State Colin Powell, at a March 6, 2001, press conference with Swedish foreign minister Anna Lindh*

In discussing the relations between the United States and South Korea, it is worth repeating the comments made by Condoleezza Rice during the presidential campaign in 2000 regarding the importance of working closely with South Korea in dealing with North Korea:

> The regime of Kim Jong Il is so opaque that it is difficult to know its motivations, other than that they are malign. But North Korea also lives outside of the international system. Like East Germany, North Korea is the evil twin of a successful regime just across its border. It must fear its eventual demise from the sheer power and pull of South Korea. Pyongyang, too, has little to gain and everything to lose from engagement in the international economy. The development of WMD thus provides the destructive way out for Kim Jong Il.
>
> President Kim Dae Jung of South Korea is attempting to find a peaceful resolution with the north through engagement. Any U.S. policy toward the north should depend heavily on coordination with Seoul and Tokyo.[1]

Rice seemed to understand that problems involving North Korea and the Korean Peninsula required a South Korean solution or, at the very least, required South Korea to buy into a U.S. solution. Because of the deadly consequences to South Korea of a North Korean military response to actions initiated by the United States, Washington is constrained in undertaking any kind of military option without the full consent of Seoul. During the run-up to North Korea's missile launch on July 4, 2006, there were suggestions that the United States should make a surgical strike on the launch pad and hope that Pyongyang would see the action as limited and having nothing to do with South Korea. That line of thinking was not only foolish, it was dangerous.

It does not take much imagination to understand that Pyongyang could not possibly distinguish between the last round of a limited attack and the beginning of a full-scale military operation to overthrow the "evil" regime of Kim Jong-il. Pyongyang's first reaction could well be to fire the significant amount of artillery it has within range of downtown Seoul. Understandably, Seoul's overwhelming preference is to resolve disputes with North Korea without risking another Korean War.

The Scramble to Be First

For Seoul, the year 2000 ended on a series of rather upbeat notes. President Kim Dae-jung had a remarkable summit meeting with North Korean leader Kim Jong-il in Pyongyang in June; President Clinton had welcomed Vice Marshal Jo Myong-nok, North Korea's envoy, to the White House; Secretary of State Madeleine Albright had traveled to Pyongyang to meet with Kim Jong-il in order to advise Clinton whether he, in turn, should have a summit meeting with Kim Jong-il in Pyongyang; and President Kim was named the 2000 Nobel Peace Prize recipient "for his work for democracy and human rights in South Korea and in East Asia in general, and for peace and reconciliation with North Korea in particular."[2]

While little was known in South Korea about President-elect George W. Bush, a lot was known about Colin Powell because of his high-profile position as chairman of the Joint Chiefs of Staff during the Gulf War and his service as a battalion commander in South Korea. In addition to approving of Bush's choice for secretary of state, the South Koreans liked what they heard from Bush's transition team. The new president was going to give priority to U.S. allies, and while the first calls and visits would be to Mexico and Canada, America's border neighbors, good allies would be rewarded next. China and Russia, on the other hand, would just have to wait. That was good news for Seoul. President Kim wanted to keep the momentum of 2000 going by being one of the very first to offer his congratulations to President Bush and, more important, by being one of the first heads of state to visit Washington as soon as possible after the inauguration.

Bush's call to President Kim Dae-jung is described in chapter 3. I was struck at the time by the sense that President Bush was going through the motions and was not especially interested in engaging Kim in conversation. I was a little surprised that he had such an indignant reaction to President Kim's call for engagement with North Korea. Whoever was responsible for briefing Bush on North Korea during the campaign and transition did such a thorough job of painting North Korea and Kim Jong-il as evil personified that Bush saw no use for those who did not share his newfound hatred of North Korea. However correct the assessment of Kim Jong-il, the intensity with which Bush categorized Kim as evil prevented development of an objective policy that factored in the legitimate views of our ally, South Korea. President Kim Dae-jung was the first but certainly not the last casualty in that regard.

The South Koreans had no way of knowing that President Kim had already made a first and lasting bad impression on President Bush. Quite frankly, I am not sure whether, three weeks into the Bush presidency, any of us who were not in the president's innermost circle realized the depth of animosity that Bush had toward North Korea and, by extension, toward those who favored engagement with North Korea. Undeterred by staff explanations that Washington was unprepared for a summit meeting between Bush and Kim, Seoul pressed until it got a commitment for a short meeting between the presidents in early March 2001.

Not every summit meeting is an occasion for an elaborate state dinner; the type of summit dictates the protocol. A state visit warrants a certain number of days in Blair House, the official guest residence of presidential visitors. Lower down the ladder is a working visit, which does not involve a state dinner but typically may involve an official meeting in the Oval Office for an hour or an hour and a half followed by working lunch in the family dining room in the residence. When Kim Dae-jung made his first visit to Washington as president in June 1997, he was treated to a black-tie state dinner in the East Ballroom, attended by a large number of guests. The South Koreans may have envisioned the same kind of reception by President Bush, but they had to settle for a working visit.

Days after the initial phone conversation between Bush and Kim, the White House spokesman announced that Bush would welcome Kim Dae-jung to Washington for a working visit on March 7, noting the alliance between their nations and their shared security objectives on the Korean Peninsula as well as a broad range of common interests in the Asia-Pacific region. The president was said to be looking forward to discussing those issues and to finding ways to strengthen the alliance and overall bilateral cooperation.[3]

Official statements issued after meetings are usually worked out in advance of the actual meeting by staff of the countries involved, and they rarely provide a true picture of the nature and direction of the relationship. The joint statement following the Bush-Kim meeting on March 7 was no different; it was designed for the domestic audiences of each partner in the alliance. The South Koreans demanded recognition of their engagement policy with North Korea, and the United States demanded an understanding that things were different now and that "new approaches to deterrence and defense," unlike those taken during the Clinton administration, would be required.[4] Such is the nature of joint statements. Given President Bush's true feelings toward Seoul's engagement policy, it is remarkable that he allowed the joint statement to be released at all.

But it does not take public comments to set back a relationship. In the case of South Korea, Seoul had hopes that the Bush administration would pick up where the Clinton administration had left off in dealing with North Korea. That is precisely what Secretary of State Colin Powell signaled to the world, first in his confirmation hearing on January 17, 2001:

> We believe that the reduction of tension between the North and the South is one of the keys to greater peace and stability on the Korean Peninsula, and the opening North-South dialogue that we have been witnessing recently is certainly a positive step in that regard.
>
> Secretary Albright has made me very well aware of the status of our recent discussions with the North Koreans, so we are mindful of all the work that has been done and we will use that work as we review our overall policy on the Peninsula. In the meantime, we will abide and agree to the commitments made under the Agreed Framework, provided that North Korea does the same."[5]

But more relevant to President Kim's visit was Powell's public statement the day before the visit:

> As I said previously, and especially in my confirmation hearings, we do plan to engage with North Korea to pick up where President Clinton and his administration left off. Some promising elements were left on the table and we will be examining those elements. We haven't begun that consultative process yet with the North Koreans because we thought it was important to first talk to our South Korean friends.
>
> And so we are not avoiding North Korea. Quite the contrary, we think we have a lot to offer that regime if they will act in ways that we think are

constructive, ways that reduce the threat of proliferation of weapons of mass destruction and missiles, and ways that help open their society and give transparency into their society. And so in due course you'll hear about our plans, but all of that will flow from the meetings with President Kim Dae Jung tomorrow.[6]

When Powell said that he had found merit in the work of the previous administration and planned to pick up where it was left off, the statement seemed genuine. In addition to whatever briefing Madeleine Albright had provided, a small group of Clinton administration officials, including Wendy Sherman, special adviser to the president and secretary of state for North Korea policy; Ambassador Charles Kartman, special envoy for four-party peace talks; Robert Einhorn, assistant secretary for nonproliferation; and I visited secretary-designate Powell at his home late one evening in December 2000, shortly after the Supreme Court had finally resolved the question of the outcome of the presidential election. The meeting was scheduled so that Condoleezza Rice, the designated national security adviser, could join after flying in from Texas that evening.

Powell invited us to sit around his dining room table, and after it became apparent that Rice had been delayed, he had us begin our presentation on the current state of affairs regarding North Korea without Rice present. We talked for more than an hour before she arrived, then summarized the presentation and answered questions after she arrived. Whether it was because it was his home, because Rice did not have the benefit of the complete presentation, or because he intended to establish a senior-subordinate relationship vis-à-vis Rice, Powell quickly asserted himself, telling us that he believed that a lot of good work had been accomplished and that he was prepared to move forward where we would be leaving off. It was clear to us that Powell was attempting to steer Rice in that direction by making commitments for the incoming administration in her presence without really giving her a chance to speak for herself.

The day after Powell publicly said that he was prepared to pick up where the Clinton administration left off, he was forced to retract his statement, and he jokingly said that he had gotten ahead of his skis.

All in all, President Kim came away from his meeting with Bush feeling humiliated. He had been given only the briefest of time with Bush, his hopes for a sympathetic hearing on his plans for robust engagement with North Korea fell on deaf ears, and whatever encouragement he had received from the appointment of Powell as secretary of state was dashed when Powell was in effect rebuked for stating that there was value in the work of the Clinton administration. In the Bush-Kim meeting, the president told Kim that the United States would not pick up negotiations with North Korea where the Clinton administration had left off.

Compounding the basic problem—that Bush and Kim were on different wave lengths when it came to handling North Korea—was the unforgivable error that President Kim made in publicly siding with President Vladimir Putin of Russia on the importance of preserving the Anti-Ballistic Missile (ABM) Treaty. One of the early policy decisions of the Bush administration was to develop a national missile defense system, an undertaking that required the abrogation of the ABM treaty. The premise of the treaty was that the United States and the Soviet Union would not challenge by developing a ballistic missile defense system the penetration capability of a retaliatory nuclear strike by the other nation. After months of preliminary talks with Russia in the hope of reaching a mutual agreement to set the treaty aside, President Bush made good on his intentions by notifying Russia on December 14, 2001, that the United States was formally withdrawing from the treaty.[7]

That the United States was seriously considering changes to the ABM treaty should not have come as a surprise to the South Koreans. Yet it seems that the seriousness of the Bush administration on this point was lost on key Foreign Ministry staffers who were in charge of preparing President Kim for the visit of President Putin in early March 2001, immediately before Kim's summit meeting with President Bush. In the joint communiqué from the Kim-Putin meeting, the two leaders described the ABM treaty as "a cornerstone of strategic stability."[8] That misstep essentially sealed the fate of the Bush-Kim summit.

Pinning Hopes on the Wrong Candidate

During the South Korean presidential election campaign of 1997, the Clinton administration was adamant about not being seen to endorse any particular candidate. At the time, I was director for Asian affairs on the National Security Council. A few South Korean presidential candidates traveled to Washington to be seen with key administration officials, but we were very clear about denying them access to the White House. However, in one instance, we were no match for the persistence of the candidates and the craftiness of President Clinton's brother, Roger.

I was called to the West Wing to explain to the deputy national security adviser why a member of the South Korean National Assembly had shown up on the president's schedule. In unraveling the mystery, we found that Roger had used his backdoor influence to get an appointment. At that point the best that we could do to maintain balance and avoid the appearance of playing favorites was to alert the chief of staff and then require, through Roger, that the National Assembly member bring two colleagues from a different political party who were traveling with him. The instructions were clear: all of the visitors were to check into the Southwest visitors' gate, where they would be met by me and cleared by the Secret Service before going in to see the president. At the appointed time, Roger and his National Assembly guest arrived, and Roger assured me that the other two had gotten the message and would be arriving separately at any moment. However, they did not show up, and the president's secretary, Betty Curry, hustled us into the Oval Office in order to maintain the president's schedule. I later found out that Roger had told the other two members to meet at the Southeast gate—ensuring that they would not make the meeting on time.

Unlike the Clinton administration in 1997, the Bush administration made no effort to hide its favorite, conservative Lee Hui-chang, as the South Korean presidential campaign season began in 2002. For the Bush administration, the prospect of working closely and harmoniously with Kim Dae-jung's government for almost two years when their fundamental approaches to North Korea were so diametrically opposed was nothing short of a nightmare. For all practical purposes, the Bush administration decided to wait until President Kim had finished his term in office in February 2003 before paying appropriate attention to the U.S.-ROK alliance. Lee Hui-chang was given full access to Washington insiders and publicly embraced when he traveled to the United States in 2002. But given what was happening in South Korea and in Washington, Washington's embrace was the political kiss of death for Lee. He lost the election.

The Bush administration's rhetoric about North Korea was very disconcerting to South Koreans. For the first time in a long time, citizens in Seoul and elsewhere in South Korea were openly talking about the prospect of a second Korean War. By the time President Bush made his first trip to South Korea in February 2002, his objective for the trip had changed from sending a strong message to Pyongyang to easing the concerns of a visibly upset ally. It was on that trip that Bush first delivered his "The United States has no intention of invading North Korea" message.

In the summer of 2002, two South Korean middle-school girls were killed in a tragic accident involving U.S. military forces. The South Koreans' culture and sense of justice demanded that someone be held accountable for the deaths. A U.S. court-martial found the servicemen involved innocent of wrongdoing, but from the Korean point of view, the United States failed to do the right thing. As much and as often as the U.S. ambassador and the president apologized, it was not enough to head off very large, emotional candlelight demonstrations, which were characterized as anti-American.

In December 2002, following this wave of incident-specific demonstrations of anti-Americanism brought on by the perception that Bush was pushing the peninsula closer to war and by anger that no one had been held accountable for the deaths of the schoolgirls, Roh Moo-hyun emerged as the eventual winner over Lee Hui-chang. In popular (and instant) mythology, Roh was seen as having been elected on a generational wave of anti-Americanism. He perpetuated that view by surrounding himself with young staffers who had little experience in dealing with the United States.

Roh Moo-hyun

In late January 2003, after Roh Moo-hyun had been elected president of South Korea but approximately one month before his inauguration, assistant secretary James Kelly and I paid a him courtesy call. President-elect Roh confided to us that his greatest fear was that he would wake up one morning to find that the United States had taken some unilateral action affecting the Korean Peninsula without his knowledge. A complex combination of factors marked the relationship between the United States and South Korea as Roh took office. The lukewarm relations between Bush and Kim Dae-jung over the previous two years, the South Koreans' increasingly public expressions of anti-Americanism, and the less-than-discreet support that the Bush administration had given to Lee Hui-chang, together with the youth and inexperience of Roh's staff, meant that Washington would closely scrutinize all of Roh's actions from the beginning of his presidency.

Early in 2003, the Department of Defense decided to announce its plans to revamp the U.S. force structure in Asia. The rationale was fairly straightforward: to make U.S. forces in Asia more flexible in a developing security environment that called for more forces to be available on shorter notice instead of being permanently earmarked, as in South Korea, for a single operational plan (the defense of South Korea). The plan had the added benefit of finally relocating the large U.S. military headquarters out of downtown Seoul. The Department of Defense also intended to consolidate a number of U.S. bases in South Korea, creating hubs from which forces could be deployed outside the region if necessary. Part of that plan called for a drawdown in the overall number of troops, from approximately 37,000 to an eventual total of 25,000.

Secretary of Defense Donald Rumsfeld sent Richard Lawless, the deputy assistant secretary of defense for East Asia and the Pacific region, to Seoul to brief the South Koreans on the U.S. decision to draw down forces. In preparation for the trip, Lawless gave a preview of his briefing at the State Department to assistant secretary Jim Kelly and several others. We were struck by the bluntness of the briefing and advised Lawless not to share the troop-reduction numbers on his first trip. We suggested that he concentrate on the intent of the troop adjustments and the U.S. commitment to enhancing U.S. military capabilities on the peninsula, demonstrated by its proposed investment there of $11 billion in new weapons and technology. He could point out that as a natural outcome of this new efficiency, there would be some adjustments to the end strength of the U.S. forces stationed in South Korea. Lawless said that he fully appreciated the advice but that Secretary Rumsfeld was adamant that the South Koreans be given the bottom line on the number of troops to be reduced. The best we could do was to get a commitment from Lawless that he would limit his briefing about the troop reductions to a couple of key advisers in South Korea's Blue House.

The reaction to the briefing was predictable. The South Koreans were stunned. All they focused on was the 33 percent reduction in the number of troops. In time, the information was leaked in both the U.S. and South Korean press and caused a public uproar among Koreans in general. Many Korean National Assembly members traveling to Washington asked me whether the troop reduction was the Bush administration's way of showing its displeasure with Roh and the anti-American sentiment attributed to his administration. The resulting crisis in the alliance was repaired by consultation and agreement at the presidential level that the Department of Defense and the Ministry of Defense would enter into Future of the Alliance (FOTA) talks to achieve consensus on the levels and disposition of U.S. forces on the peninsula. The process allowed each side to preserve its dignity and led to useful discussions on how and when to execute the final agreement. The United States got what it wanted in terms of troop reductions and consolidation, while the South Koreans were able to claim a voice in the process and a delay in the reductions.

The point here is that the Americans failed to include the South Koreans in decisions that had significant security and political ramifications. Once the information became known, the South Koreans suspected the worst—that President Bush had taken political revenge at the expense of a fifty-year security alliance. Some in South Korea, along with most in North Korea, suspected a more dire scenario—that the U.S. was preparing for a preemptive strike against North Korea. Only when both sides essentially started over and entered into active consultations did the suspicions subside.

In late 2004 President Roh made a series of speeches that raised American eyebrows. In Los Angeles in November 2004, en route to the Asia-Pacific Economic Cooperation (APEC) meetings in Santiago, Chile, Roh said, "North Korea professes that nuclear capabilities are a deterrent for defending itself from external aggression. In many cases, it is true that North Korea's claims and allegations are quite hard to believe and give credit to. However, in this particular case it is true and undeniable that there is a considerable element of rationality in North Korea's claims."[9] The United States interpreted that statement as evidence that Roh sided with North Korea. However, after a meeting between Bush and Roh in Santiago, outward appearances indicated that any hurt feelings had been salved. Then, several weeks later in Warsaw, Poland, President Roh said,

> I know that, different from the official position of the U.S. administration, there are a number of people in the United States favoring hard-line approaches. However, they will finally realize there is no other option available but dialogue, should they deal with the problem [responsibly]. Whoever takes charge of the problem will have to take the Korean people's safety and prosperity as a major premise. They cannot pursue only the nuclear dismantlement at the cost of leaving the Korean Peninsula torn into pieces."[10]

Roh's statement was a clear challenge to the Bush administration: the military option was not valid, not as long as Roh was in power. It also says something about how those around President Roh viewed the hard-line element in the Bush administration—they believed that the hard-liners were actively contemplating military options in dealing with North Korea.

When the idea of multilateral talks to resolve the current nuclear crisis, which began in late 2002, first arose, the Roh administration initially talked about playing a mediating role. However well intentioned the offer, the Bush administration reacted angrily at what it thought was an ally working too hard not to displease Pyongyang. The term "moderator" quickly fell by the wayside. In 2005 President Roh tried to define South Korea's role in the region as a "balancer." The best efforts of those around President Roh to explain what he meant by the term were largely ineffective and even confusing. Somehow the impression was created that this new concept represented a move away from the traditional alliance with the United States and an ill-conceived ambition on South Korea's part to move freely among all its neighbors, perhaps playing them off each other and seeking Seoul's interests in the ensuing "balance." Such inferences are misleading and tend to obscure the real intention of South Korea's policymakers.

The best explanation that I have heard of this matter was given to me by a veteran Korea hand.[11] A recreation of that explanation would be something along the lines of the following:

> The inspiration for this new attempt to articulate Korea's role is a robust and strengthening Korean nationalism and specifically a determination that Korea will hold its own among more powerful neighbors— including the United States—in shaping the future of inter-Korean relations and pursuing reunification. The assertion of a leading, or at least a major, role on these issues does contain more than a strain of bristling independence, even truculence, but it represents an adjustment, not a reinvention, of current security and diplomatic arrangements in the region.
>
> Seoul has made it very clear, both in words and actions, that it views its interests, now and in the future, as closely bound up in its core alliance with the United States. For the Koreans, this alliance is necessary but not sufficient to protect their interests. The additional element required is a U.S. strategy that recognizes Korea's desire for continued stability on the peninsula and comity among all nations in the region. Next to conflict on the peninsula, Koreans most fear a division of Northeast Asia into two or more hostile camps. Because Korea is the smallest nation in the area, the Koreans are convinced that their interests would be lost in large-power rivalries under such circumstances. So their objective, given their intention to preserve their close alliance with the United States, is that U.S. power and influence be deployed in a manner that maintains balance and communication among the nations of Northeast Asia. As one Korean leader has often said in meetings with high-ranking visitors from other countries, Korea is always the loser when larger nations quarrel. Korea's security and room for maneuver are served, however, when these powers are in equilibrium and dealing with one another. Korea's hope is that the United States will engineer such a situation.
>
> The Koreans acknowledge the key role of the U.S.-Japan alliance in maintaining regional stability, although Seoul would emphasize the value in containing Japan through such ties. In fact, Seoul's willingness to risk strained bilateral relations with Tokyo and to quarrel over issues from textbooks to Dokto demonstrates that Koreans believe that it is not up

to them to maintain the regional balance. The real Korean fear, however, is that the United States and China will find themselves in a stand-off, with the United States and Japan on one side and perhaps China, North Korea, and Russia on the other. The Koreans believe that such a situation would dash hopes of inter-Korean engagement, reunification, Seoul's eventual mastery of North Korea, and Seoul's ability to take a mature, active role in international diplomacy. Seoul again would be left as a clearly subordinate nation taking direction from stronger countries.

It is to prevent such a development and to preserve space for its own initiatives that Seoul sought to describe a regional dynamic in which it would have positive relations with China and (ideally) North Korea through positive U.S. engagement with these countries. In theory, that scenario could also include Japan, but Seoul believes that in any event the United States will bring Japan into the equation in a useful and not too disruptive manner.

In practice, what this kind of thinking hopes to produce is the avoidance of a division of Northeast Asia into competing camps; the preservation of South Korea's ties to all neighbors; and the reflection of this ideal circumstance, which serves Seoul's interests so well, in the approach of a key ally—the United States—to the countries in the area. In essence, Seoul cannot create this situation, but it can play a role of advocate and lobby others to support its vision.

South Korea cannot maintain balance in Northeast Asia without the United States and knows it. Seoul does not always hear the rhetoric that it wishes to hear about balance in Asia from other quarters, however, and so it has tried to articulate this as its own policy and objective. But the point is to convince others—primarily the United States—who have the power to implement the vision. Seoul's policymakers are not so foolish as to imagine that they alone can create the world that they want if they cannot convince others. That is the objective to which their statements about "balance" are really directed.

The Importance of the Alliance

Most Americans who follow the U.S.-ROK relationship believe that, for all the reasons cited in this chapter and more, the relationship is in serious trouble. Members of the Bush administration bristle at those kinds of remarks, saying that the relationship is solid. In the recent past South Korean officials would privately confide their concerns about the direction of the relationship, but at some point in 2005, Seoul appears to have made a decision to take steps to improve relations. The naming of Ambassador Song Min-soon as deputy foreign minister and chief negotiator in the six-party talks was a positive step that resulted in a true partnership when the United States named Ambassador Christopher Hill as assistant secretary of state and chief negotiator for the United States. Both Hill and Song served as ambassadors in Warsaw at the same time, and their partnership in the six-party process has been humorously referred to as the "Warsaw Pact." Subsequently, Song was promoted to the position of foreign minister. In other personnel moves, Vice Minister Lee Tae-sik became ambassador to the United States and Yu Myung-hwan, second vice minister for foreign affairs, assumed the duties and title of senior, or first, vice minister. About the same time as Lee Tae-sik was appointed ambassador to the United States, Seoul hired a public relations firm to help it get its policy message more clearly across in the United States.

When President Bush traveled to South Korea in mid-November 2005 to attend a meeting of APEC leaders in Busan, he met separately with President Roh. Coming out of that summit was a mutual agreement to hold strategic consultations at the ministerial level. The first meeting was held in Washington on January 19, 2006, between Foreign Minister Ban Ki-moon and Secretary of State Rice. Marring an otherwise gallant attempt to showcase an alliance on the mend was the unfortunate and uncoordinated announcement in Seoul the following day by the governing Uri Party that Seoul would reduce its troop commitment in Iraq of 3,200 soldiers by 1,000 during 2006. Apparently the possibility had been discussed at a lower level between the Ministry of Defense and the Department of Defense, but the information had not made its way to more senior staff who would have recognized the potential political embarrassment and adequately prepared President Bush for the possibility that the information would become public during his trip. According to well-placed South Korean sources, the Ministry of Defense had briefed Uri Party politicians of the planned withdrawal as part of the process to extend legislative authority to keep the remainder of the South Korean force in Iraq for another year. The politicians went directly to a news conference to announce what they had heard without coordinating their actions with President Roh, to the embarrassment of President Bush.

In early December 2005, I visited Seoul and met with several senior government officials. While in the past they had expressed private concerns about the U.S.-ROK relationship, each official went out of his way to convince me that the relationship—from the South Korean point of view—had significantly improved and was indeed on solid ground. It was almost as if President Roh had gathered his senior ministers and outlined a public relations campaign to improve the image of the U.S.-ROK relationship. In fact, the actual campaign had started two years earlier, with the selection of Ban Ki-moon as foreign minister. At the end of 2005, Prime Minister Lee Hae-chan said the relationship was "more stable than ever before." A story in the government-controlled newspaper *Yonhap* citing Lee's comments indicated that the credit should go to Foreign Minister Ban.[12]

In June 2006, amid great angst and speculation that North Korea was on the verge of launching its first long-range missile since 1998, President Bush made several phone calls to key allies and players in an attempt to have them dissuade Pyongyang from going through with the launch. The South Korean press immediately picked on the exclusion of President Roh Moo-hyun from the list of leaders that Bush had consulted. The obvious question on everyone's mind was how Bush could fail to consult with South Korea if he hoped to take coordinated action on North Korea. The concern was that Bush discounted Seoul's ability to dissuade Pyongyang—or worse, that Bush simply did not want to talk to Roh. When the story surfaced in the media, the Blue House moved immediately to downplay the political faux pas by coordinating and announcing a summit meeting between Roh and Bush in mid-September 2006.

In late August 2006, Foreign Minister Ban Ki-moon described the alliance as undergoing an adjustment "unlike any [at any] other time in the past. But the process is going without strain."[13] Ban acknowledged that Washington might have some regrets over the changing situation since many of the issues (wartime control of its forces) were being brought up for the first time in the fifty-year history of the relationship.

Kaesong Industrial Complex

One of the more interesting issues on which Seoul and Washington have not seen eye to eye is the Kaesong industrial park, a South Korean–North Korean joint venture in North Korea. Currently it is in its initial stage, with twenty small and medium-size South Korean businesses operating modern factories that employ approximately 11,000 North Korean workers under South Korean management. Eventually, Seoul envisions a much-expanded complex employing hundreds of thousands of North Korean workers. Seoul sees the success of the Kaesong industrial complex as beneficial in maintaining stable relations with North Korea and considers it a key to the eventual reunification of the peninsula. Seoul has negotiated the right to pay North Korean workers directly, but until regulations and banking facilities are in place at Kaesong, funds are being funneled through official North Korean channels to the workers. To help prevent funds being kept by North Korean officials without the workers' knowledge, South Korean businesses at Kaesong have the workers sign a monthly pay sheet acknowledging the amount that they are supposed to receive. North Korea does keep a percentage for social services, like the taxes deducted from American paychecks. Washington, on the other hand, views wages going to North Korea as money that can be used for Pyongyang's nuclear program. Jay Lefkowitz, the Bush administration's special envoy for human rights for North Korea, has expressed concern that the North Korean workers are little more than slave labor, receiving less than $2 a day even before Pyongyang extracts its social security fees.

The Kaesong disconnect has spilled over to free trade agreement (FTA) negotiations. Seoul wants products manufactured at the Kaesong industrial complex using South Korean content, equipment, and management to be treated as "South Korean" for the purposes of the FTA. Getting the United States to acknowledge Kaesong products as South Korean would entice additional small and medium-size businesses to begin operations at Kaesong. Washington's position, however, is that products made in North Korea by North Korean labor (under slave labor conditions) cannot be accepted as South Korean–made for FTA purposes.

The irony of the U.S. position is that labor conditions at Kaesong are first rate. North Korean employees work in a clean, well-lighted, and comfortable South Korean business environment that has only the most modern equipment, in absolutely stark contrast to anything that they have ever experienced in North Korea. If the unspoken U.S. policy is to undermine the regime of Kim Jong-il, there can be no better and faster way than to rapidly expand the North Korean workforce at Kaesong to hundreds of thousands of workers. That number would have to be drawn from all over North Korea, not just from the isolated area around Kaesong. It would not take long before North Korean workers at Kaesong began to seriously question the workers' paradise that they have been led to believe exists in North Korea. Logic would suggest that the Bush administration should be admonishing Seoul for going so slowly in developing Kaesong, welcoming Kaesong products as made in South Korea within FTA negotiations, and generally be doing everything in its power to see that Kaesong succeeds. But no.

6

The Players

Because the U.S. and some Western nations are thinking the North Korean regime must eventually collapse, Pyongyang feels a greater sense of insecurity and crisis. Problems don't get solved if you make value judgments about the North Korean regime. This is key.

—President Roh Moo-hyun of South Korea, on a state visit to France,
December 6, 2004

In chapter 4, I described how Secretary Powell had said to the Chinese that, of the potential hosts, they were in the best position to organize and hold multilateral talks to resolve the North Korean nuclear crisis. Powell was inspired to make that comment during a stopover in Tokyo en route to Beijing, when Japanese diplomats told him that they could organize and host a multilateral meeting. While Powell liked the idea of an Asian capital hosting the talks, he knew that Pyongyang would not be enticed by Japan's offer of leadership. Even though Prime Minister Junichiro Koizumi had made a historic visit to Pyongyang in September 2002, during which North Korean leader Kim Jong-il admitted to the kidnapping of Japanese citizens in the 1980s, there had been an unexpected public backlash in Japan over the unaccounted-for deaths of several of the abductees. That turn of events precipitated a rupture in the emerging renewal of normalization talks between the two countries.

The United States urged China to take a leadership role in getting North Korea to multilateral talks. Up to that point, playing a sustained leadership role in Asia seemed out of character, at best, for China. Beijing was generally passive in diplomatic situations and far more comfortable reacting to events than taking an active role in guiding others toward resolution. Given China's diplomatic preferences, it would have been quite reasonable if Beijing had simply withdrawn from an active role once the initial trilateral talks in April 2003 failed. It would have been perfectly understandable, and no one would have blamed Beijing, especially considering how the United States had pulled the rug out from under the fragile diplomatic house of cards that Beijing had constructed in hopes of getting Washington and Pyongyang to talk to each other. But immediately after the failure of the April 2003 trilateral session, the Chinese sought to initiate another trilateral event rather than walk away from the process. Washington had received approval from Seoul and Tokyo of the first trilateral sessions, from which they had been excluded, but only with the understanding that the talks would be expanded to include them as soon as possible. The United States was concerned that Seoul and Tokyo would be excluded from talks again.

In late July 2003, Beijing sent Vice Foreign Minister Dai Bingguo to Pyongyang and then to Washington to gauge the possibilities and to try to convince Secretary Powell that it was premature to move directly into five-party talks. The Chinese thought that taking a more flexible approach and meeting with the North Koreans in a trilateral setting was the best and perhaps only way to move forward. Out of deference to China for assuming the leadership role that Washington had thrust on Beijing, Powell sought the understanding and permission of his counterparts in Seoul and Tokyo for the United States to attend trilateral meetings once again. Tokyo and Seoul agreed. Powell acquiesced to the Chinese request for trilateral talks, but only on condition that Beijing persuade Pyongyang to expand the talks immediately to include Tokyo and Seoul. Determined that the trilateral and the five-party sessions be seen as and function as a single set of talks, Powell insisted that five-party sessions take place within a day or two of the beginning of the trilateral session. He was afraid that if the trilateral talks were a stand-alone set of talks with a clearly defined end, Pyongyang might not return for five-party talks.

In a telephone conversation with his Russian counterpart, Igor Ivanov, Powell explained how his plan for the transition from trilateral to five-party talks would work. When the Russian foreign minister pointedly asked, "Whose idea was it to exclude Russia?" Powell quickly reformulated his plan to include Moscow as the sixth player.

When this three-, five-, and six-party two-step process was explained to North Korea, Pyongyang simplified matters by making the countersuggestion that we move directly to six-party talks. In doing so, Pyongyang also claimed authorship of the six-party process.

There have been six rounds of talks to date: preliminary three-party talks (April 23–25, 2003) and initial six-party talks (August 27–29, 2003), followed by four more rounds of six-party talks: round 2 (February 25–28, 2004), round 3 (June 23–26, 2004), round 4 (July 26–August 7 and September 13–19, 2005), and round 5 (session 1, November 9–11, 2005; session 2, December 18–22, 2006;

and session 3, February 8–13, 2007). Additional rounds and working groups were scheduled as a result of the February 13, 2007, agreement (see chapter 10).

Japan

Japan has been both a significant and a marginal player in the current nuclear crisis. Its focus on the domestically important abduction issue has led to two visits by Prime Minister Koizumi to Pyongyang and, at one time, to the prospect of a breakthrough in Japan-DPRK relations. Japan's support of the Bush administration's mostly hard-line approach to North Korea on the nuclear issue has sharpened the distinction between the U.S.-Japan and the U.S.-ROK relationship. In contrast to Seoul, which has been seen as opposing Washington's hard-line policy, Tokyo has been able to coordinate with Washington more effectively and reinforce U.S. policy toward North Korea because of strong Japanese public revulsion over the abduction issue.

It is, however, Tokyo's almost total focus on the abduction issue that has marginalized it in the six-party process. During the fourth round of talks—by all measures the most robust and productive to date—North Korea's head of delegation refused to hold bilateral talks with Japan's head of delegation because the subject inevitably would have been abductions rather than meaningful (and independent) discussion on ways to resolve the nuclear crisis.

During the Clinton administration, when Tokyo and Pyongyang were not talking to each other, the United States would periodically raise with North Korea issues of concern to Tokyo, including the abductions. Tokyo wanted Washington to make any removal of North Korea from the State Department's terrorism list contingent on the resolution of the abduction issue, fearing that if Washington removed Pyongyang from the list then Tokyo would have little, if any, leverage in its attempts to resolve the issue. Inexplicably, Pyongyang has not been motivated to address Japan's concerns by the prospect, once normalization is achieved, of large Japanese reparations for Japan's annexation and occupation of Korea from 1910 until 1945. Toward the end of 2000, as relations between Washington and Pyongyang began to warm, Washington made clear to Tokyo that it would not consider the abductions a constraint to removing Pyongyang from the terrorism list. The rationale was fairly straightforward: North Korea's abduction of Japanese citizens was not part of the initial justification for placing North Korea on the list. That decision was reversed during the Bush administration's first term. Tokyo convinced Washington to officially require resolution of the abduction issue before Pyongyang could be removed from the list.

As good an ally as Tokyo has been to the United States, Tokyo was very secretive when it came to sharing information on its developing relationship with Pyongyang. While at the National Security Council as director of Asian affairs, I made sure that I fully debriefed both my Japanese and South Korean colleagues whenever I had contact with North Korean diplomats. Late in the Clinton administration, I found out from the North Koreans that the Japanese minister for political affairs in Washington had opened a channel of communication with the North Korean mission to the United Nations. In essence, Tokyo had established its own "New York channel." When I asked my Japanese colleagues at the Japanese embassy in Washington about the contact, they were not forthcoming, even though I had openly shared information with them regarding U.S. contact with North Korea. This secrecy continued during the Bush administration.

We knew that Japanese diplomats were periodically meeting with their North Korean counterparts in Beijing throughout the latter part of 2001 and the first half of 2002; however, we did not know the nature of the talks or, as it turned out, the frequency. Occasionally we would ask Hitoshi Tanaka, the director general of the Asian and Oceanian Affairs Bureau, about the contacts, but he would simply say that nothing of interest had transpired and that we could expect him to tell us if anything did. Tanaka further refused to tell us exactly which North Korean he had been meeting with, referring instead only to a mysterious "Mr. X." In mid-summer 2002, Tanaka met with assistant secretary James Kelly over lunch. Tanaka revealed that he had been regularly and secretly meeting with Mr. X in Beijing for almost a year, and he told Kelly that if there was progress in those talks he would need Washington's support.

It was obvious to me from Tanaka's manner and language that something major was about to take place and that Tokyo needed Washington's unconditional support to avoid any political embarrassment. However, in replying to Tanaka, Kelly gave a circumscribed description about the atmosphere in Washington and, whether he meant to or not, threw cold water on Tanaka precisely when, in my opinion, Tanaka was about to reveal the scope and objective of Japan's year-long contacts with North Korea. Tanaka, a seasoned American hand, replied bluntly to Kelly, "What I hear you telling me is that you will not support us." His remark was unusually direct for a Japanese diplomat and caught Kelly off guard. Kelly did his best to undo the damage, to no avail. Tanaka reversed course. Instead of sharing information about what Tokyo had planned, he deflected further discussion about the Japan–North Korea meetings and "promised" to keep us informed if anything important came up.

When deputy secretary of state Richard Armitage was in Tokyo in late August 2002, he was told that Tanaka had arranged a summit meeting between Prime Minister Koizumi and Chairman Kim Jong-il. I believe that Tanaka had intended to tell us of the planned trip six weeks earlier but was turned off by his perception of a lack of unqualified trust and support from the United States. Because of the personal relationship that had developed between Koizumi and Bush, Bush chose to endorse Koizumi's trip to Pyongyang. In a telephone call, Bush was supposed to have given Koizumi enough warning about new U.S. intelligence about North Korea's highly enriched uranium program to prevent him from being blindsided when it eventually became public and Koizumi was questioned about why he traveled to Pyongyang to deal with Kim Jong-il knowing that North Korea had embarked on a secret program to gain nuclear weapons. It is more likely that Bush expressed generalized concern and promised that Ambassador Howard Baker would provide more explicit details in meetings in Tokyo.

Between the announcement of Koizumi's trip to Pyongyang and the actual trip, I had occasion to talk to Hitoshi Tanaka. I told him that in my opinion he would not have set up the meeting between Koizumi and Kim Jong-il unless the outcome had been pre-negotiated and it would be favorable to Tokyo. Tanaka remarked, "You know how these things work," but he refused to reveal the intended outcome of the trip in advance of Koizumi's visit to Pyongyang. Even though I assumed that Pyongyang had agreed to address Japanese concerns over past abductions, I am not sure that Tanaka would have guessed that Kim Jong-il would apologize for the abductions, which had taken place while his father, the Great Leader, was in charge.

The exuberance that all of Japan felt following Koizumi's trip over the prospect of a final accounting regarding the abduction cases did not last long. North Korea's claim that only five abductees remained alive; that the others had died, some on the same day; and that some of the graves had been washed away during severe storms led to a public backlash and a hardening of attitudes in Japan toward North Korea. Just as there was a hard-line element in the Bush administration that affected U.S. policy toward North Korea, there developed a similar hard-line element in Koizumi's administration that pushed for containment of and confrontation with North Korea. Koizumi, for his part, continued to look for ways to achieve normalization of relations between Tokyo and Pyongyang.

After his second trip to Pyongyang in May 2004, Koizumi advised President Bush during the June G-8 meeting at Sea Island, Georgia, to formulate a concrete proposal that could serve as the basis for a negotiated settlement of the nuclear crisis during the third round of six-party talks. Koizumi's advice, combined with the political reality that the U.S.–North Korea policy failure could become an issue in the U.S. presidential campaign, led Bush to authorize the presentation of the first U.S. proposal in Beijing during the third round of talks. During the twenty days of negotiations that marked the fourth round of six-party talks (July–September 2005), Japan insisted that its lead negotiator bring up the abductions in its bilateral sessions with North Korea, leading Pyongyang to refuse any such meetings. In stark contrast, numerous bilateral meetings were being held between all other parties involved in the talks. Perhaps it was the absolute lack of contact and progress between Tokyo and Pyongyang at the fourth round that led Japan to modify its approach and reopen the dialogue on normalization with North Korea following the abbreviated fifth round of talks in November 2005. Japanese and North Korean diplomats met in Beijing on December 25, and they agreed "on a new format for bilateral negotiations in which three working groups will separately address diplomatic normalization, the abduction issue and North Korea's nuclear and missile programs."[1]

The on-again, off-again nature of Japan's talks with North Korea and its usefulness in the six-party talks are tied specifically to how well Tokyo believes Pyongyang is responding to its primary domestic concern—resolution of the abduction issue. Unless the Japanese public sees what it considers significant progress on the abductions, the only course of action that Japan is able or inclined to take is to threaten support for the hard-line tendencies of the more conservative elements in its government and in Washington.

China

Each of the participants in the six-party process has different reasons for wanting a successful diplomatic resolution of the North Korean nuclear crisis. In some cases the reason is as simple as the desire to avoid the consequences of diplomatic failure. A person comparing the top five national interest priorities of each nation, except North Korea, could conclude that they were remarkably similar, although the rankings might be different. Of course, each nation develops its own priorities based on its particular situation and objectives. The top priority for the United States is shaped by security concerns in general and concerns about proliferation of weapons of mass destruction in particular. In the post 9-11 environment, the United States is most concerned about the potential threat posed by a nuclear North Korea. While some try to make the case that the United States must look to the future, when North Korea may pose a credible nuclear threat to U.S. territory and interests, the primary concern is that North Korea might transfer nuclear weapons, material, or technology to others, including terrorists, today. Closing down the North Korean nuclear program, therefore, is the top priority of the United States in the six-party talks.

The fact that North Korea successfully detonated its first nuclear device on October 9, 2006, which is discussed in greater detail in chapter 10, does not automatically mean that it now poses a credible nuclear threat to the United States. North Korea still has a way to go in refining its nuclear weapons program. It must fully master the technology necessary to detonate a device of sufficient yield, miniaturize that device in order to mate it to a reliable long-range ballistic missile, and ensure the reliability of its longest-range ballistic missile—something that the July 4, 2006, Taepodong-2 ballistic missile launch failed to do.

In the case of China, proliferation is a concern in general, but because of its long-term relationship with Pyongyang and its assessment of the likelihood that North Korea will transfer nuclear weapons, material, or technology, proliferation is not China's top priority. However, the longer-term consequences of failure to resolve the nuclear issue could conceivably move the issue to a higher position on Beijing's list of vital national interests. For example, if it appeared that Pyongyang intended to maintain its nuclear weapons program indefinitely, causing Tokyo to reconsider its decision not to develop a nuclear weapons program, Beijing might adjust its own approach to North Korea and begin to exert a level of pressure on Pyongyang that it is currently unwilling to exert. If the situation in North Korea led to Taiwan's entry into the nuclear weapons field, Beijing would most certainly act to prevent it by taking measures to quickly end Pyongyang's nuclear program—and by extension, Taiwan's consideration of a nuclear weapons program.

In the aftermath of Pyongyang's October 9 nuclear test, there were calls in Japan for Tokyo to review its self-imposed prohibition concerning the possession and manufacturing of nuclear weapons. By most accounts, the call for a serious discussion of Tokyo's nuclear options has been more academic than policy oriented; as a result, Beijing's calculus of the consequences of a North Korean nuclear program and its impact on China's national interest priorities have not changed.

The relationship between Beijing and Pyongyang is complicated and evolving. Over the years, it often has been described as being as close as "lips and teeth," but the reality is somewhat different. There are, however, elements of closeness between the senior cadre in both militaries, and the party organs of each nation are sympathetic to the other's cause. For example, senior members of the International Department of the Chinese Communist Party with whom I met during a trip to the region immediately before 9-11 told me that basically they understood North Korea's suspicions of the United States. Because North Korea was a small country and the United States was a powerful country, they said, it was incumbent on Washington to make concessions. I had occasion to meet many of the same people three years later, after North Korea's HEU program came to light and after North Korea had withdrawn from the Nuclear Non-Proliferation Treaty and completed the reprocessing of its spent fuel into plutonium. The attitude of the officials was essentially the same: North Korea was the little guy, and they understood the actions that Pyongyang had taken.

My contacts at the Chinese Foreign Ministry did not share the views of their colleagues from the party. They found dealing with Pyongyang exasperating. It was China that had come to the aid of North Korea during the Korean War. It was China that provided significant oil and food aid to North Korea. It was China that was a regional power with international influence, while North Korea was a small, bankrupt, dependent neighbor. Yet Chinese diplomats had to tread cautiously around their North Korean counterparts, who did not take kindly to the slightest pressure from Beijing. Chinese diplomats consistently have described the relationship as important for historical and geographical reasons. They acknowledge that Beijing has some leverage over Pyongyang but note that once that leverage is applied, it is lost.

After North Korea's nuclear test, I met again with many of the same Chinese officials that I had met with in previous visits en route to Pyongyang. Even though the Foreign Ministry officials were annoyed with Pyongyang, the views and attitudes of the party officials had changed very little, suggesting that my analysis of China's relationship with North Korea remained valid even after the nuclear test.

Any conclusion that Beijing does not hold significant leverage over Pyongyang is not quite accurate. However, Beijing may avoid applying too much leverage on Pyongyang for what is only a second-tier national security priority for China (North Korea's nuclear weapons program) because it fears that doing so could have a negative impact on its top national security priority (regional stability).

Nevertheless, Pyongyang is careful not to push Beijing too far, for fear of exhausting Beijing's patience. In early February 2005, when most observers were anticipating resumption of six-party talks, Pyongyang announced that it had no intention of returning to the talks and admitted for the first time that it was manufacturing nuclear weapons. But when Beijing sent a high-level envoy to Pyongyang a few weeks later, Kim Jong-il said that in fact he was prepared to return to talks, under the right circumstances. However, following the fifth round of talks in November 2005, official North Korean statements indicated that as long as the United States continued to impose financial sanctions on Pyongyang, there was no hope for holding another round of talks.

The July 4 missile test and subsequent Chinese participation in the unanimous approval of UN Security Council Resolution 1695 did not alter the fundamentals of the Beijing-Pyongyang relationship. However, prior to North Korea's October 9 nuclear test, it was assumed that such a test would change Pyongyang's relationship with Beijing. China's national security interests would be threatened, and Beijing would act accordingly—something that Pyongyang fully understood. Conventional wisdom suggested that therefore North Korea would not cross the Chinese "red line" and test a nuclear weapon. Unfortunately, Pyongyang apparently decided that the risks were worth taking. Perhaps believing that its survival was in jeopardy—that the pressure from the United States was unrelenting and that it could cause significant economic and political damage to the regime—North Korea may have conducted its October 9 nuclear weapons test in order to get some level of relief and to demonstrate its declared nuclear deterrent capability. Pyongyang may have judged that the inevitable consequences (cessation of Chinese and South Korean aid) would be temporary or that in the final analysis China would never let North Korea collapse. In any case, Pyongyang made the decision to proceed with both a long-range missile test and a more provocative nuclear test in the face of Chinese public and private opposition to both.

It also appears that Pyongyang correctly predicted that Beijing's ire would not lead to regime-threatening actions. While Beijing did vote to impose mandatory sanctions on North Korea in UN Security Council Resolution 1718 (October 14, 2006), it also prevented the Security Council from considering the possibility of military action should North Korea fail to respond to the resolution. In his remarks conveying China's decision to support the resolution, Ambassador Wang Guangya reiterated that sanctions were not the end in themselves and that if Pyongyang complied with the resolution, the council would suspend or lift the sanctions. He then urged other countries to adopt a prudent and responsible attitude and refrain from taking any provocative steps that could intensify the tension.[2]

In mid-January 2006, Kim Jong-il made an unannounced visit to China, where in discussions with President Hu Jintao he repeated his continued support for the six-party talks and his willingness to return "under the right circumstances." What Kim was doing was creating room to maneuver. His purpose in traveling to southern China and visiting high-tech areas was twofold. He had a genuine interest in the Chinese technology sector and wanted his large entourage to see it firsthand, presumably in preparation for any future economic reforms that he may want to initiate. But Kim also was sending a clear signal to Beijing. He was saying, in effect, "I'm on path to emulating Chinese reforms, which is what you wanted, so there is no need for you to join forces with the Americans, who may be looking to change my regime. I also publicly acknowledge your stake in leading the six-party process and will return to talks once you get the Americans back on the reservation."

With his January trip, Kim bought significant time and continued neutrality from the Chinese. Any hope that the United States could use North Korea's obstinacy to garner support in the near term to "punish" Pyongyang for failing to return to talks evaporated. Because of its differences with the United States on relative priorities regarding North Korea's nuclear weapons program and its active leadership role as host of the talks, Beijing is careful to maintain balance in its dealings with Washington and Pyongyang. Favoring either camp could well spell the end of the talks and the beginning of a new phase of confrontation that Beijing might not be able to contain.

South Korea

For South Korea the issue of resolving the North Korean nuclear crisis becomes more complex all the time. It is perhaps a bit simplistic to explain differences in views of the issue in South Korea as the difference between those who experienced the Korean War and those who did not, but the thinking of many Americans about Korea has been shaped by the highly successful television series *M*A*S*H*, which was set during the Korean War. There is a general understanding of deprivation and sacrifice and an appreciation of the U.S. contribution to South Korea among the older generation of Koreans that coincides with what a larger and more diverse demographic segment of the United States perceives to be their nation's due.

But the Korean War ended fifty-four years ago, and the succeeding generations have built a new South Korea. Politically, South Korea has gone from being a military dictatorship to being a firmly established democracy. The country has matured to the point that the Roh Moo-hyun administration has sought to establish a national foreign policy that is more independent of the United States while still staying closely allied to Washington. That has led to some confusion in the United States, where any deviation from close adherence to Washington is seen as ingratitude for all that the United States did during the

Korean War. That simplistic point of view is being replaced by the more serious realization that the Korea of *M*A*S*H* has become the tenth-largest economy in the world, has world-class consumer product companies, and is a leading technology hub. The changes in South Korea affect how it ranks its national security interests. Because tension on the peninsula has a direct influence on South Korea's creditworthiness, Seoul understandably makes maintaining stability a top priority. Moreover, older South Koreans' memories of wartime deprivation and suffering are not shared by today's younger generations, who take their country's affluence for granted, so fewer and fewer Koreans see North Korea as a threat, especially when they cannot comprehend their elders' experiences. However, even with the changing sense of the North Korean threat and the maturing of its foreign policy, Seoul sees overwhelming value in its strategic relationship with the United States.

Nevertheless, an unscientific assessment of how South Koreans and Americans view the health of the alliance reveals a telling difference. In the United States there is a general sense among nongovernment types that the alliance is adrift and headed in the wrong direction. An example of this view was provided by Kurt Campbell, vice president of the Washington-based Center for Strategic and International Studies (CSIS), when he spoke at a seminar hosted by the Korea Economic Institute on February 27, 2006. Campbell said that he was worried about the relationship between the two countries, comparing it to that of a king and queen who live separate lives within their marriage but still make public appearances on the balcony, waving to their subjects below. Campbell explained that ending the alliance was too painful for both Seoul and Washington and that neither side wanted to face that prospect.[3] Though colorful, his example was probably a bit of an exaggeration; nonetheless, it serves to illustrate a general sense among Americans that something is amiss. At the same seminar, Lee Tae-sik, South Korea's ambassador to the United States, acknowledged the relationship had run into problems but maintained that, in a testament to the strength and resilience of the relationship, the problems had been fully addressed and resolved.

This difference in approach to and perception of the alliance is significant. South Korea has, as all sovereign nations do, an obligation to pursue its own national objectives, balancing them, when possible, with the interests of its allies. Maintaining stability on the peninsula and promoting healthy economic development while ensuring national security top Seoul's national objectives. Preserving the nonproliferation regime in general and walking back the North Korean nuclear weapons program in particular are also relatively high on Seoul's list of priorities. In that regard, Seoul seeks to implement an engagement strategy of its own with North Korea that supports its top priorities while simultaneously working with the United States to achieve the common alliance goal of resolving the problem of North Korea's nuclear weapons program. The key to the South Korean approach is balance. In trying to maneuver between its foreign and its domestic policies, Seoul periodically comes into conflict with the United States over specific policy elements. The fact that Seoul and Washington can acknowledge a problem and ultimately find a solution is, according to the Lee Tae-sik view, healthy for the alliance. The same experience, however, may not be viewed in such a mature manner by American officials who fail to understand Seoul's top priorities and demonstrate that failure in their response to issues involving North Korea. Instead of seeing the resolution process as a strengthening of the alliance, Washington views every policy difference as another irritant. The result is a tacit, unacknowledged, drifting apart.

Russia

Russia's participation in the six-party process is rather straightforward. As a former superpower, Moscow is interested in preserving as many of its former prerogatives as possible; being left out is not an attractive option. In addition, President Vladimir Putin has some undefined personal stake in an ill-defined relationship with the DPRK's Kim Jong-il. Putin traveled to Pyongyang and met with Kim in July 2000 en route to the Okinawa round of the G-8 summit, and Kim reciprocated by taking a long train trip across Russia to Moscow in August 2001.

While Russia wants to be seen as a player, its actual performance in the six-party talks has been lackluster. Privately, Russian participants have complained about North Korean intransigence; in public, however, Russia has more often than not appeared to side with Pyongyang or at least to express sympathy for its position. During the recess of the fourth round of six-party talks, a month before agreement had been reached on the inclusion of an light-water reactor in the joint agreement, deputy foreign minister Alexander Alexeyev, Moscow's head of delegation, said that "Russia has always insisted that the DPRK, as a sovereign state, can develop its peaceful nuclear program in keeping with international law."[4] At the time of Alexeyev's remarks, Washington was adamantly opposed to the idea.

Two months earlier, U.S. lawmakers had been questioning the role that Russia was playing in the talks, suggesting that more was expected. In testimony at a Senate hearing, U.S. lead negotiator Chris Hill rhetorically asked, "Are they using all of their leverage?" In an article in the *Wall Street Journal*, Russian officials were quoted as saying that Russia could serve as intermediary, but they insisted that they had far less clout than China. "We're prepared to lend a helping hand to all parties around the table," said a Russian diplomat. "But," he added, "We can't do as much as the Chinese. We are able to explain to our North Korean friends the U.S. approach and position."[5]

North Korea

What Pyongyang has been able to do well has been to play one party off the other, even though the United States, Japan, and South Korea have been on guard to prevent just such an occurrence. On one hand, an element of the Bush administration has taken a hard-line approach to North Korea and Japan has generally accepted that approach; on the other, Seoul has favored a more cautious tack that protects the prospects for longer-term engagement. Pyongyang, therefore, has been able to exploit the policy seams. Pyongyang has been equally adept at assuming a recalcitrant independence throughout the six-party process, yet it knows precisely when and how to reassure Beijing of its fundamental commitment to the denuclearization of the Korean Peninsula while placing the blame for lack of meaningful progress at Washington's doorstep. After the substantive fourth round of talks in September 2005 and a pro-forma three-day fifth round of talks in November, Pyongyang boycotted the process while proclaiming its willingness to return to talks once the United States changed its hostile policy and withdrew financial sanctions associated with the Banco Delta Asia in Macau.[6] In response, Beijing, notwithstanding a certain amount of frustration that it may feel regarding Pyongyang, called on Washington to show more flexibility in order to entice Pyongyang back to the talks.

Keeping track of the national interests and strategic goals that each player has in the six-party process can be a bit confusing, especially when casual observers tend to impose their personal views of what the goals ought to be as they judge the interplay between the players. A simplified "cheat-sheet" listing each nation's desired outcome might look something like the list in the box on page 97.

Comparing Positions

UNITED STATES
—Eliminate North Korea's nuclear weapons program
—Punish North Korea for violations of previous agreements
—Effect regime change

SOUTH KOREA
—Prevent any increase in tension on the peninsula
—Preserve North-South rapprochement gains
—Eliminate North Korea's nuclear weapons program

CHINA
—Preserve peace and stability in the region
—Prevent escalation of tensions outside of six-party talks (that is, keep the United States from taking unilateral action against North Korea)

JAPAN
—Maintain access to North Korea to pursue the abduction issue
—Maintain alliance solidarity with the United States regarding North Korean weapons proliferation

RUSSIA
—Be seen as a Pacific player
—Be positioned, as a supplier of goods and services, to take advantage of economic incentives offered to North Korea in a negotiated settlement

NORTH KOREA
—Manage or limit potential damage from the United States
—Seek direct talks with the United States
—Manipulate China and South Korea to gain objectives with regard to the United States
—Seek security guarantee and economic benefits in exchange for concessions on nuclear weapons program.

PART III
Six-Party Talks

7

Six-Party Talks: A Scorecard

The American policy towards DPRK—this is the main problem we are facing.

—Vice Foreign Minister Wang Yi of China, to reporters after a disappointing first round of six-party talks, September 2, 2003

Almost immediately after the failure of the preliminary three-party talks in April 2003, the Chinese sought to resurrect the process, repeating the three-party formula. By that time, the United States was insisting that any future rounds include the Republic of Korea and Japan. Washington had received approval from Seoul and Tokyo of the first trilateral session, which had excluded them, but with the understanding that the talks would be expanded to include the ROK and Japan as soon as possible. At Moscow's insistence, the United States quickly added Russia to the list of future participants in any multilateral talks. In consultations with Secretary of State Colin Powell in late July 2003, Chinese vice minister Dai Bingguo pushed Washington to accept another round of three-party talks in view of Pyongyang's insistence that it would not attend five- or six-party talks. In consideration of Beijing's efforts, the United States compromised: it could attend an initial three-party session if the session were followed immediately by a full six-party round of talks.

By that time, Secretary Powell had gained the president's approval for the U.S. delegation to have direct contact with North Korea's delegation in a multilateral setting. On August 1, the state-run Korean Central News Agency (KCNA) responded publicly to various formulas that had been proposed to restart talks in Beijing: "Some time ago, the U.S. informed the DPRK through a third party that the DPRK-U.S. bilateral talks may be held within the framework of multilateral talks. At the recent DPRK-U.S. talks, the DPRK put forward a new proposal to have six-party talks without going through the three-party talks and to have the DPRK-U.S. bilateral talks there. The DPRK's proposal is now under discussion."[1]

Six-Party Talks: The First Round

During the first round of six-party talks in late August 2003, the U.S. and DPRK delegations did meet for approximately thirty minutes in a corner of the room used for plenary talks. However, the plenary talks did not go well, and, unable to reach agreement on a joint statement from the six parties, Chinese vice minister Wang Yi was forced to issue a chairman's statement instead:

> The major result coming out of the talks is that all parties share a consensus with the following main points:
>
> — All parties are willing to work for peaceful settlement of the nuclear issue on the Korean Peninsula through dialog, and to safeguard peace and stability and bring about lasting peace on the Peninsula;
>
> — All parties maintain that while a nuclear-free Peninsula should be realized, the DPRK's security concerns and other areas should be considered and solved;
>
> — All parties agree, in principle, to explore and decide on an overall plan for solving the nuclear issue in stages and through synchronous or parallel implementation in a just and reasonable manner;
>
> — All parties agree that in the process of peace talks, any action and word that may escalate or intensify the situation should be avoided;
>
> — All parties agree that dialog should continue to establish trust, reduce differences, and broaden common ground;
>
> — All parties agree that the six-party talks should continue, and the date and venue for the next round of talks should be decided through diplomatic channels as soon as possible."[2]

A couple of days later, when Wang was asked by reporters in Manila what he considered the biggest obstacle to holding the next round of talks, he replied, "The American policy towards DPRK—this is the main problem we are facing."[3] Continuing its active shuttle diplomacy, Beijing attempted to send Vice Premier Wu Bangguo to Pyongyang to convince the North Koreans to continue the multilateral process; however, China was asked twice to postpone his visit until after October 20, 2003. Pyongyang did not want to meet with Beijing before it knew the outcome of President Bush's trip to Asia, which was associated with the Bangkok Asia-Pacific Economic Cooperation (APEC) meeting.

On October 19, President Bush said that he was willing to put in writing the statements that he had been making about not invading North Korea—in other words, that he was willing to examine a possible multilateral, written security guarantee. An unofficial response from Pyongyang came on October 21 in a KCNA broadcast commentary: "It would be a laughing matter, which isn't worth even a glance, if the United States gives us a certain security assurance within the multilateral framework in return for an end to our nuclear weapons program."[4]

By October 25, KCNA carried the official response of the DPRK Foreign Ministry to a question regarding President Bush's intentions: "We are ready to consider Bush's remarks on the 'written assurances of nonaggression' if they are based on the intention to coexist with the DPRK and aimed to play a positive role in realizing the proposal for a package solution on the principle of simultaneous action."[5]

North Korea's statement put Pyongyang in a position to accept Wu Bangguo's request to accede to another round of six-party talks in Beijing without being seen as giving in to Chinese pressure. Beijing began a new round of shuttle diplomacy in November in an attempt to create consensus for a joint statement to be issued at the conclusion of the next round of talks. After failing to get consensus for a joint statement following the August talks, Beijing wanted to ensure success in advance of the next round. The process came to an abrupt halt on December 12, when Vice President Cheney is said to have intervened, insisting that the draft joint statement include certain language calling for the "irreversible" dismantling of North Korea's nuclear program and "verification" that it had been done. He reportedly said, "I have been charged by the president with making sure that none of the tyrannies in the world are negotiated with. We don't negotiate with evil; we defeat it." Any chance that a statement could be agreed upon was in effect killed.[6]

It took another two months before Pyongyang agreed to participate in the February 25–28, 2004, talks. At that time, Pyongyang was uncertain of Washington's motivation and goals for the six-party talks. The case can be made that had Pyongyang believed that Washington could indeed "coexist" with Pyongyang, a negotiated settlement to walk back North Korea's nuclear weapons program might have been a possibility. For North Korea, a security guarantee without a U.S. commitment to normalizing relations would have been meaningless.

Round Two

The first two days of the February 2004 round of talks appeared to take a more positive tone, but on the third day talks again began to break down, over the specifics of a new Chinese proposal for a joint statement. The plenary session on day three broke up after an hour and a half, with the remainder of Friday and Saturday devoted to trying to salvage a statement that could highlight the success of the talks. In the end, there was no agreement, and once again Beijing had to issue a chairman's statement, which included the following elements:

—The Parties agreed that the second round of the six-party talks had launched the discussion on substantive issues, which was beneficial and positive, and that the attitudes of all parties were serious in the discussion. While differences remained, the Parties enhanced their understanding of each other's position through the talks.

—The Parties expressed their commitment to a nuclear-weapon-free Korean Peninsula, and to resolving the nuclear issue peacefully through dialogue in a spirit of mutual respect and consultation on an equal basis, so as to maintain peace and stability on the Korean Peninsula and the region at large.

—The Parties expressed their willingness to coexist peacefully. They agreed to take coordinated steps to address the nuclear issue and the related concerns.

—The Parties agreed to continue the process of the talks and agreed in principle to hold the third round of the six-party talks in Beijing no later than the end of the second quarter of 2004. They agreed to set up a working group in preparation for the plenary session. The terms of reference of the working group will be established through diplomatic channels.[7]

After the conclusion of the February 2004 round of talks, the Russian head of delegation noted the lack of any "practical movement forward so far" and warned that the situation could "assume a dangerous nature": "If the negotiating process is stalled, a number of countries could take certain measures against North Korea, for example, a blockade, which could further exacerbate the political and even military atmosphere on the Korean Peninsula."[8]

In an article in the March 4, 2004, edition of the *Washington Post*, President Bush is cited as having "instructed the U.S. delegation to say the administration's continued support of the six-party process rested on North Korea's commitment to completely, verifiably and irreversibly dismantle its program." The article went on to highlight the implication that all options were still on the table—a not-so-subtle hint that military action was possible if Pyongyang did not admit to its HEU program and commit to dismantling both its plutonium and HEU nuclear weapons programs.

In an apparent effort to keep the prospects for talks alive, Vice Foreign Minister Wang Yi, head of the Chinese delegation, said that all parties should make concerted efforts in three areas:

—First, they should carefully study key standpoints of substantial issues and solutions proposed during the talks, from which they could summarize positive factors.

—Second, a working group should be formed as soon as possible to prepare for the third round of talks.

—Third, the parties should maintain a peaceful environment for the process of talks and avoid words or actions that might intensify differences or provoke other parties.[9]

Round Three

The third round of six-party talks, in late June 2004, was shaping up as critical to further progress. The South Koreans were making progress in their own talks with Pyongyang, Japanese prime minister Koizumi had made a second trip to Pyongyang, and the Chinese had made public comments about the need for greater U.S. flexibility in dealing with North Korea. Had the June round of talks followed the pattern of the previous two, many observers believe that it might have been the end of the multilateral process. However, the Bush administration's concern over continuing international criticism of the U.S. stance, the prospect that North Korea might become an election issue, and, most important, Prime Minister Koizumi's personal appeal to President Bush during the G-8 meeting in early June 2004 at Sea Island, Georgia, led the United States to make its first concrete proposal to resolve the nuclear crisis during the third round of talks.

While Pyongyang eventually rejected the specifics of the U.S. proposal, it initially declared that positive progress had been made. In testimony before the Senate Committee on Foreign Relations, assistant secretary of state James Kelly described the proposal as one in which the United States envisioned giving North Korea a short period of three months to prepare for the dismantling and removal of its nuclear programs. According to Kelly, in that initial period the

DPRK was to provide a complete listing of all its nuclear activities and cease all nuclear operations; permit the securing of all fissile material and the monitoring of all fuel rods; and publicly disclose all nuclear weapons, weapon components, and key centrifuge parts and permit observation of their disablement. Kelly emphasized that North Korea's declaration had to include its uranium enrichment program and existing weapons. Under the U.S. proposal, other parties would take corresponding steps as the DPRK carried out its commitments. One of the provisions of the proposal that Pyongyang found troubling (among many) was that the United States was not to take part in providing heavy fuel oil to North Korea even if Pyongyang agreed to the U.S. approach.[10]

Pyongyang replied, "Clearly expressing once again that the denuclearization of the Korean peninsula is our ultimate goal, we once again made it clear that if the United States gives up its hostile policy against us through action, we will transparently renounce all our nuclear weapons-related programs. We presented a concrete plan on nuclear freeze, on the premise that if the United States withdraws the CVID [complete, verifiable, irreversible dismantlement] demand and accepts our demand for reward."[11] The North Korean proposal for a freeze included all facilities related to nuclear weapons and the plutonium obtained through reprocessing. Pyongyang said that the proposal meant that nuclear weapons would no longer be manufactured, transferred, or tested. The third round ended with both the United States and the DPRK having made proposals but without serious discussion of either.

8

Rounds Four and Five: False Start or Cause for Optimism?

Assistant Secretary Hill did have a bilateral meeting with the North Korean representative. They, I think, he would describe the atmosphere as businesslike. I think that he also pointed out the fact that this was not a negotiating session. We have in the past met with the North Koreans in the context of the six-party talks. That's how I would describe this meeting.
—Sean McCormack, assistant secretary of state for
public affairs, July 25, 2005

After a hiatus of thirteen months, Pyongyang announced on July 8, 2005, that it was ready to return to six-party talks. During that period of inactivity it was generally thought that Pyongyang was waiting to see whether President Bush would lose his reelection bid in November 2004. In September 2004 I met with Pak Gil-yon, the North Korean ambassador to the United Nations, and expressed my belief that because of the U.S. presidential election Pyongyang was not following through on its commitment to meet for a fourth round of talks by the end of September. The ambassador denied any connection between Pyongyang's reluctance to return to the talks and the election.

The rejuvenated talks that took place over a twenty-day period in Beijing beginning in late July 2005 were the result of three critical changes that had occurred within the administration. The first change involved the president and probably a small group of close advisers, who reassessed the administration's North Korea policy over the previous couple of years and reached the obvious conclusion that it had failed. That led to the second change, which was extraordinarily important: the appointment of Condoleezza Rice as secretary of state. In her former role as national security adviser, Rice was not in charge of implementation of the president's foreign policy. But as secretary of state that responsibility and public accountability for the results are part of the job. It is clear that she wanted to succeed in her public role of chief diplomat. The combination of the talks that she had with the president and her ability to understand that the administration had to take a new direction before new results could be expected led to the third change, which for tactical reasons was ultimately the most important: the appointment of Ambassador Chris Hill as the assistant secretary for East Asia and Pacific affairs at the State Department and as the head of delegation for discussions with North Korea on the six-party process.

Chris Hill is a professional diplomat, a career Foreign Service officer whose most recent previous assignment was as ambassador to the Republic of Korea. Previously he had served as ambassador to Poland (2000–2004), ambassador to the Republic of Macedonia (1996–99), and special envoy to Kosovo (1998–99). He also served as special assistant to the president and as senior director for Southeast European affairs in the National Security Council.[1] On February 14, 2005, he was named head of the U.S. delegation to the six-party talks. Hill's qualifications for the job come from his experience in some difficult assignments in Eastern Europe, where he was in charge of or participated in some extraordinarily tough negotiations, including the Dayton Accords. But he has at heart the instinct of a professional negotiator to engage, to look for ways around problems, to seek solutions, to support the policies of the administration as he has been given them, and also to influence the development of those policies.

In addition to the policy review and personnel changes, other events contributed to making the fourth round of talks possible. Constant pressure from China and the need for North Korea to manage its relationship with the Chinese are the fundamental reasons why the North Koreans chose to come back to the talks when they did. Maintaining a relationship with China is fundamental to the national well-being of North Korea. Without it, the very survival of Kim Jong-il's regime would be in question.

I believe that Pyongyang made the decision to announce its return to six-party talks long before Kim Jong-il met with Chung Dong-young, the South Korean unification minister, in June 2005; the North Koreans were simply looking for a way to justify that decision. During his meeting with Chung, Kim Jong-il said that it was his father's deathbed wish that the peninsula be denuclearized. That was extraordinarily important information that he did not have to make public; he chose to do it. Had he not already decided to come back to the talks, he would not have invoked his father's name. He also said that they were prepared to come back to the Nuclear Non-Proliferation Treaty (NPT) and to accept IAEA inspectors. Another event that some point to as an inducement for North Korea to return to talks was South Korea's decision to offer, as part of a potential nuclear settlement, 2 million kilowatts of electricity. While it certainly got the attention of the North Koreans, I do not think that it was an essential part of their decisionmaking process. The South Koreans' provision of 500,000 metric tons of food also was useful, but it was not a significant part of the calculus.

More important is the question of why the North Koreans remained involved at that point. It is one thing to come back to the talks; it is quite another to stay fully engaged. Without doubt, their engagement can be attributed to Chris Hill's conduct and the latitude that he was given to negotiate, which resulted in the first-ever two-week period of talks during the Bush administration. In the previous rounds of talks, the United States had held only cursory meetings with the North Koreans. The trilateral session involving the United States, China, and North Korea in April 2003 and the first three rounds of six-party talks cannot be considered negotiations; actual negotiations can reasonably be described as beginning only with the fourth round. But what changed? If you listened to Secretary Rice when she appeared on the *NewsHour with Jim Lehrer* in the middle of the fourth round of negotiations, you would conclude that the administration had had a consistent policy of direct bilateral dialogue with North Korea throughout:

> *Mr. Lehrer:* Much is being made today over the fact that Secretary Hill has had three one-on-one—at least three one-on-one conversations with the North Korean representative. And this is being seen as a breakthrough policy change by you, that you said, "Okay, it's all right to talk to the North Koreans, one-on-one," and it hadn't been before. Is that a correct reading?
>
> *Secretary Rice:* Jim, I don't know where this comes from because we have always talked to the North Koreans within the context of the six-party talks, one-on-one if necessary in bilaterals. We had bilaterals also with the South Koreans. We have had bilaterals with the Chinese. It is not unusual in a negotiation that is multi-partied as this one is to have breakout sessions in which people talk directly. But we have always said that contacts and discussions with the North Koreans, bilaterally in the context of the six-party talks, were just fine. And I believe Jim Kelly had done that on occasion, too.[2]

Rice's remarks lead one to conclude that the administration felt that to accept a compliment on its new, realistic approach to negotiating, it first had to admit to the failure of its North Korea policy over the previous four years. Admitting failure is not in the nature of the Bush administration. And, of course, Secretary Rice's appearance on the *NewsHour* was not meant to be a cross-examination. If it had been, Rice would have been reminded of the National Security Council instructions to Jim Kelly (signed by her deputy, Stephen Hadley, on her behalf) in April 2003 that forbade Kelly from meeting his North Korean counterpart bilaterally under any circumstance.

The decision to engage Pyongyang meant that the administration had to control its rhetoric. When the president referred to North Korean leader Kim Jong-il as "Mister" Kim Jong-il rather than some of the derogatory terms that he had used in the recent past, such as "dictator" and "tyrant," the North Koreans took notice. The United States uses what is referred to as the New York channel for communications between the special envoy for six-party talks or the head of the Korea desk at the State Department and their counterparts at the North Korean UN mission in New York, Pak Gil-yon, the North Korean ambassador to the UN, and Han Song-ryol, the deputy permanent representative. While members of the administration periodically and publicly recite "no hostile intent" or some other catch phrase meant to convey a sense of commitment to diplomacy, Pyongyang routinely dismisses those utterances as lacking authority. Once the decision was made to change administration policy and seriously engage North Korea, Ambassador DeTrani, the special envoy, used the New York channel to convey in an official manner statements that had previously been made in public. Most important, DeTrani repeated, in an official communication, the U.S. recognition of the sovereignty of North Korea. It was one thing to say it; it was another to package it in an official message and present it through official channels to the North Koreans.

In the past the North Koreans have complained bitterly about the lack of direct communications. Too often Pyongyang has had to settle for information from the United States that has been filtered through the Chinese or with hearing about U.S. policy in some public forum. What followed from the DeTrani-Pak meeting was an initiative by Ambassador Hill to create an opportunity for direct contact prior to the announcement of the fourth round of talks.

At the end of June 2005, Li Gun, the DPRK deputy six-party negotiator, participated in a conference organized by Donald Zagoria, a trustee of the National Committee on American Foreign Policy in New York. In a press briefing on June 29, the State Department spokesman had the following exchange with a reporter regarding the possibility of a substantive meeting between DeTrani and Li Gun:

> *Question:* Do you expect them [DeTrani and Foster] to have any dealings with North Korean official Li Gun at the meeting, any substantive exchanges, if I can put it that way?

Mr. McCormack: There are no meetings scheduled with Mr. Li outside the context of the conference. I suspect, since they will be at the conference, that they will be in the same room together but there are no planned meetings or exchanges.[3]

For public relations purposes, DeTrani and Li Gun appeared together on stage during the conference, but unseen was the room set up off stage in which the two met privately two or three times. When DeTrani and Li were meeting privately, Hill telephoned DeTrani on his cell phone at a prearranged time. DeTrani then passed the phone to Li Gun. It was during this "impromptu" telephone call between Hill and Li that the groundwork was set for Hill to meet with his counterpart, Vice Minister Kim Gye-gwan, in Beijing on July 9 in advance of the opening of the fourth round of six-party talks.

That Hill had taken the initiative to get to know his counterpart struck a positive chord with the North Koreans. Until then, they had only second-hand information about Hill. They had followed what he had to say publicly, but now they were going to have an opportunity to meet with him on a professional basis and form their own first-hand impressions. Until that point, the North Koreans were sending mixed signals about the future of the six-party process. On one hand, Kim Jong-il had signaled his readiness to return to talks, but he also was hedging his bets when he confided to South Korean unification minister Chung Dong-young on June 17 that he wanted to wait out the remaining three years of the Bush administration. That attitude seems consistent with more recent revelations about Kim's views on President Bush that were reported in July 2006. In comments to Chinese president Jiang Zemin in September 2001, Kim reportedly said, "I'm weighing whether to make a return visit to South Korea. My visit to the South would show the world that Koreans can settle issues related to the Korean Peninsula by themselves. But the international political atmosphere has changed after the U.S presidential election. It's difficult to forecast what results my return visit would bring."[4]

The relationship between China and North Korea is a complicated one that is not especially well understood by many in the United States. One example of that misunderstanding was the April 26, 2005, suggestion by Ambassador Hill that China shut down its oil pipeline to North Korea to pressure Pyongyang to return to talks. A senior Chinese official rejected the idea outright.[5] The Chinese have their own national security interests, which include a nuclear-weapons-free Korean Peninsula, but that is not their top priority; maintaining stability along their border and in the region is a higher concern. As President Hu Jintao of China said on October 28, 2005, during his first visit to Pyongyang, "China stresses the need to stick to the objective of a nuclear-free peninsula, and stick to a course of dialogue and peaceful resolution, so as to preserve peace and stability on the peninsula and in the region."[6] Beijing has used and will continue to use its influence on Pyongyang to achieve denuclearization, but not at the expense of its top priority. Pushing Pyongyang too far or cutting off oil and food assistance risks creating a dangerous and unstable situation—something that Beijing will not do. In the six-month period from January to June 2005, when Pyongyang had declared itself to be a nuclear weapons state and Washington was sharply criticizing Beijing to increase pressure on Pyongyang, China was, in fact, increasing its exports of oil and food to North Korea—crude oil exports by 45 percent and cereal exports by 96 percent.[7]

The manner in which Ambassador Hill went about his business in both the plenary sessions and the bilateral sessions with the North Koreans during the fourth round of talks kept the North Koreans engaged over the initial thirteen-day period. Before the start of the fourth round, Li Gun, Pyongyang's deputy negotiator, complained bitterly to me in a July 3 meeting in New York about the format of the first three rounds of the six-party talks. The plenary session of the six parties, with their delegations of eight to twelve members and a total of twenty-four interpreters, spent little time in actual negotiations. Each head of delegation, in turn, gave an opening speech. Li Gun and his colleagues, describing how they hated the plenary sessions, said that they were beside themselves: "They just bore us to tears. We know what everybody's position is in terms of their formal statements. We want to get beyond that."

Maintaining the six-party structure but minimizing nonproductive time coincided directly with Ambassador Hill's view of what ought to be done. As a result, the fourth round opened with a thirty-minute meeting, and then the parties moved directly into substantive bilateral discussions. The North Koreans were impressed with this approach and began to talk positively about it.

One of Hill's priorities was to create a statement of basic principles to guide the process that, once agreed to, would not have to be constantly renegotiated or redefined as the talks proceeded. He believed that if everyone could agree on what was important, then what followed in the serious negotiations would come far more rapidly.

After an unprecedented thirteen days of a series of mostly bilateral talks, a recess was called. The Chinese, as hosts, acted as secretariat, producing four drafts of the statement of principles in which they tried to find common language incorporating the points that each of the delegations had emphasized. Toward the end of the first part of the fourth round, around day 10 or 11, Vice

Minister Kim Gye-gwan, North Korea's head of delegation, introduced Pyongyang's demand for a light-water reactor (LWR). Up to that point, the talks had bogged down on the theoretical right of North Korea to have a peaceful nuclear energy program. The initial U.S. position was stated in stark terms: North Korea did not have the right to any kind of nuclear program, peaceful or otherwise. Toward the end of the session, the U.S. position had shifted to the point that the United States accepted North Korea's sovereign right to peaceful nuclear energy once it had dismantled its nuclear weapons programs, rejoined the NPT, and complied with IAEA safeguards; ultimately, however, the United States did not want North Korea to exercise that right—ever.

In the discussions during the first half of the fourth round of talks, the United States downplayed the highly enriched uranium (HEU) issue. In the past, HEU drove the U.S. policy toward North Korea. In this round, the United States briefed the North Koreans and others on the information that it had received from Pakistani scientist A.Q. Khan through the Pakistani government. In a subtle shift, the State Department stopped referring to *highly* enriched uranium and began instead to describe the problem as enriched uranium. From a technical standpoint, enriching uranium to any degree is a violation of the 1992 North-South agreement and would be a violation of Pyongyang's commitment under the NPT. However, the information that the United States received in the summer of 2002 that led to the confrontation with North Korea that October was based on an analysis that found that Pyongyang's uranium enrichment program would lead to an alternative way to produce nuclear weapons. Producing nuclear weapons through the enriched uranium route requires that the uranium be highly enriched. One interpretation of the change in terminology is that the United States was leaving the door open for North Korea to continue to deny having a highly enriched uranium program designed to produce nuclear weapons while allowing it some technical leeway to explain its uranium enrichment equipment in non–nuclear weapons terms. So far Pyongyang has resisted acknowledging any kind of uranium enrichment program. Han Song-ryol, DPRK deputy permanent representative to the United Nations, reiterated Pyongyang's denial when asked about it in an October 27, 2005, interview: "No, it doesn't exist."[8]

Subsuming the explicit U.S. demand that Pyongyang give up its HEU program in generic language requiring the North to give up "all" of its nuclear weapons–related programs is a far better tactic to keep the momentum of the talks moving in the right direction. The time will come when Pyongyang will be required to declare or explain its uranium enrichment program before it can expect to receive any benefits under a settlement.

At the time of the recess of the fourth round, U.S. opposition to Pyongyang's (eventual) right to peaceful nuclear energy placed it in a minority of one and threatened to erase the positive gains that Ambassador Hill had achieved. The more that the United States found itself isolated from its four allies and friends on the issue, the more Pyongyang dug in its heels, demanding the right to generate nuclear energy for peaceful purposes. With little prospect of preventing the emerging deadlock, a recess was called on August 7, with all parties agreeing to resume talks during the week of August 29.

Recess Trip to Pyongyang

John Lewis, a professor emeritus at Stanford University, organized a trip to Pyongyang during the recess, although the trip had been planned in advance of the decision to resume talks. Once the talks got under way, we assumed that they would be over before our trip began. Because the talks were in progress, Lewis sought and received Secretary Rice's "blessing" for the trip. Considering my past experience with and resignation from the administration, I was a little surprised that Rice gave Lewis an unqualified green light for Lewis, Siegfried Hecker, and me to travel to Pyongyang and engage the very negotiators that assistant secretary Hill was negotiating with. My anticipation of reservation on Rice's part was based in part on observations that the same Lewis "team" made in January 2004 on a similar trip to Pyongyang, during which we were allowed to visit North Korea's nuclear facilities at Yongbyon. We were given unprecedented access to the facilities and scientists and shown what the director of the facilities described as plutonium from their most recent reprocessing activities. Hecker later testified before Congress that he believed that the material was in fact plutonium.

When I returned from the January 2004 trip, I published an opinion piece in the *New York Times* in which I said (in part):

> In December 2002 North Korea was suspected of having one or two nuclear weapons that it had acquired before agreeing in 1994 to freeze its known nuclear program and to allow it to be monitored. More than a year later, North Korea may have quadrupled its arsenal of nuclear weapons. During the intervening period, the Bush administration has relied on intelligence that dismissed North Korean claims that it restarted its nuclear program at Yongbyon with the express purpose of reprocessing previously sealed and monitored spent fuel to extract a "nuclear deterrent."

American policy on North Korea is hardly better than American intelligence. At best it can be described only as amateurish. At worst, it is a failed attempt to lure American allies down a path that is not designed to resolve the crisis diplomatically but to lead to the failure and ultimate isolation of North Korea in hopes that its government will collapse. Having a discussion with North Korea does not mean abandoning the multilateral framework agreed to in 1994. Nor does direct communications mean capitulating to North Korean demands. It simply means serious exploration of what is possible and acceptable to all parties.[9]

I knew that the opinion piece would cause the administration discomfort, so I sent an advance copy to then Secretary of State Colin Powell through Larry Wilkerson, his chief of staff. I was later told by Wilkerson that Powell was furious, which might explain some inaccurate remarks about me that Powell later made in an interview with the *Washington Times*.[10] According to Wilkerson, Powell believed that my opinion piece undermined his North Korea policy. So when Secretary Rice approved the August 2005 trip that included me, I was pleasantly surprised.

When our group traveled to Pyongyang, we spent several days in Beijing consulting with key Chinese officials concerning their views on where the six-party process stood. One Chinese official confirmed what we had heard in Washington from U.S. officials involved in the negotiations regarding the collapse of the deputies' working group. Toward the end of the first thirteen days of negotiations, the latest Chinese draft of a statement of principles contained four areas that had been bracketed by either the United States or the North Koreans—meaning that one or both parties had not yet agreed to proposed language in those areas. Joseph DeTrani, the U.S. deputy, and Li Gun, his North Korean counterpart, met on instructions from their respective heads of delegation in an effort to eliminate or reduce the areas of nonagreement. By the end of the deputies' session (which did not include the other deputies from the six parties), the instances of bracketed language had grown exponentially, from four to ten areas of disagreement. Items that had previously been agreed on, or supposedly agreed on, were reopened for debate. U.S. officials blamed an uncooperative Li Gun and North Korean officials blamed the United States for the reversal.

Just before a recess was agreed on, the U.S. negotiator, Chris Hill, upset at what he perceived to be a sleight of hand by Kim Gye-gwan, his North Korean counterpart, refused to meet bilaterally for two days. Kim initially agreed to language encompassing "all nuclear weapons programs," but then changed his definition, informing Hill that North Korea's programs were to be dual use because of hostile U.S. policy. When rumors surfaced that Hill had been prohibited by Washington from meeting with Kim (he had not), Hill resumed bilateral meetings and Kim returned to the original formula, which was that "all meant all." In Pyongyang, Kim gave us a slightly different account of the event:

> In the last several days of the last session, we have accomplished much through direct conversations with the U.S. Just two days before the end of the first session of the fourth round of the talks, however, the direct talks with the U.S. ended. Direct talks are not a gift given to us by the U.S. Hill told me that there was no further reason to have direct talks. I said to him, "Do you want to go back to the starting point? Do you want a go-between? Do you see direct talks as a trick?" When I said this, Hill was embarrassed. In fact, the direct talks allowed us to find out what we had to solve. Our demands became well understood and vice versa. We have—both of us have—a good idea of the ceiling on our demands. I do appreciate Chris Hill. He does want to solve the problem between our two countries.[11]

When we were planning our trip, we did not know that it would occur in the middle of a recess. The group had some concerns about proceeding, but in the end we thought that the trip might be of some use to the administration. When asked for my thoughts about the timing, I wrote to my colleagues:

> As a former negotiator, I would welcome a report from a group of disciplined professionals talking with the North Koreans before the next round of six-party talks. As long as we remember that we are not authorized and should not attempt to negotiate anything on our own, our observations and conversations with key North Koreans may be useful to Ambassador Hill as he prepares and refines his approach to his next official encounter with Kim Gye-gwan. I think we all understand that Pyongyang may try to manipulate our visit to their advantage, but as long as we know that and simply report what is said and add our own observations, Ambassador Hill will be able to separate the wheat from the chaff of any North Korean attempt at manipulation.[12]

We also had a desire to learn as much as we could about Pyongyang's nuclear program in light of the extraordinary access that we were given to their nuclear facilities at Yongbyon in January 2004. Even though we had asked in advance to revisit Yongbyon, we knew from experience that we would not know before we arrived in Pyongyang whether our request would be honored, but because of Sig Hecker's presence on the team, we were hopeful that the response would be positive. When the North Koreans approved Hecker, a former director of the Los Alamos National Laboratory and a plutonium expert, as a member of the January 2004 team, I was reasonably confident that Pyongyang had made a deliberate decision to allow us to visit Yongbyon then; otherwise it made little sense to permit him to travel to North Korea. However, when we arrived in Pyongyang this time, we were told that we could not visit Yongbyon. Instead, we were told that Ri Hong Sop, the director of the nuclear facilities—the same individual with whom we had met in January 2004 and who had shown us almost everything that we asked to see—would come to Pyongyang to meet with us.

Although we were disappointed about not being able to return to Yongbyon, we soon learned the reason why we were denied access. When we met with Ri Hong Sop, he came straight to the point. He would not allow nonstaff personnel to visit the site because of the elevated radiation levels resulting from the reprocessing activities that were then under way. Ri explained that the fuel rods from the five-megawatt electric (5 MWe) reactor, which had run successfully for more than two years starting in January 2003, were unloaded in early April 2005 and reloaded in late May with the remaining fresh fuel that North Korea had kept on hand since the fuel fabrication facilities were shut down under the 1994 Agreed Framework. The reactor began operating again in mid-June at full power. According to Ri, they had begun reprocessing the 8,000 fuel rods, which had spent approximately three months in the cooling pool, in order to extract plutonium in late June and would soon be finished. That was information that the U.S. government did not have, and we immediately conveyed it to Washington when we returned to Beijing on August 27.

It became clear in our discussions with Vice Minister Kim Gye-gwan that Pyongyang was using the recess to harden its negotiating position and wanted to try out—on us—a new formula emphasizing its right to peaceful nuclear energy in general and to a light-water reactor in particular. It also became clear during the first phase of the fourth round of six-party talks that the U.S. insistence that North Korea not have any kind of nuclear program, peaceful or otherwise, was a going-in negotiating position that would not prevail over the long term. While undoubtedly some in the Bush administration held firmly to a core belief that North Korea could not be trusted with any kind of peaceful nuclear program, reality dictated that Washington realize that it was isolated in that view and could not, in the end, prevail.

Shortly after the talks recessed on August 7, 2005, two events occurred that Pyongyang used to justify not returning to the talks on the agreed-to schedule. The first was the announcement by U.S. Forces Korea that an annual joint exercise, Ulchi Focus Lens, would be held from August 15 until September 2. When we first met with Vice Minister Kim on August 24, he intimated that because of the "surprise" announcement of the military exercise, the North Korean delegation would have to wait until the exercise was over before returning to the talks. In Kim's words, they could not be seen as being coerced into attending the talks by the threat posed by U.S.-ROK war games. According to Kim, the Korean People's Army (KPA) took the issue seriously and the Foreign Ministry would have to wait until the conclusion of the exercise to return to talks. I cautioned Kim that whatever goodwill North Korea had accrued over its professional engagement in the talks and its public decision to return to the talks the week of August 29 would be negated by his contrived delay. I went to great lengths to express my disappointment that anyone in the KPA would actually pretend to be surprised by the announcement of a regular exercise that took place each year at the same time.

The other event that displeased Pyongyang was the announcement during the recess of the appointment of Jay Lefkowitz as special envoy on human rights in North Korea. I sarcastically told Kim that he was directly responsible for the appointment of Lefkowitz because the administration had no alternative under the terms of the North Korean Human Rights Act, which had been passed by members of Congress that Kim continued to invite to Pyongyang. (The act required the naming of a human rights envoy and provided for humanitarian funds for nongovernmental organizations that aid North Korean refugees, among other things.)

By the time we met again with Kim on August 26, the KPA had enjoined the Foreign Ministry from returning to six-party talks until the end of a ten-day "penalty" period following the Ulchi Focus Lens exercise. Kim thus was prevented from returning to talks until after September 12. I again complained to Kim that the rationale for delaying the return did not make much sense. I chided him for using the KPA's contrived surprise at the announcement of Ulchi Focus Lens when it was the United States that should have been offended by Pyongyang's decision to reprocess its spent fuel from the 5 MWe reactor to extract plutonium just before and during the fourth round of talks. Kim replied, "You know me to be a reasonable person." I said that I wished that he would be "reasonable sooner rather than later." Nonetheless, the second phase of the fourth round of talks began on September 13.

The most significant discussion that we held with Vice Minister Kim was on the DPRK's energy needs. Kim continued to press Pyongyang's desire for an LWR. He framed it in terms of a negotiating formula: North Korea is a sovereign nation; as a sovereign nation, the DPRK has the right, now and in the future, to peaceful nuclear energy; the United States has expressed its recognition of North Korea's sovereignty; the provision of an LWR by the United States would be proof of U.S. respect for North Korea's sovereignty. Kim stressed that the LWR was the "key to everything." We spent considerable time during the three days of talks presenting our own argument, which held not only that the DPRK did not need an LWR but also that by pursuing an LWR, which would take years to construct, Pyongyang would forgo sources of conventional energy, which could be supplied much more quickly and would be available to support light industry or economic reform projects that much sooner. Our arguments eventually produced a frustrated response from Kim— that the demand for an LWR was a political decision.

Kim Gye-gwan repeatedly emphasized North Korea's "right" to peaceful nuclear energy and said that unless the United States provided Pyongyang with an LWR there would be no deal. I believed that if the DPRK was serious about negotiating away its nuclear weapons program, the LWR would not be the deal breaker that Kim tried to portray it to be. We believed that Kim was using our presence to overemphasize Pyongyang's early (going-in) negotiating position. The LWR may be the only leverage that North Korea has and can link to a "reasonable" demand for peaceful nuclear energy that would resound well with China, Russia, and the ROK. I fully expected that the resumed fourth-round talks would be difficult and possibly end less than ideally.

Round Four, Resumed

When Christopher Hill met with the press before traveling to Beijing for the reconvened fourth round of talks, a reporter asked him, "If it is only a theoretical issue, do you see any possibility that you will agree to disagree and set aside this topic during this round or must it be included in the so-called statement of principles?" Hill was fairly clear in his response: the administration was not interested in entertaining the prospect of a North Korean civilian nuclear program. He said, "Well, I think it has to be addressed and what we're not interested in is really creating ambiguity. Nuclear weapons, nuclear programs are not something that one should leave in an ambiguous state, so—no pun intended. But anyway, the—we have to address these things and we will."[13]

Once the talks began, Hill began to signal a slight change in U.S. policy. When asked about a potential North Korean peaceful nuclear program, he said, "When we can achieve an agreement on that [the dismantlement of the North's nuclear weapons program], and when we do that, we can look at some of these other questions."[14] But by Friday, September 16, the *Washington Post* was reporting that "U.S. and North Korean diplomats acknowledged an irreconcilable deadlock Thursday in long-stalled nuclear disarmament talks, casting doubt on the future of Chinese-sponsored six-party negotiations."[15] The Chinese set a deadline for the negotiators to agree to the latest (fifth) draft of joint statement of principles, but things did not look promising.[16] North Korea held to its demand for an LWR, rejecting South Korea's offer of conventional energy and purportedly threatening to extract additional plutonium if its demands were not met.[17] Frustration was rising. Hill commented, "It has been very obvious to us they are not interested in economic assistance, they seem to be interested in a light water reactor as a sort of trophy."[18]

The Chinese had, in good faith, attempted to find common ground throughout the twenty days of negotiating and on the content of the five drafts. By Friday, September 16, the Chinese were at a crossroads. It seemed as though the North Koreans and the Americans would continue their circular discussion without ever coming to closure, threatening the future of the talks. Beijing has always viewed the six-party process as a commitment, recognizing that it would require many rounds of discussions and perhaps years to yield a successful conclusion, but the prospect of failure loomed large. According to reports coming out of Beijing, the Chinese were prepared to force the hand of both the United States and North Korea, telling the U.S. delegation that it was isolated in its opposition to a future North Korean peaceful nuclear energy program and that if the U.S. did not sign the latest draft—without changes—the United States would be blamed for the breakdown of the talks.[19] The Chinese gave essentially the same message to the North Koreans.

Faced with the prospect of being blamed for its intransigence and the potential failure of the talks, the administration reviewed its options. It would have to come to grips with its opposition to North Korea's demand for an LWR, because the draft declaration included direct reference to an LWR in the first of six points: "The DPRK stated that it has the right to peaceful uses of nuclear energy. The other parties expressed their respect and agreed to discuss at an appropriate time the subject of the provision of light-water reactor to the DPRK."

Secretary Rice was in New York City meeting with her counterparts on the margins of the UN General Assembly meeting. Faced with a tough decision, she came up with a solution that would allow the United States to sign on to the Chinese draft and maintain the momentum of the talks but still allow the United States to parse the diplomatic language publicly in a way that suited its own needs. Rice got her Japanese and Korean counterparts to agree to that approach, although, according to the *New York Times,* the South Koreans were concerned that an explicit U.S. statement (see appendix C) would "sour" the atmosphere.[20]

The case can be made that the South Koreans were correct. A day after the joint statement was agreed to and released in Beijing, Pyongyang issued its own statement:

> As clarified in the joint statement, we will return to the NPT and sign the Safeguards Agreement with the IAEA and comply with it immediately upon the U.S. provision of LWRs, a basis of confidence-building, to us. What is most essential is, therefore, for the U.S. to provide LWRs to the DPRK as early as possible as evidence proving the former's substantial recognition of the latter's nuclear activity for a peaceful purpose. The U.S. should not even dream of the issue of the DPRK's dismantlement of its nuclear deterrent before providing LWRs, a physical guarantee for confidence-building. This is our just and consistent stand. . . . We have so far shaped our policies towards the U.S. hardliners and will do so in the future, too.[21]

In response, assistant secretary Hill said, "They knew exactly what was in the deal. They didn't like some of the aspects of it, but they knew it was a good deal for them and they took it. The fact that they continue to negotiate after the deal is hardly surprising. . . . They're sort of spouting off to internal audiences."[22] There was a certain amount of playing to the domestic audience in the North Korean statement, just as there was in the U.S. statement. I believe that the North Koreans understood the U.S. position, which was that discussion of an LWR would come at an appropriate time and that the appropriate time would come after denuclearization had been verified and Pyongyang had reentered the Non-Proliferation Treaty and was in good standing. What the North Koreans did not understand or expect were much the same things that Chris Hill did not expect when he was given the U.S. statement as a fait accompli.

While the joint statement had no explicit reference to North Korea's uranium enrichment program, an implied reference was embedded in the language. Certainly, "all nuclear weapons and existing nuclear programs" and the reference to the 1992 joint declaration, which explicitly prohibited enriching uranium, were meant to hold North Korea accountable for its uranium enrichment program.

It appears that the U.S. statement was actually written by the more hard-line element in the administration, which was opposed to meaningful engagement with Pyongyang, while Hill was busy negotiating behind the scenes with the Chinese, Russians, Japanese, and South Koreans. Hill was trying to achieve the understanding that if the United States signed the draft joint statement, the others would not undermine the United States by discussing or providing an LWR until after Pyongyang had rejoined the NPT. While Hill was occupied with negotiations in Beijing, Bob Joseph, the under secretary of state for arms control and international security, took the lead in crafting the U.S. statement. The statement defined "appropriate time" as occurring only "when the DPRK has come into full compliance with the NPT and IAEA safeguards, *and has demonstrated a sustained commitment to cooperation and transparency and has ceased proliferating nuclear technology* [emphasis added]." That loophole suggests that the United States alone determines when Pyongyang has reached the appropriate level of "sustained commitment." In other words, not only does North Korea have to return to the NPT and comply with IAEA safeguards, it has to satisfy an arbitrary—and unspecified—goal set by the United States before even a discussion of the subject of the provision of an LWR can take place. The U.S. statement also makes clear that "the DPRK's statement concerning its 'right' to the peaceful uses of nuclear energy should be premised upon completion of verification of the DPRK's elimination of all nuclear weapons and existing nuclear programs and full compliance with the NPT and IAEA safeguards." [23]

The Japanese and South Korean statements reflected the behind-the-scenes diplomacy that Hill was working on. The Japanese statement, issued by Sasae Kenichiro, head of the Japanese delegation, mirrored the basic U.S. definition of what "appropriate time" meant:

> In this regard, let me take this opportunity to clarify the position of my delegation regarding "at an appropriate time" in paragraph 6 of section 1. We believe that it is imperative that the DPRK in the first place abandon all nuclear weapons and existing nuclear programs under credible international verification in order to implement the commitments expressed by the DPRK in this joint statement. It is also imperative that the DPRK fully comply with all the international agreements and norms regarding the use of nuclear energy including the NPT and IAEA safeguards, and build confidence in the international community. When all of the above are met, we will be ready to discuss the subject of the provision of LWR. [24]

The South Korean statement was similar: "An appropriate time related to the provision of LWR . . . will arrive naturally when nuclear weapons and existing programs are dismantled and Pyongyang returns to the NPT and comes into full compliance with IAEA safeguards."

A review of the U.S., Japanese, and ROK statements shows common language where Ambassador Hill worked to reach agreement on the need for Pyongyang to return to the NPT and permit IAEA safeguards to be put in place before an LWR could be discussed. What is prominently different is the added language, written without Hill's input, that is found at the end of the U.S. statement—and not found in any of the other statements—spelling out how the United States defined the term "appropriate time" employed in the September 19 joint statement:

> When the DPRK . . . has demonstrated a sustained commitment to cooperation and transparency and has ceased proliferating nuclear technology.
>
> When these conditions have been met, I want to be very clear—we will support such a discussion.
>
> The United States notes that the NPT recognizes the right of parties to the Treaty to pursue peaceful uses of nuclear energy in the context of compliance with Articles I and II of the Treaty. Foremost among the Treaty's obligations is the commitment not to possess or pursue nuclear weapons. The Treaty also calls for its parties to adhere to safeguards agreements with the IAEA. Thus, the DPRK's statement concerning its "right" to the peaceful uses of nuclear energy should be premised upon the completion of verification of the DPRK's elimination of all nuclear weapons and existing nuclear programs and full compliance with the NPT and IAEA safeguards.
>
> The Joint Statement accurately notes the willingness of the United States to respect the DPRK's sovereignty and to exist with the DPRK peacefully together. Of course, in that context the United States continues to have serious concerns about the treatment of people and behavior in areas such as human rights in the DPRK. The U.S. acceptance of the Joint Statement should in no way be interpreted as meaning we accept all aspects of the DPRK's system, human rights situation or treatment of its people. We intend to sit down and make sure that our concerns in these areas are addressed.
>
> The Joint Statement sets out a visionary view of the end-point of the process of the denuclearization of the Korean Peninsula. It is a very

important first step to get us to the critical and urgent next phase—implementation of DPRK commitments outlined above and the measures the United States and other parties would provide in return, including security assurances, economic and energy cooperation, and taking steps toward normalized relations. [25]

During my tenure as special envoy for negotiations with the DPRK, I repeatedly found instances in which those opposed to engagement with North Korea would try to create policy through talking points or statements without getting explicit approval by the Principals Committee, which is charged with setting U.S. policy. It appears that the U.S. statement issued on September 19 was a successful example of "policy by statement." The compounding result was that Hill was compelled to issue it and then to incorporate it in all future official comments. In his appearance before the House International Relations Committee on October 6, 2005, Hill elaborated on the U.S. understanding of the joint statement, using much of the same language that he used on September 19.

For the first time, the DPRK committed to abandoning all nuclear weapons and existing nuclear programs and returning, at an early date, to the Treaty on the Non-Proliferation of Nuclear Weapons and to IAEA safeguards. The new DPRK commitment is broader in scope than was the case under the Agreed Framework, under which the DPRK agreed to cease a series of defined nuclear activities at specific facilities. While North Korea did freeze its graphite-moderated reactor programs, it subsequently violated the Agreed Framework and the 1992 inter-Korean joint declaration on denuclearizing the Peninsula by pursuing a clandestine uranium enrichment program. Although the DPRK's new pledge to dismantle is unambiguous, the proof of its intent will of course be in the nature of its declaration of nuclear weapons and programs, and then in the speed with which it abandons them.

In my closing statement at the talks, Mr. Chairman, I specified that the DPRK must comprehensively declare, and then completely, verifiably and irreversibly eliminate, all elements of its past and present nuclear programs—plutonium and uranium—and all of its nuclear weapons, and not reconstitute those programs in the future. I made clear that to return to the NPT and come into full compliance with IAEA safeguards, the DPRK would, among other things, need to cooperate on all steps deemed necessary to verify the correctness and completeness of its declarations of nuclear materials and activities. My counterparts from all the other parties to the Six-Party Talks stipulated in their own closing remarks that the signal achievement of the fourth round was the DPRK's commitment to undertake full denuclearization. All my counterparts stressed that it was incumbent on the DPRK to abandon its nuclear status, return to the NPT and abide by IAEA safeguards.

There has been much comment on the DPRK's future right to a civilian nuclear program. The DPRK, in the Joint Statement, asserted that it has the right to peaceful uses of nuclear energy. The other parties took note of this assertion and agreed to discuss, at an appropriate time, the subject of the provision of a light water reactor to the DPRK. We have been crystal clear with respect to when the "appropriate time" would be to discuss with the DPRK. The U.S. will only support such a discussion:

—after the DPRK had promptly eliminated all nuclear weapons and all nuclear programs, and this had been verified to the satisfaction of all parties by credible international means, including the IAEA; and

—after the DPRK had come into full compliance with the NPT and IAEA safeguards, had demonstrated a sustained commitment to cooperation and transparency, and had ceased proliferating nuclear technology. [26]

In a press conference the day after the joint statement was signed, Qin Gang, the Chinese Foreign Ministry spokesman, defined "appropriate time" as requiring further consultation among all six parties.

Question: The joint statement issued yesterday states that the provision of [a] light-water reactor to the DPRK will be discussed at an appropriate time. When will be an "appropriate time" in China's opinion? Now or in the future?

Answer: In the joint statement adopted yesterday, all parties agreed to discuss the issue of providing the DPRK with [a] light-water reactor at an appropriate time. It requires further consultation among the six parties to define when will be the appropriate time. [27]

The Russians were straightforward in their statement concerning North Korea's right to peaceful nuclear energy and did not attempt to clarify what it understood to be an appropriate time.

During the fourth round, the Russian delegation has repeatedly pledged its respect for the right of the DPRK to peaceful nuclear programs and consent to discuss at an appropriate time the subject of the provision of a light-water reactor to Pyongyang. We are satisfied with the fact that, owing to the efforts and goodwill of all the delegations, we have arrived at a compromise formula which guarantees the DPRK's future right to peaceful nuclear programs.[28]

The North Korean position regarding its sovereign right to peaceful nuclear energy was clear during the talks. Pyongyang asserted that as a sovereign nation it had a right then and in the future to peaceful nuclear energy and that that right did not depend on its status in the NPT—much as India, a non-NPT nation, had the right to peaceful nuclear energy. Pyongyang also cited U.S. support to India's peaceful nuclear energy program to bolster its claim.

Compromising on core principles is not conducive to resolving an issue in terms that the compromising party will later find agreeable. While it may have jeopardized the momentum that the Chinese were so desperate to maintain, the appropriate negotiating approach regarding North Korea's demand for an LWR would have been the following:

> *The United States recognizes the right of the DPRK to have peaceful nuclear energy programs, but the United States has no obligation or intention of providing or supporting the provision of LWRs to the DPRK. When the DPRK has denuclearized to international satisfaction and rejoined the NPT in good standing, the United States will not interfere in North Korea's attempt to arrange financing through international financial institutions to build its own LWR— as long as the DPRK remains in good standing with the NPT.*

What the Bush administration has done in agreeing to discuss the provision of LWRs, albeit at an unspecified future date to be determined solely by the United States, is to make North Korea a false promise and give Pyongyang continued negotiating ammunition throughout the six-party talks. My own assessment of Pyongyang's position regarding U.S. provision of an LWR, formulated during discussions with Vice Minister Kim Gye-gwan during our August 2005 trip to Pyongyang, was that it was a tough negotiating ploy that ultimately would be discarded. I conveyed that assessment to Chris Hill on my return to Washington.

Another issue that, without creative interpretation, defies logic is the U.S. agreement in the joint statement to discuss the provision of an LWR at an appropriate time while declaring in the U.S. statement its intent "to terminate KEDO by the end of the year," as it did.[29] The purpose of the Korean Peninsula Energy Development Organization (KEDO) was to build two LWRs for North Korea when certain nonproliferation conditions were satisfied. LWRs are proliferation resistant but not proliferation proof; it is possible to extract fissile material from an LWR. However, the volume of fissile material necessary to create a nuclear weapon would be too great to be delivered by a ballistic missile. Terminating the LWR projects while declaring support for discussion of the provision of an LWR does not make a lot of sense—unless the United States has defined discussion of the provision of an LWR as an academic or diplomatic exercise that will not result in the actual provision of an LWR.

What would have made more sense would have been to preserve KEDO, an international consortium with a track record of negotiating tough protocols with the DPRK. As part of the 1994 Agreed Framework required, KEDO organized the purchase and delivery of heavy fuel oil to North Korea pending the completion of the first of the LWRs. KEDO and its South Korea component in particular might have a role to play in the delivery of conventional energy to North Korea as part of a final solution produced by the six-party talks. Had KEDO not been terminated, it would have been best positioned to complete work on one of the currently suspended LWRs if the six parties ultimately agreed to provide an LWR to North Korea. Terminating KEDO seems to have been more a Bush administration effort to wipe the slate clean of any vestiges of the "Clinton" 1994 Agreed Framework than anything else.

Round Five: Or a False Start?

At the conclusion of the fourth round of talks, Hill made it clear that he would like to visit Pyongyang before the fifth round of talks got under way in November. There were initial rumors that Pyongyang had set conditions that Hill would have to meet before he would be invited to visit. That sounded very unlikely, but in the end it turned out that conditions indeed had been set; unfortunately, they were set by Vice President Cheney. According to usually reliable sources, Hill was told that he had to get something in return for—and in advance of—his visit: Pyongyang had to shut down its operations at Yongbyon. That message was conveyed to the North Koreans through the New York channel. The response from Pyongyang was that shutting down Yongbyon was not an option but that Hill was welcome to visit without preconditions. Hill chose to drop the matter, but he did pick up the new talking point from the vice president's office: Pyongyang should shut down its reprocessing activities at Yongbyon. "The time to stop reprocessing, time to stop that reactor, is now, and once that stops we look forward to the DPRK making a declaration on what it has for nuclear programs and get on to the task of ridding the Korean Peninsula of the very dangerous material," Hill said.[30] By that time, North Korea may well have produced enough plutonium for ten nuclear weapons.

On June 1, 2006, a spokesman for the DPRK Foreign Ministry issued a statement commenting on the deadlocked six-party talks interspersed with comments critical of the United States. Embedded in the statement was Pyongyang's reaffirmation of the September 19 joint statement and a new invitation for Hill to visit Pyongyang:

> The DPRK remains unchanged in its stand and will to sincerely implement the joint statement of the six-party talks and denuclearize the Korean Peninsula. We will not need even a single nuclear weapon once we get convinced that the U.S. does not antagonize us and confidence is built between the DPRK and the U.S. and, accordingly, we are no longer exposed to the U.S. threat. This is what we have already clarified more than once. The DPRK has already made a strategic decision to abandon its nuclear program and this was reflected in the above-said joint statement. If the U.S. has a true political intention to implement the joint statement we kindly invite once again the head of the U.S. side's delegation to the talks to visit Pyongyang and directly explain it to us."[31]

The call for Pyongyang to stop reprocessing was a bit confusing since in late August or early September 2005, North Korea completed reprocessing the last of the spent fuel that was removed from the 5 MWe reactor in April and May 2005. The reactor was reloaded in late May 2005 with the last of the new fuel that remained from the Agreed Framework freeze of 1994. May 2006 was the earliest that North Korea could extract through chemical reprocessing even one more weapon's worth of plutonium. In general, it takes a year for fuel in the 5 MWe reactor to be irradiated enough to produce plutonium for approximately one nuclear weapon.

The U.S. demand that North Korea give up one of its strongest negotiating cards in advance of actual negotiations in exchange for a visit by Hill was doomed from the beginning. It amounted to tough talk without much thought behind it. In practical terms, North Korea had stopped reprocessing and would not be conducting any activities that might be embarrassing to the administration during a potential visit by Hill. However, asking Pyongyang to officially freeze its activities at Yongbyon was essentially an attempt to get something important, which North Korea was withholding to use in actual negotiations, in exchange for a visit, something commonly viewed as part of the normal diplomatic process.

After the conclusion of the fourth round, the administration for the first time formally accused North Korea of manufacturing high-quality counterfeit $100 "supernotes."[32] As a part of an action focused on counterfeiting, the

Department of the Treasury issued a warning to U.S. banks about doing business with Banco Delta Asia, based in Macao, because of its money-laundering activities on behalf of North Korea.[33] In addition, in October, under Executive Order 13382, a new order freezing the assets of proliferators of weapons of mass destruction (WMD) and their delivery vehicles, the Treasury Department prohibited all transactions between eight North Korean companies and any U.S. person and froze any assets that the companies had under U.S. jurisdiction.[34]

In describing these and other efforts, Bob Joseph, the under secretary of state for arms control, said that the measures were "necessary for our defense and the defense of our friends and allies." He also said that the measures were "independent of the diplomatic efforts that we are pursuing" with the North, which also included China, Russia, Japan, and South Korea, adding that he believed that the measures would "reinforce the prospect for the success of those talks."[35]

However appropriate the measures were independent of the six-party talks, they did not appear to reinforce the prospect for success during the fifth round, which took place November 9–11, 2005. That round ended without significant progress and little substantive discussion of nuclear dismantlement. Vice Minister Kim Gye-gwan emphasized the need for simultaneous action in the implementation of the September 19 joint statement. What he probably heard rather than an unambiguous reaffirmation of the joint statement's fifth point ("The six parties agreed to take coordinated steps to implement the aforementioned consensus in a phased manner in line with the principle of 'commitment for commitment, action for action.'") was the comment by national security adviser Stephen Hadley, aboard Air Force One en route to Asia with the president, when he reiterated that the United States would continue to adhere to a policy of no economic aid for North Korea before it gave up its nuclear programs.[36] That statement was followed the next day by Secretary Rice's remarks criticizing what the South Korean unification minister described as North Korea's five-point proposal during the fifth round. Purportedly, Kim Gye-gwan had presented a roadmap that would suspend nuclear tests, ban nuclear relocation, ban further nuclear production, verifiably stop nuclear activities and dismantle facilities, and return the DPRK to the Nuclear Non-Proliferation Treaty and IAEA inspections in exchange for aid and normalization of relations as spelled out in the September 19, 2005, joint statement.[37] The South Korean newspaper *Chosun Ilbo* reported that "in a meeting with South Korean Foreign Minister Ban Ki-moon on the sidelines of the APEC forum in Busan, Rice said the North's demand at six-nation talks now in recess to be given aid in five stages as it dismantles its nuclear program was not helpful and could take up a lot of time."[38]

The fifth round ended with a brief chairman's statement that reaffirmed that the parties would fully implement the joint statement in line with the principle of "commitment for commitment, action for action."[39] What the parties did not do was set a date for the next round of talks. When a date or time frame is not set, it usually means that Pyongyang is unhappy with the process and intends to use the date for the next round as leverage. In this case, Pyongyang's unhappiness was explicitly expressed by Vice Minister Kim Gye-gwan when he told Ambassador Hill that the actions levied against Banco Delta Asia and the eight North Korean companies were an embodiment of U.S. hostile intent and that talks on denuclearization could not proceed without first removing the new obstacle that those actions created. Kim proposed holding bilateral negotiations with the United States following the fifth round. Hill agreed to a meeting but insisted that there would be no negotiations. Hill told Kim that the United States would provide a briefing of the U.S. law that triggered the actions against Banco Delta Asia and the other companies and let Pyongyang know what it needed to do to have the sanctions removed. From Hill's perspective, he was talking about two distinct meetings: one involving Kim Gye-gwan and another involving a technical briefing to North Korean experts. Kim Gye-gwan, however, thought that he would be taking a single trip to the United States to discuss a full range of issues, including the financial "sanctions" related to Banco Delta Asia.

The North Koreans proceeded to make travel arrangements (and line up financing for the trip) for Kim Gye-gwan. Hill, who had remained in Asia for about a week, returned to Washington, where he was met with stiff opposition from well-organized hard-liners who were opposed to any bilateral meetings with the North Koreans. On November 25, 2005, the invitation to Kim was "withdrawn," resulting in Kim believing that Hill had broken a pledge. Kim's deputy, Li Gun, was invited to lead a technical group to hear from Treasury Department officials about the U.S. actions against Banco Delta Asia. State Department officials could attend as observers, but they would not be allowed to meet bilaterally with the North Korean delegation. Pyongyang decided not to send any delegation to the United States for a planned December 11 meeting.[40]

What is clear about the fifth round is that because the APEC leaders' meeting was being held in South Korea at about the same time, a serious discussion was not going to take place in what turned out to be a return to the pre–fourth round schedule of three-day meetings. What is also clear is that there are two distinct U.S. policy tracks regarding North Korea operating simultaneously.

What is unclear is whether the two tracks are well coordinated. Track one, represented by the good-faith effort of Hill, is committed in the short run to a negotiated settlement that takes into account the concerns of the other players. Track two, represented by under secretary Bob Joseph, is bent on cracking down on North Korea's illegal activities as well as enhancing the capabilities of the Proliferation Security Initiative (PSI), a program announced by President Bush May 31, 2003, that builds on existing nonproliferation activities worldwide and calls on nations to cooperate in interdicting traffic suspected of carrying weapons of mass destruction. The second track is in the enviable position of being able to justify its actions solely on the basis of North Korea's illegal actions. It is difficult, therefore, to argue within or outside the administration that the second-track measures are inappropriate.

The most chilling aspect of this reemerged bifurcation of U.S. policy toward North Korea after Hill's success in engaging Pyongyang during the fourth round of talks is that since Hill has lost a skirmish or two within the administration, he has adopted some of the philosophy and language of the track-two advocates in an effort to achieve his goal of best-effort negotiating. He has repeated as U.S. policy the added language in the U.S. statement—which goes beyond the common language that he negotiated with the United States, Japan, and South Korea—requiring Pyongyang to demonstrate a sustained commitment to cooperation and transparency and to cease proliferating nuclear technology. He has also repeated the purported requirement by the vice president for North Korea to shut down Yongbyon voluntarily, since the Bush administration is opposed to negotiating a freeze of the facilities.

What remains to be seen is whether Bob Joseph has succeeded in capturing the lead in North Korea policy, as he did in the first term, or whether Hill can rebound from events that began to slip out of his control beginning with the U.S. statement of September 19, 2005. An analysis of events described in chapter 9 suggests that the answer, unfortunately, is that the administration's commitment to negotiating a settlement with North Korea through the six-party process exists in name only. North Korea policy has been fully captured by those in the administration who seek regime change.

9

Consequences and Accountability

We have the opportunity to secure a system for stopping the proliferation of weapons of mass destruction. I think this kind of opportunity will not come again. Under current conditions, where there is no trust, how can we give up our weapons first?

—*North Korean vice minister Kim Gye-gwan in an interview with Dan Rather, 60 Minutes, January 15, 2006*

It is hard to imagine that the quote that opens this chapter captures a North Korean diplomat making the case to Dan Rather for saving the Nuclear Non-Proliferation Treaty, from which Pyongyang withdrew in January 2003.[1] But, of course, there are many parts to the basic message that Kim Gye-gwan relayed to Dan Rather. First, it is an attempt to focus attention on the stakes involved in the six-party talks. Second, it is an attempt to put the other parties to the negotiations on notice that what they have may be a once-in-a-lifetime opportunity, not likely to come again. Third, it is an attempt to rationalize North Korea's decision to stay away from the talks until conditions are more favorable to Pyongyang. Finally, Kim makes a plea for his audience to understand the logic of Pyongyang's position: ". . . how can we give up our weapons first?"

In discussions with me after I visited North Korea's nuclear facilities at Yongbyon two years earlier, in January 2004, Kim had said, "Time is not on your side," referring to Pyongyang's continued work on its nuclear weapons program pending satisfactory resolution of the current crisis. Months later, Vice President Cheney echoed Kim's words, saying, "Time is not on our side." That may have been the only time that the vice president agreed with a North Korean.

In practical terms, both Kim and Cheney are correct. The biggest losers in this protracted crisis have been the nonproliferation regime and the potential

132

security of the United States. Since the latest nuclear weapons crisis began in October 2002, North Korea has sped through any semblance of a Clinton-era "red line" by ejecting in December 2002 the International Atomic Energy Agency (IAEA) inspectors who had been monitoring North Korea's frozen plutonium program facilities at Yongbyon, removing IAEA monitoring devices, unsealing previously locked nuclear facilities, withdrawing from the Nuclear Non-Proliferation Treaty (NPT), shutting down a five-megawatt electric reactor, removing 8,000 spent fuel rods from the previously monitored cooling pond, chemically reprocessing the spent fuel and extracting plutonium, converting the plutonium into a metal that can be used to create a nuclear weapon, informing the world on February 10, 2005, that it had in fact manufactured nuclear weapons, and ultimately conducting a nuclear test on October 9, 2006. North Korea reloaded the five-megawatt electric reactor with fresh fuel in 2003. In mid-2005, just before and during the critical fourth round of six-party talks, Pyongyang again unloaded the spent fuel from the reactor and extracted additional plutonium in order to increase its nuclear weapons arsenal.

Scientists always hedge their bets when asked how many nuclear weapons North Korea might possess. Their first (and absolutely correct) response is to state how much plutonium North Korea has; if pressed, they may translate that into numbers of weapons. But they always pose a question in return: How much plutonium does North Korea need for a single weapon? The point of that little dance is to make it clear that a nuclear weapon does not require a set amount of plutonium. The amount depends on the sophistication of the nuclear weapons design, the process, and the technology involved; the more sophisticated, the less the amount of plutonium needed. But to generalize, one can say that a full load of fuel in North Korea's five-megawatt electric reactor potentially allows for extraction of one bomb's worth of plutonium each year that it remains in the reactor running at or near full capacity. That is to say, North Korea probably extracted enough plutonium in 2003 to create about six nuclear weapons and extracted enough plutonium in 2005 to add another two weapons to their arsenal. Those eight weapons are in addition to the one or two that North Korea was suspected of having before the freeze under the 1994 Agreed Framework took effect. Pyongyang may then possess approximately ten nuclear weapons; if it has not actually manufactured that number, it certainly has enough plutonium to do so.

Whether Pyongyang has manufactured a nuclear weapon is not the most disturbing question. Pyongyang may not and probably does not have the ability to mate a weapon to a missile—yet. But that is of little comfort to those who believe that Pyongyang is capable of selling anything for the right price. Nuclear technology, plutonium, or an actual nuclear weapon in the hands of North Korea should elicit much more than a rhetorical "That's unacceptable." For the United States, especially in a post 9-11 environment, the prospect of an unmonitored, unaccountable North Korean nuclear weapons program should demand an urgent effort to resolve the crisis as quickly as possible. Instead, one could make the case that the United States sees little or no actual threat from a North Korean nuclear weapons program, does not believe that Pyongyang would proliferate under any circumstances, and, contrary to Vice President Cheney's admonition, believes that in fact time *is* on its side. The lack of U.S. urgency could easily reinforce North Korea's perception that the only logical explanation for U.S. inaction is that the administration prefers to avoid a solution that extends the longevity of Kim Jong-il's regime and to pursue one that seeks regime change.

Consequences of a Two-Track Approach

In chapter 8, I questioned whether the diplomacy-negotiation track represented by assistant secretary Chris Hill and the isolate-and-confront track nominally represented by under secretary Bob Joseph were well coordinated. Months after I wrote that chapter, it remains clear to me that the public policy of the Bush administration is to be seen working with regional friends and allies to address the North Korean nuclear issue diplomatically but that the administration does not believe that Kim Jong-il will ever give up his nuclear weapons program voluntarily.

Some of the best publicly available insight into the administration's thinking has come from Aaron Friedberg, former deputy national security adviser to Vice President Cheney. In a panel presentation at the American Enterprise Institution (AEI) on February 2, 2006, Friedberg explicitly said that Kim Jong-il would not give up his nuclear weapons unless the alternative was so unattractive that it left him no choice. Friedberg defined that alternative as a sufficient personal threat to Kim Jong-il's hold on power; he then went on to say that while entering into discussions with the Kim regime, the United States should pursue a robust policy of pressuring Kim until he decides to give up his nuclear weapons.

Friedberg described what he viewed as one of the worst outcomes of a failed six-party process—the continuation of the Kim regime. That struck me as odd, since the success of the six-party talks, by design, would result in the continuation of Kim's regime. Presumably the president has made a fundamental decision: that even though he cannot stand Kim Jong-il as a person or leader, he is prepared as it were to hold his nose and strike a deal that would end North Korea's nuclear weapons program. I have long had doubts about whether President Bush would ultimately agree to any deal that prolonged the Kim regime. Bush has defined his presidency in terms of eliminating tyranny throughout the world. He points to his accomplishments in removing the Taliban from Afghanistan and Saddam from power in Iraq, and he takes credit for Libya's decision to give up its nuclear weapons program. Given his priorities, the idea that Bush could "stomach" a deal that kept in power a man who is responsible for large-scale human rights abuses and who "starved his people" is neither logical nor a reasonable assessment of Bush's ability to be flexible.

The deal that the United States struck with Libya resulted in the United States accepting that Qaddafi would remain in power in exchange for giving up his nuclear weapons program. A parallel deal does not seem to apply in Kim Jong-il's case. While the United States would like Pyongyang to follow the Libyan model and forsake its nuclear weapons program, it is unlikely that President Bush would then accept Kim in the same manner that he has accepted Qaddafi.

In wrapping up his presentation, Friedberg acknowledged the difficulty for the United States of "going it alone" in its effort to apply significant decision-altering pressure on Kim Jong-il. He cited the "unhelpful" assistance that China and South Korea are providing to North Korea, saying that if the talks and pressure fail, there will be recriminations—that the United States would review its alliance with South Korea as a consequence.

The idea that the United States would hold its ally South Korea responsible for the failure of its uncoordinated and unacknowledged dual-track approach toward North Korea suggests that the United States does not fully understand or appreciate the national security objectives of its friends and allies in the region. Or worse, that it fully understands and does not care.

In early March 2006, North Korea reversed its earlier decision not to attend a December technical meeting (see chapter 8) and sent Li Gun, its director general for North American affairs, to New York City to meet with Treasury officials regarding actions that the United States took when it charged Banco Delta Asia of Macau with being involved in money laundering; the meeting also dealt with U.S. sanctions against the North Korean companies that the United States charged with being involved in the transfer of weapons of mass destruction (WMD) or the associated technology, specifically the sale of missiles. Washington has taken its "fig leaf" explanation that its actions regarding North Korea's illegal activities have no relationship to the diplomatic track of six-party talks to an extreme. No person involved in the six-party process was permitted to travel to New York to meet with Li Gun. The administration reverted to a rationale that it employed after the third round of talks when Pyongyang refused to return to Beijing for talks for thirteen months. If the North Koreans wanted to talk about the six-party process or nuclear weapons, they could just show up in Beijing, where U.S. negotiators would be happy to talk to them, but pending Pyongyang's return to the formal six-party process, U.S. participants were forbidden to go to New York to talk to Li Gun. The State Department managed to win a small concession in getting permission for Kathleen Stephens, principal deputy secretary of state for East Asian affairs, to meet with Li Gun because she was not "technically" a six-party negotiator.

U.S. Strategy in 2006

The March 2006 National Security Strategy addresses North Korea in the following manner:

> The North Korean regime also poses a serious nuclear proliferation challenge. It presents a long and bleak record of duplicity and bad-faith negotiations. In the past, the regime has attempted to split the United States from its allies. This time, the United States has successfully forged a consensus among key regional partners—China, Japan, Russia, and the Republic of Korea (ROK)—that the DPRK must give up all of its existing nuclear programs. Regional cooperation offers the best hope for a peaceful, diplomatic resolution of this problem. In a joint statement signed on September 19, 2005, in the Six-Party Talks among these participants, the DPRK agreed to abandon its nuclear weapons and all existing nuclear programs. The joint statement also declared that the relevant parties would negotiate a permanent peace for the Korean peninsula and explore ways to promote security cooperation in Asia. Along with our partners in the Six-Party Talks, the United States will continue to press the DPRK to implement these commitments.
>
> The United States has broader concerns regarding the DPRK as well. The DPRK counterfeits our currency; traffics in narcotics and engages in other illicit activities; threatens the ROK with its army and its neighbors with its missiles; and brutalizes and starves its people. The DPRK regime needs to change these policies, open up its political system, and afford freedom to its people. In the interim, we will continue to take all necessary measures to protect our national and economic security against the adverse effects of their bad conduct.[2]

The negotiating track in 2006 all but lost out to a resurgent view from the first term of the Bush administration—that North Korea is an evil place and its bad behavior should not be rewarded. On March 10, 2006, President Bush repeated for the first time in a long time his charge that North Korea, along with Iran, was part of an "axis of evil," a phrase that first appeared in his 2002 State of the Union speech. It is part of the rhetoric that Bush had set aside at the urging of South Korea and China in the spring of 2005 as assistant secretary Chris Hill maneuvered to establish the primacy of diplomacy in U.S. policy toward North Korea. That painstakingly created atmosphere devoid of charged rhetoric made Pyongyang's return to the fourth round of six-party talks possible. But that was when the administration was prepared to give Hill a legitimate amount of room to maneuver to see whether diplomacy would succeed.

A combination of factors contributed to the relative demise of diplomacy and negotiations in 2006. First, the administration viewed North Korea's statement of September 20, 2005, as backing off Pyongyang's commitments in the joint statement of a day earlier. The administration chose to ignore that North Korea's response (however over-the-top it was) was a direct response to what Pyongyang perceived as the United States reneging on its commitments in the joint statement by issuing—at the time that the joint statement was issued— a unilateral explanation of its understanding of the joint statement.

The Metamorphosis of Chris Hill

In late March 2006, Ambassador Chun Yung-woo, South Korea's new chief negotiator for six-party talks, traveled to Washington to meet a number of U.S. officials influential in determining North Korea policy. He said after his trip that he had heard little to encourage diplomatic resolution of the nuclear crisis. One thing that he suggested to Chris Hill was having a trilateral meeting of the U.S., Japanese, and South Korean heads of delegation on the margins of the upcoming Northeast Asia Cooperation Dialogue (NEACD), which was being held in Tokyo the week of April 10.[3] If North Korea's head of delegation, Kim Gye-gwan, were also to attend the NEACD conference, there would be an opportunity for bilateral and trilateral meetings involving the United States and North Korea. The suggestion appealed to Hill, who said that he would try to get the approval of Secretary of State Rice. The Chun recommendation came a few weeks after a similar proposal by Li Gun, North Korea's director general for North American affairs, who had come to New York for a technical briefing by the Treasury Department on the U.S. counterfeiting charge and the U.S. response. Li Gun differed in his approach in that he told a State Department official that if Hill were to attend the NEACD meeting, Kim Gye-gwan would also attend and would be prepared to meet bilaterally with Hill. Li Gun's straightforward proposal was a "bridge too far," and it was rejected out of hand.

The Chun proposal presented the opportunity for a "chance" informal gathering of the six-party negotiators who also happened to be participating in the previously scheduled NEACD meeting in Tokyo. Any meeting on the margins of NEACD would be seen within the broader context—as taking advantage of the presence of other heads of delegations, not as a separate attempt to arrange a bilateral meeting between the United States and North Korea.

Of course, the presence of the heads of delegations at the NEACD conference was in itself a significant deviation from the norm. In the past, the highest-ranking U.S. participant had been a deputy assistant secretary—a step below assistant secretary Hill—and in some years the U.S. representative was an office director or Navy captain. While North Korea was a founding member of NEACD, which was established in 1993, Pyongyang did not begin to participate on a regular basis until October 2002, at NEACD's thirteenth meeting, and then only at the level of the section chief of the DPRK Institute for Disarmament and Peace—significantly below the level of Vice Minister Kim Gye-gwan. In other words, the only reason that the heads of delegation of each country involved in the six-party process attended the NEACD conference was to participate in an "impromptu" six-party meeting. The stagnation that set in after the fourth round of talks in September 2005 and the various "non-related" measures to protect U.S. currency taken by Washington against Pyongyang (through the Banco Delta Asia in Macau) had given rise to open speculation that the death of the six-party process was close at hand. The prospect of using the NEACD conference as the rationale for bringing the parties together to breathe life into the moribund process was especially appealing to each of the heads of delegation, or so it seemed.

When assistant secretary Chris Hill arrived in Tokyo he told the press, "I will meet everybody participating in the six-party talks. But he [Kim] is not participating in the talks. Mr. Kim needs to decide whether he wants to participate in the six-way talks."[4] The sound of air escaping from the "balloon of expectation" was audible. Outside observers were extremely disappointed, but Hill had in fact already communicated his intention to avoid any contact with Kim Gye-gwan before he arrived. In that brief moment, Chris Hill confirmed what many had suspected but hoped would not happen: Hill had completed his metamorphosis into Jim Kelly, his predecessor, who had been completely hamstrung by onerous instructions from officials opposed to a negotiated settlement with Pyongyang.[5]

One consequence of that forgone opportunity to advance the diplomatic effort was, unfortunately, the continued loss of U.S. credibility—and loss of credibility for Chris Hill personally. However, because Kim Gye-gwan knew in advance that Hill would not meet with him in any format but chose to travel to Tokyo anyway, speculation arose that the North Koreans understood that they would be seen as having taken the high road and that failure to move diplomacy forward would be blamed on the United States.

Nonetheless, an opinion piece in the *Chosun Ilbo* summed up the general reaction best:

> Hill has snubbed North Korea's second-ranking diplomat, who was willing to meet him without any conditions attached, humiliating the man and forcing him to return home empty-handed. Kim is left with no good explanation when he reports to the North Korean leadership. The episode has also left a sour taste in the mouths of the other nations in the talks, all of whose delegation chiefs were in Tokyo, sending a message that their influence counts for little in Washington's eyes.[6]

Other press coverage of the event, which homed in on the fact that a widely expected meeting between the two sides foundered on Hill's refusal, confirmed that perception. Up to that point, sulking had been a North Korean specialty. Now it seems that the United States has decided to give it a try.

Another suggestion in play in Tokyo was Japan's proposal to hold informal six-way talks since all heads of delegations would be there at the same time, but Hill inexplicably refused. Up to that point, Washington had given positive consideration to most of Tokyo's suggestions concerning six-party talks. President Bush had heeded Prime Minister Koizumi's call for the United States to put together a concrete proposal for the third round of talks in June 2004, and Bush had given his personal support to Koizumi's trips to Pyongyang. But this time, Hill rejected the Japanese proposal outright. Knowing that nothing was going to come of the track 2 NEACD conference, Russia's head of delegation, who had been in Tokyo a few days before the opening of the conference, went home.

Making the Six-Party Process Work

Despite the title of this book, which suggests that I believe that the six-party talks failed to prevent North Korea from becoming a nuclear weapons state, I have an obligation to suggest what I thought might have worked. Nevertheless, recommending ways to resolve the current North Korean nuclear crisis may be a fairly useless exercise, because far too many caveats have to be attached. What might have worked when the joint statement of principles was issued on September 19, 2005, may no longer be a viable option or a much better one than the February 13, 2007, agreement.

In devising a strategy to revive diplomacy, one is faced with an artificial choice: put together a recommendation that stands a chance of being adopted by the Bush administration or create a scenario that stands a chance of being accepted by Pyongyang. Of course, the reality is that no approach to the current crisis is, on the surface, acceptable to both parties. But that is precisely what negotiations are for—the parties work to achieve an acceptable compromise.

I have already described what I believe to have been the administration's actual policy toward North Korea in 2006, best exemplified by repeating this excerpt from the March 2006 National Security Strategy:

> The United States has broader concerns regarding the DPRK as well. The DPRK counterfeits our currency; traffics in narcotics and engages in other illicit activities; threatens the ROK with its army and its neighbors with its missiles; and brutalizes and starves its people. *The DPRK regime needs to changes these policies, open up its political system, and afford freedom to its people* [italics added]. In the interim, we will continue to take all necessary measures to protect our national and economic security against the adverse effects of their bad conduct.[7]

If in fact President Bush views North Korea and its leader, Kim Jong-il, as irredeemably evil, there will be no negotiated solution to the nuclear crisis. The obvious problem arising from such a moral perspective is that it provides no opportunity to address the far more dangerous issue of nuclear security. While the Bush administration may abhor North Korea's disregard for human rights, despise its trafficking in illegal and counterfeit substances, and have every right to take action against its currency counterfeiting, none of those activities remotely approaches the level of threat to U.S. security that an unconstrained North Korean nuclear weapons program does. Yet, given the lack of urgency that the administration has displayed in addressing the nuclear problem, logic demands that we believe that it considers Pyongyang's narcotics trafficking or provision of refuge to a few North Koreans dissatisfied with their new life in South Korea as a more urgent problem. Failure to tackle the nuclear crisis with an appropriate sense of urgency resulted in North Korea first launching a series of missiles on July 4 (U.S. time) and then conducting a nuclear test on October 9, 2006.

Not choosing to accept the logic (or illogic) that I have just described, I suggest the following as a possibility for resolving the nuclear crisis and as a down payment on a broader dialogue on normalization of relations that would address other areas of U.S. concern.

Any scenario that has as its outcome a peaceful, negotiated settlement that ensures the security of the United States and its friends and allies in Northeast Asia must begin with a fundamental, strategic decision by the president of the United States to accept that normalization of relations with the current North Korean regime is acceptable. That is to say, the president must be able to agree to a negotiated settlement in which Kim Jong-il remains in power. That is not President Bush's position, as perceived by North Korea and supported by the evidence of the first six years of his presidency. The first step toward a negotiated resolution requires appointment of a presidential envoy to travel to Pyongyang with a personal message from the president that conveys the essence of the president's strategic decision to negotiate in good faith and to live with Kim Jong-il's regime.

Section 1211 of the National Defense Authorization Act for fiscal year 2007 calls for the appointment of a senior coordinator for North Korea policy, an individual envisioned by the authors of the act as a senior statesperson who has the confidence of the president and the stature to build interagency and bipartisan consensus.[8] The act thereby provides the president with the political cover to take the necessary steps to reverse a policy that has not worked for six years. Compounding the current situation, however, is the unfortunate acceleration of Pyongyang's drive to create a viable nuclear deterrent. The missile launches of July 4, 2006, and the underground nuclear test on October 9, 2006, have eliminated any ambiguity about North Korea's intention to become a declared and demonstrated nuclear weapons state. It is therefore all the more important that the president make a strategic choice between his desire to end North Korea's nuclear weapons program and his desire to end the regime of Kim Jong-il.

The proximate cause of the current nuclear crisis is the U.S. discovery of North Korea's attempt to circumvent the 1994 Agreed Framework by creating a highly enriched uranium (HEU) program to make nuclear weapons. Since late 2002, the United States has demanded that Pyongyang admit to the HEU program and reveal its extent as a necessary first step toward resolution of the crisis. In spite of its initial verbal acknowledgement of its HEU program on October 4, 2002, Pyongyang has since then adamantly denied involvement in any aspect of an HEU program; Vice Minister Kim Gye-gwan specifically denied that Pyongyang had any program-related scientists, facilities, equipment, or materials. The denial was not unexpected; it was the original acknowledgment that was unusual.

We have now come full circle on how best to address the HEU issue. In late 2002, the United States should have immediately engaged Pyongyang in serious bilateral discussions about its concerns just as it confronted Pyongyang in 1998 over suspicions that North Korea was replicating its nuclear facilities in an underground facility at Kumchang-ri. By the third round of six-party talks in June 2004, it was clear that our friends and allies had doubts about the accuracy of our intelligence about North Korea's HEU program, and we should have clarified the matter by making the HEU case within the context of the six-party talks. That did not happen either. Now, four years after the United States first confronted Pyongyang with its suspicions about HEU, it is time to reconsider private, bilateral discussions with North Korea as the first step toward resolving U.S. concerns.

U.S. public highlighting of the HEU program and Pyongyang's very persistent and public denial have most likely impeded the program to the extent that it may no longer be a serious or perhaps even a potential threat to U.S. security. The approach that the United States should take with Pyongyang in the proposed private discussions should be straightforward: the United States must demand that Pyongyang resolve to U.S. satisfaction, as it did in the Kumchang-ri case, that it no longer has an HEU program. That initial step is all the more important in light of North Korea's nuclear test. Resolving our concerns over HEU would clear the underbrush that has hampered serious talks in the six-party process and serve as a tangible indication of Pyongyang's stated desire to denuclearize. In return, the United States would resume its responsibility under the Agreed Framework of providing 500,000 metric tons of heavy fuel oil (HFO) to North Korea. With the first shipment of HFO, Pyongyang would shut down operations at its Yongbyon nuclear facility, making all plutonium processed since January 2003 available for IAEA inspection. As an initial monitoring step pending the full return of IAEA inspectors, any additional plutonium that Pyongyang has weaponized should be placed under Chinese inspection or control within North Korea and certification to that effect made to the IAEA. Pyongyang would also have to account for the amount of plutonium used in the October 9, 2006, nuclear test.

These reciprocal actions would defuse the current crisis and lead to serious, final negotiations under the auspices of the six-party process. While it may be tempting to describe such actions as a return to the status quo ante of the 1994 Agreed Framework, the reality is that the Agreed Framework no longer exists. The most identifiable program of the Agreed Framework ended in May 2006 when the Korean Peninsula Energy Development Organization (KEDO) formally terminated all work on the two light-water reactors (LWRs) that were an integral part of the agreement. Without implementation of the KEDO project, there no longer exists a reciprocal action-forcing mechanism to get Pyongyang to remove all spent fuel from North Korea, dismantle its remaining gas-moderated reactor, or fully account for its pre-1994 plutonium with the IAEA. U.S. provision of HFO is essential to prove to Pyongyang that the United States is invested in the process and not simply sitting on the sidelines while others provide energy assistance to North Korea.

Any private discussion with Pyongyang would include the U.S. claim that because North Korea broke out of the Agreed Framework by pursuing its HEU program, a penalty is in order. The penalty would be the loss of the U.S.-supported LWRs promised under the Agreed Framework, although the United States would honor its pledge in the 2005 joint statement of principles to "discuss the subject of the provision of a Light Water Reactor to North Korea at an appropriate time."[9] Simply said, the United States would not object to North Korea obtaining elsewhere a program designed for the peaceful use of nuclear energy—at an appropriate time.

Of course, neither North Korea nor the United States is likely to begin the process outlined above unless both are relatively sure that it would lead to a meaningful negotiation of North Korea's entire nuclear program and commensurate reciprocal actions to normalize relations. Each country would have an incentive to carry out its respective commitments regarding implementation of the HEU agreement while negotiating the larger issue of the entire nuclear program and normalization of relations. U.S. discovery of hidden HEU components would trigger six-party condemnation and the end of HFO deliveries to North Korea. U.S. failure to provide North Korea with heavy fuel oil would result in the expulsion of IAEA and Chinese inspectors by Pyongyang.

To enter negotiations toward achieving normalization requires Washington to make a strategic decision—which it has not yet made—to accept North Korea's system of government and leadership much as it has the Chinese, Vietnamese, Russian, and numerous other nondemocratic or near-totalitarian governments. Normalization of relations with Pyongyang does require the United States to refrain from efforts to change the regime, but it does not mean that the United States must forgo serious engagement on the humanitarian issues and monetary security concerns that cause it trouble. I would expect that we would demand robust talks on North Korea's missile, chemical, and biological programs as well as on counterfeiting and humanitarian issues.

Current U.S. actions not directly related to North Korea's counterfeiting of U.S. currency are punitive, related to the administration's desire for regime change. Pyongyang views the U.S. "illegal activities" actions as sanctions, while the United States declares that they are not. However, the United States has indeed applied a new economic sanction against North Korea. On April 6, 2006, the Treasury Department's Office of Foreign Assets Control (OFAC) amended foreign assets control regulations authorized under the Trading with the Enemy Act, which established economic sanctions against North Korea, by adding a provision prohibiting U.S. persons from owning, leasing, operating, or insuring any vessel operating under the North Korean flag.[10] The provision, which became effective May 8, 2006, provides criminal penalties ranging from ten years in prison to $1,000,000 in corporate fines. No rationale was provided for the sanction.

Once Washington has demonstrated that it has made a strategic decision regarding normalization of relations with North Korea (by taking reciprocal steps such as providing heavy fuel oil) and Pyongyang has demonstrated that it is prepared to get completely out of the nuclear weapons business (by satisfactorily resolving the HEU issue and placing its plutonium under inspection), serious negotiations on the larger issues of denuclearization and normalization could begin. At the same time, the United States could initiate a separate set of negotiations with North Korea—as a subset of the six-party talks—to regulate North Korea's longer-range missile program, which would be prohibited by the Missile Technology Control Regime (MTCR) if Pyongyang were a member.

Pyongyang undoubtedly would seek developmental assistance in return for placing its nuclear weapons and missile programs on the table. That assistance would come from all partners in the six-party process, but its cost would be borne primarily by South Korea, Japan, and, to a lesser extent, the United States. China and Russia would have to make a contribution in order for the process to be seen as truly a six-party affair. Once nuclear weapons and missiles were addressed satisfactorily, attention would turn to North Korea's chemical and biological programs. The end result would be a resolution of the WMD issue that would be deserving of an ironclad U.S. security guarantee, backed by China, Russia, South Korea, and Japan. Among other options, China and Russia could pledge veto action if the United States ever sought UN sanctions involving the threat of or use of military force, while Japan and South Korea could pledge that they would not allow use of their territory for U.S. military action of any kind against North Korea. The specific reciprocal steps to be taken would be the function of the negotiations, but in principle, the steps would evolve from those that are easiest to verify (and that possibly could be reversed) to those that are the most difficult to verify (and most likely irreversible).

In an opinion piece in the *Washington Post*, July 31, 2006, former secretary of state Henry Kissinger reminded us that "we must learn from the North Korean negotiations not to engage in a process involving long pauses to settle disagreements within the administration and within the negotiating group, while the other side adds to its nuclear potential. If the six-nation forums dealing with Iran and North Korea suffer comparable failures, the consequence will be a world of unchecked proliferation, not controlled by either governing principles or functioning institutions."[11]

10

Missiles, Nukes, and Talks

The DPRK will not use nuclear weapons first, nor give them to terrorists like al Qaeda. We make these expensive weapons to defend our right to survive.
—*Colonel General Ri Chang-bok, to Jack Pritchard during a visit to Pyongyang, October 31–November 4, 2006*

Life has a way of getting in the way of the theoretical. The possibility of finding a negotiated resolution to the ever-growing North Korean nuclear crisis was complicated by the North Korean missile launch that occurred on July 4, 2006, and the nuclear test that followed on October 9—nine and thirteen months after the fourth round of six-party talks in September 2005, during one of the long pauses in negotiations that Henry Kissinger warned against.

The July Fourth Fireworks

A good part of June 2006 was filled with reports, speculation, and plenty of opinions about North Korea's missile program and the question of whether Pyongyang would test a Taepodong-2.[1] Along with concerns about Pyongyang's intent was an equally strong concern about the danger of proliferation of a flight-tested ICBM. Those who were most concerned about a possible North Korean long-range missile test believed that a test would represent Pyongyang's ultimate desire to have a weapon of mass destruction and the means to deliver it over a great distance. Pyongyang's thinking may have been based in part on its belief that the combination of weapon and delivery system would be a strong deterrent against the United States.

In response to reports that North Korea was preparing to test fire a Taepodong-2, the international community issued a unanimous call for

Pyongyang to stop. UN secretary-general Kofi Annan asked North Korea to halt test preparations and avoid the escalation of tensions, saying, "I hope that the leaders of North Korea will listen to and hear what the world is saying. We are all worried." President Bush and Secretary of State Rice warned North Korea not to launch a missile. Japan's prime minister, Junichiro Koizumi, and foreign minister, Taro Aso, warned that Japan would consider imposing economic sanctions in the event of a launch. South Korea's foreign minister, Ban Ki-moon, and China's foreign minister, Li Zhaoxing, met in Beijing and jointly called on North Korea to halt its test preparations. The ROK's unification minister, Lee Jong-seok, declared, "The government has made it clear that a missile launch would have an impact on the South's assistance to the North." Despite the international community's unanimous agreement that North Korea had to reverse the course that it appeared to be taking, Pyongyang test fired the Taepodong-2 on July 4, shortly after the United States launched the space shuttle. North Korea also launched five Scud and Nodong shorter-range missiles around the time of the Taepodong-2 launch, and a seventh missile was reported fired on July 5 (U.S. time).

On July 15, the UN Security Council unanimously passed Resolution 1695. As often happens, the council's action entailed both good news and bad news. The obvious good news was that the Security Council had arrived at a unanimous decision on how to respond to the missile launch; the bad news was that foreseeable and unnecessary collateral damage to the U.S.-ROK alliance resulted from the manner in which the resolution came about.

There was never the remotest possibility that the original draft resolution sponsored by Tokyo and strongly encouraged by Washington would be adopted. Beijing and Moscow both vowed to veto any resolution that included the provisions of chapter VII, article 42, of the UN charter, which would make sanctions mandatory and enforcement by military means possible. Seoul also opposed any such resolution, which it believed might be destabilizing. Washington well understood Seoul's concerns and could not pretend to be surprised when Seoul publicly objected to the Tokyo-Washington push for a chapter VII, article 42–type resolution. Ultimately, China and Russia prevailed (Seoul was not a member of the Security Council and did not have a vote), sponsoring a compromise resolution without any chapter VII, article 42 provisions.

The 15-0 resolution that finally was adopted, under the "special responsibility for the maintenance of international peace and security" provision found in the preamble of the UN charter, could have been achieved at the very beginning. However, in defense of the Bush administration, one former official claimed that it was necessary to push the chapter VII, article 42 proposal to get

Beijing and Moscow to ultimately accept the final compromise, even though the administration knew that there would be "collateral" damage to the U.S.-ROK relationship.

Rather than accept the inevitability of collateral damage, the Bush administration should have taken Seoul into its confidence early and worked out a mutually agreeable plan of action that would have resulted in Seoul adopting moderate language that indicated its support of the eventual UN resolution. Washington, for its part, could have worked more effectively behind the scenes with Beijing rather than bluster about not accepting anything that did not have "teeth" in it. At the end of the day, Beijing and Moscow made it clear that they would not allow Washington to run rough shod over their interests. Washington was left to backtrack on what it had declared to be acceptable, and Seoul scrambled to repair damage to the alliance before the scheduled meeting of President Roh Moo-hyun and President Bush in September. When confronted by a universal call not to launch its missiles, Pyongyang saw no face-saving way to back down and chose instead to go ahead with the launch. What it did not bargain on was the rather swift and unanimous action by the UN Security Council. Rather than heed Resolution 1695's demand to "suspend all activities related to its ballistic missile programme, and in this context re-establish its pre-existing commitments to a moratorium on missile launching" and "return immediately to the Six-Party Talks without precondition," Pyongyang denounced the resolution and vowed not to return to six-party talks until the United States lifted economic sanctions.[2]

Missile Moratorium Primer

It is worth taking a few minutes to review the facts regarding North Korea's missile program and the missile moratorium that Pyongyang voluntarily agreed to in 1999, particularly since Resolution 1695 seems to imply that once a conditional, voluntary commitment is made, a country is forever bound to it, as though it were a permanent, legally binding agreement. A brief timeline follows:

—On August 31, 1998, North Korea fired a multistage Taepodong-1 missile in an attempt to orbit a small communications satellite. The satellite, however, failed to achieve orbit—a fact that did not deter Pyongyang from issuing stamps and commemorative coins depicting "Artificial Earth Satellite Kwangmyongsong 1 (98.8.31)" orbiting above the Korean Peninsula. At the time of the launch, U.S. negotiators led by Ambassador Charles Kartman were meeting in New York City with a delegation from the Foreign Ministry led by

Vice Minister Kim Gye-gwan (now the head of the North Korean delegation to six-party talks). Kartman interrupted his presentation of U.S. concerns about reports of a possible secret underground nuclear facility—which would be a violation of the 1994 Agreed Framework—to warn Kim that any launch of a long-range missile would be met with condemnation by the United States and the international community. Pyongyang fired the Taepodong-1 over Japan the following day.

The Japanese immediately cut off funding for the Korean Peninsula Energy Development Organization (KEDO), which was charged with implementing the terms of the 1994 Agreed Framework. In an effort to walk back the North Korean missile program to the extent possible until a final resolution could be found—and to get the Agreed Framework back on track—Kartman engaged in a series of negotiations with his North Korean counterpart.

Missile moratorium negotiations concluded in Berlin in September 1999. On September 17, 1999, the United States announced its intention to remove certain sanctions that had been imposed against North Korea under the Trading with the Enemy Act of 1950. One week later, on September 24, 1999, Pyongyang replied, "In response to the U.S. demand, the DPRK will have high-level talks with the U.S. for the settlement of pending issues as an immediate task. It will not launch a missile while the talks are under way with a view to creating an atmosphere more favorable for the talks."

—In late October 2000, Secretary of State Madeleine Albright traveled to Pyongyang to meet with DPRK leader Kim Jong-il to assess whether it would be prudent for President Bill Clinton to travel to North Korea. Albright also attempted to determine what a final missile deal between Clinton and Kim might look like, but Kim was unwilling to discuss the issue in detail with Albright, insisting that he reserve that discussion for Clinton. In a final attempt to clarify the missile issue, Albright arranged for a meeting between Bob Einhorn, the assistant secretary of state for non-proliferation, and a North Korean counterpart, which was to occur in Kuala Lumpur the first week of November 2000. Unsurprisingly, the North Korean negotiator was unauthorized and unwilling to discuss a subject that Kim Jong-il had reserved for himself.

—In May 2001, Swedish prime minister Göran Persson, heading a European Union delegation, met with Kim Jong-il, who reportedly told him that Pyongyang would not conduct any ballistic missile tests for the next two years while waiting to see whether the Bush administration was interested in better relations.

—On September 17, 2002, Japanese prime minister Junichiro Koizumi and DPRK leader Kim Jong-il issued what is called the DPRK-Japan Pyongyang

Declaration. In it "the DPRK side expressed its will to extend its moratorium on missile tests beyond 2003 in the spirit of the declaration."[3]

—On March 2, 2005, the DPRK Ministry of Foreign Affairs issued a memorandum attacking President Bush for what it called his failure in his State of the Union address to mention the six-party talks and the peaceful resolution of the nuclear issue and for calling North Korea an "outpost of tyranny." The memorandum specifically proclaimed, "We are also not bound to any international treaty or law as far as the missile issue is concerned. In September 1999, the period of the previous U.S. administration, we announced the moratorium on the missile launch while dialogue was under way but the DPRK-U.S. dialogue was totally suspended when the Bush administration took office in 2001. Accordingly, we are not bound to the moratorium on the missile launch at present."

The Nuclear Test

Essentially the same set of events witnessed in June and July with the missile test were repeated after Pyongyang announced on October 3, 2006, that it intended to conduct a nuclear test and then made good on its announcement by conducting its first nuclear explosion on October 9. The North Koreans have been remarkably consistent in their own rationale—however faulty and misguided the United States may believe it to be—for developing their nuclear weapons program. In its October 3 announcement, Pyongyang described the "daily" pressure by the United States that resulted in its decision to test a nuclear device, its no–first use policy, and finally, its continuing commitment to denuclearize the Korean Peninsula:

> The Foreign Ministry of the Democratic People's Republic of Korea issued the following statement Tuesday solemnly clarifying the DPRK stand on the new measure to be taken by it to bolster its war deterrent for self-defence: The U.S. daily increasing threat of a nuclear war and its vicious sanctions and pressure have caused a grave situation on the Korean Peninsula in which the supreme interests and security of our State are seriously infringed upon and the Korean nation stands at the crossroads of life and death.
>
> The U.S. has become more frantic in its military exercises and arms build-up on the peninsula and in its vicinity for the purpose of launching the second Korean war since it made a de facto "declaration of war"

against the DPRK through the recent brigandish adoption of a UNSC resolution.

At the same time it is making desperate efforts to internationalize the sanctions and blockade against the DPRK by leaving no dastardly means and methods untried in a foolish attempt to isolate and stifle it economically and bring down the socialist system chosen by its people themselves.

The present Bush administration has gone the lengths of making ultimatum that it would punish the DPRK if it refuses to yield to the U.S. within the timetable set by it. Under the present situation in which the U.S. moves to isolate and stifle the DPRK have reached the worst phase, going beyond the extremity, the DPRK can no longer remain an onlooker to the developments.

The DPRK has already declared that it would take all necessary countermeasures to defend the sovereignty of the country and the dignity of the nation from the Bush administration's vicious hostile actions.

The DPRK Foreign Ministry is authorized to solemnly declare as follows in connection with the new measure to be taken to bolster the war deterrent for self-defence:

Firstly, the field of scientific research of the DPRK will in the future conduct a nuclear test under the condition where safety is firmly guaranteed.

The DPRK was compelled to pull out of the NPT as the present U.S. administration scrapped the DPRK-U.S. Agreed Framework and seriously threatened the DPRK's sovereignty and right to existence.

The DPRK officially announced that it manufactured up-to-date nuclear weapons after going through transparent legitimate processes to cope with the U.S. escalated threat of a nuclear war and sanctions and pressure.

The already declared possession of nuclear weapons presupposes the nuclear test. The U.S. extreme threat of a nuclear war and sanctions and pressure compel the DPRK to conduct a nuclear test, an essential process for bolstering nuclear deterrent, as a corresponding measure for defence.

Secondly, the DPRK will never use nuclear weapons first but strictly prohibit any threat of nuclear weapons and nuclear transfer. A people without reliable war deterrent are bound to meet a tragic death and the sovereignty of their country is bound to be wantonly infringed upon. This is a bitter lesson taught by the bloodshed resulting from the law of the jungle in different parts of the world.

The DPRK's nuclear weapons will serve as reliable war deterrent for protecting the supreme interests of the state and the security of the Korean nation from the U.S. threat of aggression and averting a new war and firmly safeguarding peace and stability on the Korean peninsula under any circumstances.

The DPRK will always sincerely implement its international commitment in the field of nuclear non-proliferation as a responsible nuclear weapons state.

Thirdly, the DPRK will do its utmost to realize the denuclearization of the peninsula and give impetus to the world-wide nuclear disarmament and the ultimate elimination of nuclear weapons.

As the DPRK has been exposed to the U.S. nuclear threat and blackmail over the past more than half a century, it proposed the denuclearization of the peninsula before any others and has since made utmost efforts to that end.

The U.S., however, abused the idea of denuclearization set out by the DPRK for isolating and stifling the ideology and system chosen by its people, while systematically disregarding all its magnanimity and sincerity.

The ultimate goal of the DPRK is not a "denuclearization" to be followed by its unilateral disarmament but one aimed at settling the hostile relations between the DPRK and the U.S. and removing the very source of all nuclear threats from the Korean Peninsula and its vicinity.

There is no change in the principled stand of the DPRK to materialize the denuclearization of the peninsula through dialogue and negotiation. The DPRK will make positive efforts to denuclearize the peninsula its own way without fail despite all challenges and difficulties.[4]

Speculation about the timing of the nuclear test centered on the anniversary of Kim Jong-il's appointment as general secretary of the Korea Workers' Party (October 8), the anniversary of the establishment of the Korea Workers' Party (October 10), or, just to annoy the United States, Columbus Day (October 9). The specific date, however, has little or no meaning. What is important is the fact that North Korea's nuclear weapons program had advanced from a state of suspended animation in 2000 to the point six years later that Pyongyang could choose a date to conduct a nuclear test, having calculated that it could withstand any adverse consequences.

Resolution 1718

When Pyongyang announced its intention to conduct a nuclear test, the international community, again, unanimously voiced its objections and loudly warned Pyongyang not to go through with the test. Shortly after the test, the UN Security Council debated whether to impose sanctions that carried the threat of military force (chapter VII, article 42) or to agree on something without a military force provision (chapter VII, article 41). In the end, the council unanimously passed Resolution 1718, which carried no threat of military force, on October 14, 2006. The terms of the resolution, enforcement of which is mandatory for UN members, prohibits the provision of large-scale conventional arms, nuclear technology and related training, and luxury goods to North Korea. It also imposes a travel ban on persons related to Pyongyang's nuclear weapons program.

John Bolton, then the U.S. ambassador to the United Nations, declared that Pyongyang's nuclear test posed the gravest threat to international peace and security that the Security Council had ever had to confront. The Chinese representative to the UN, Ambassador Wang Guangya, condemned North Korea's actions but said that the Security Council's response should not only indicate the firm position of the international community but also help create conditions that would enable the final peaceful resolution of the DPRK nuclear issue through dialogue. He urged countries to adopt a prudent and responsible attitude toward inspecting North Korean cargo and to refrain from taking provocative steps that could intensify tensions.[5]

November 2006 Trip to Pyongyang

In chapter 8, I talked about a trip to Pyongyang that John Lewis, a professor at Stanford University; Siegfried Hecker, director emeritus of Los Alamos National Laboratory; and I made in 2005 during the recess of the fourth round of six-party talks. The same delegation, with the addition of Robert Carlin, a long-time intelligence analyst on North Korea and now a visiting scholar with Stanford University's Project on Peace and Cooperation in the Asian-Pacific Region, made a similar trip to Pyongyang from October 31 until November 4, 2006. We made plans for the trip at a time when little or no contact was taking place between U.S. and North Korean diplomats. On September 25, 2006, we were told by the North Koreans that our request to travel to Pyongyang for the purpose of holding discussions on U.S.-DPRK relations had been approved.

We were a little concerned that Pyongyang might, at the last moment, reject Bob Carlin's visa application. On September 14, at an event sponsored by the Brookings Institution and the Stanford University Asia-Pacific Research Center, Carlin had made a presentation on North Korean views toward the United States. He captured his audience's attention by claiming to have come into possession of a letter smuggled out of Pyongyang describing First Vice Minister Kang Sok-ju's comments to an assembly of North Korean ambassadors. Carlin's presentation was clever, and even though he revealed that in fact he was the author of the letter, a number of people initially were fooled into believing that he had a copy of a North Korean document. Because of Carlin's extensive study of North Korea over thirty years, he was able to fabricate a speech that in substance and tone could easily be mistaken for the real thing. In fact, a South Korean newspaper ran the gist of Carlin's presentation in a story describing it as an accurate representation of Kang's comments, a copy of which Carlin had obtained.

Shortly thereafter Carlin and I made separate offers to host a farewell lunch for Han Song-ryol, North Korea's deputy permanent representative to the United Nations, in New York City. Han told Carlin that, reluctantly, he had to decline Carlin's offer, but he accepted my invitation to lunch. On October 12 I met with Han at the Ambassador Grill at the UN Plaza Millennium Hotel. Because of our concern about Carlin's visa for the upcoming October 31 trip to Pyongyang, I asked Han why he had not accepted Carlin's invitation. Han told me that First Vice Minister Kang had in fact delivered remarks so similar to those that Carlin had presented that Pyongyang, on reading the South Korean story, suspected that one of its ambassadors had leaked the information. It took a while before officials in Pyongyang realized that Carlin's presentation was a fabrication rather than an actual leak. Because of the sensitivity of naming senior North Korean officials in the manner that Carlin had done, Pyongyang was less than amused by his prank and the fact that they had fallen for it. But it appeared that the only damage was the cancellation of the Han-Carlin lunch.

The point of retelling the Carlin story is to highlight the value in having experienced Korea watchers on a team. Bob Carlin was a valuable asset to previous administrations in their negotiations with North Korea. He could use his accumulated knowledge about North Korea to forecast how Pyongyang would receive a certain message, explain how to craft a better message, and most important, decipher what North Korea's response actually meant in the context of the history of U.S.–North Korean relations. Such a valuable asset is missing from the Bush administration's diplomatic and policy toolbox.

When Pyongyang detonated its nuclear device on October 9, our delegation had a decision to make. Should we proceed with our planned trip to Pyongyang or cancel it? Ultimately, we decided that it was now even more important to open a channel of communication with the North Koreans so that they could hear our thoughts and reactions to the test directly from us and, equally important, so that we could listen and report on what they had to say. Although we were undertaking our trip as private citizens, we made sure to inform the Bush administration in advance of our plans, and when we concluded our trip our first order of business was to report key observations to the administration.

Unknown to our delegation was the fact that the Air Koryo aircraft that we boarded in Beijing on October 31 was the same one that Vice Foreign Minister Kim Gye-gwan had deplaned minutes earlier to meet with assistant secretary Chris Hill. When we arrived in Pyongyang and sat down with a Ministry of Foreign Affairs representative to negotiate a final schedule, we were disappointed that Kim Gye-gwan was not listed as our main discussion counterpart, as he had been during the previous two visits. All we were told was that everything would be made clear to us when we met with Li Gun, the director general for North American affairs. One significant change at the Koryo Hotel since I had last stayed there four years earlier was the addition of one Japanese, three Chinese, three Russian, and, most important, a BBC channel to the previously meager two North Korean television channels. By the time our group met for dinner, we had heard the news on BBC that the United States and North Korea had met in Beijing and that Pyongyang had agreed to return to the six-party talks. That explained Vice Minister Kim's absence from our schedule.

In our talks over the next few days we were told that North Korea had tested a nuclear device because of U.S. political pressure and because it was only natural for a nuclear state to test. Even though Pyongyang had conducted a nuclear test, it was still committed to the denuclearization of the Korean Peninsula. The rationale for staying away from the six-party talks for the last year was because of the so-called sanctions that the United States had imposed on the Banco Delta Asia (BDA) in Macau. In point of fact, the U.S. Department of the Treasury had issued a statement of concern that BDA was involved in money laundering and handling of counterfeit U.S. currency for the North Korean government. The effect of the notice was to persuade others to stop using

BDA; in addition, the Macanese froze certain North Korean BDA accounts valued at $24 million.

According to the North Koreans, Hill and Kim Gye-gwan worked out an understanding that would allow the BDA issue to be brought up and resolved in the next round of six-party talks. Specifically, Pyongyang understood that a technical working group would be formed to discuss financial sanctions and that China (Macau) would unfreeze the BDA accounts. The U.S. responsibility in the arrangement was to not interfere with the unfreezing of the assets. I found this "understanding" to be uncharacteristic of the Bush administration's approach to North Korea, especially so since the meeting between Hill and Kim lasted only two hours, one of which was taken up with translation. Equally puzzling was the fact that Hill did not have with him the normal complement of political minders. Whether Hill actually said what the North Koreans claimed that he said is questionable. Other U.S. officials, although they were not in the room with Hill and Kim, doubt that Hill intended to convey such a specific agreement. More likely, the North Koreans recognized that when they detonated a nuclear device, giving the Chinese only two hours' notice, they pushed Beijing a bit too far.

Following the October 9 nuclear test, Chinese state counselor Tang Jiaxuan traveled to Pyongyang to meet with North Korean leader Kim Jong-il. Kim is reported to have told Tang that North Korea would return to the six-party talks but that it needed some type of bilateral meeting with the United States before making the announcement. If this particular version is true—and it sounds far more likely than Hill and Kim Gye-gwan reaching an agreement in a two-hour meeting that neither had seriously prepared for—then the more probable rationale for why Pyongyang announced its intention to return to six-party talks was North Korea's desire to manage its relationship with China after the international community had unanimously condemned the North's nuclear test and imposed mandatory sanctions through Resolution 1718.

In addition to engaging in political and security talks in Pyongyang, we met with Ri Hong Sop, director of the Yongbyon nuclear facilities. Going into the meeting we believed that North Korea's five-megawatt reactor had been experiencing problems during the year, causing the North Koreans to shut down the reactor from time to time. In our discussions with Ri a year earlier, we had been told that an assessment of the fifty-megawatt reactor, construction of which had been frozen under the 1994 Agreed Framework, had been finished and that a plan was in place to restart construction. In 2006, Ri revealed that technical difficulties were slowing down resumption of full-scale construction of the fifty-megawatt reactor. We also learned that the uranium fuel-rod fabrication facility would not be fully operational until sometime in 2007, another delay in the schedule given a year earlier. Hecker wrote a complete report of what we learned from Ri, which is available in appendix D.

Second Session, Fifth Round

Weeks after Hill met with Kim in Beijing, the United States developed what it referred to as the Early Harvest proposal, which was described publicly as including a number of conditions that North Korea would have to accept before talks could resume and the United States would be willing to discuss Pyongyang's concerns over "financial sanctions." The conditions included full disclosure of all North Korean nuclear facilities, closure of the nuclear test site, return of IAEA inspectors, and shutting down of the reactor and plutonium-processing facility. Hill is reported to have told the North Koreans in bilateral talks over November 28–29 that the United States would provide an economic benefits package if Pyongyang agreed to the measures. Hill also told the North Koreans that the United States would move to further isolate and punish Pyongyang if they failed to accept the proposal. Hill's counterpart, Kim Gye-gwan, did not make any real attempt to probe for clarifications. Kim simply said that he would take the U.S. proposal back to Pyongyang for further consideration. A U.S. official described the proposal as comprehensive, saying that in exchange for North Korea's acceptance of a specific set of incentives, the United States was willing to engage Pyongyang at an accelerated pace over eighteen months in hopes of resolving the nuclear issue.

Even though North Korea's acceptance of the Early Harvest proposal was supposed to be a precondition for beginning the next round of six-party talks, the talks—which were termed the second session of the fifth round, which ended in November 2005—convened on December 18, 2006, without any indication from Pyongyang that it would accept the proposal. The talks concluded on December 22 with no tangible sign of progress. During five days of meetings in Beijing, Kim Gye-gwan refused to talk about the DPRK's nuclear weapons program. He insisted that the United States remove the financial sanctions that it has imposed on the regime. Japan's chief negotiator, Sasae Kenichiro, questioned whether the talks would survive as a forum if they again failed to make any progress, noting that "there will be opinions questioning the credibility of the six-party talks." Assistant secretary Hill was more blunt, accusing North Korea of not addressing the nuclear issue. "When the [North] raises problems, one day it's financial issues, another day it's something they want but they know they can't have, another day it's something we said about them that hurt their feelings," Hill said. "What they need to do is to get serious about the issue that made them such a problem . . . their nuclear activities."[6]

The separate technical talks on the financial issues of concern to Pyongyang that were held for two days concurrent with the six-party talks also ended without results. Additional technical talks were agreed to, as was continuation of the six-party talks. However, no date was set for the next round of six-party talks.

Third Session, Fifth Round

One of the dangers of writing about an issue that has not been resolved is that there may be new twists and turns before final publication. While this volume was being edited, a number of things happened. In November 2006, the Democrats won control of both the House of Representatives and the Senate, handing the president and the Republican Party a significant defeat. John Bolton, the U.S. ambassador to the United Nations, resigned, knowing that his recess appointment would expire when the new Congress was organized in January and that there was no chance that President Bush would or could send his nomination to a Senate controlled by Democrats. Secretary of Defense Donald Rumsfeld resigned. The trial of I. Lewis "Scooter" Libby, former chief of staff to the vice president, began in January 2007, and Bob Joseph, under secretary of state for arms control, announced his resignation. The hard-line influence that did the most to shape President Bush's North Korea policy rapidly diminished at the end of 2006 and the beginning of 2007.

Historians will debate whether U.S. participation in the third round of six-party talks was approved because President Bush was so shaken by the November election, the public demand to end U.S. involvement in Iraq, and his very low opinion poll ratings that he was looking to lay the groundwork for his legacy by seeking success wherever he could find it or because he was finally free of the inane influence of the recently departed or attention-diverted hard-liners. The result, however, was the reemergence of Chris Hill as negotiator-in-charge. Hill was able to get the approval of Secretary Rice and the president to meet in Berlin bilaterally with Kim Gye-gwan in January 2007 following the failed second session of the fifth round of six-party talks in Beijing in late December 2006. The significance and symbolism of the Berlin meeting cannot be underestimated. Berlin was the site for many Clinton-era bilateral negotiations with North Korea, the last being the highly successful missile moratorium agreement in September 1999. The administration tried to portray the Hill-Kim meeting as being within the context of the six-party talks and as nothing unusual, but in truth it was from the North Korean perspective an important bilateral meeting. Hill and Kim produced an outline of an initial step that would lead back to negotiations to settle the nuclear crisis. In Beijing, at what was labeled the third session of the fifth round of six-party talks, an agreement was announced on February 13.

North Korea and the other members of the six-party talks agreed to take parallel actions in two phases. For its part, Pyongyang agreed to shut and seal its nuclear facilities at Yongbyon, to allow IAEA inspectors to return to monitor compliance and conduct inspections as agreed between the IAEA and North Korea, and to discuss compiling a list of all its nuclear programs. In return, Pyongyong and Washington are to begin bilateral talks aimed at resolving bilateral issues and moving toward full diplomatic relations. The United States is to start the process of removing North Korea from its list of state sponsors of terrorism and advance the process of terminating the application of the Trading with the Enemies Act (sanctions imposed on North Korea because of the Korean War). The five other parties agreed to cooperate in providing North Korea with 50,000 tons of heavy fuel oil within sixty days. Five working groups were set up to discuss five topics: denuclearization of the Korean Peninsula; normalization of DPRK-U.S. relations; normalization of DPRK-Japan relations; economy and energy cooperation; and a Northeast Asia peace and security mechanism. The working groups are to convene within thirty days and report to a meeting of the six-party heads of delegation. Once the initial actions are completed, a meeting of foreign ministers will be held. During the next phase of the agreement, North Korea is to submit a complete declaration of all its nuclear programs and to disable all nuclear facilities. In return, Pyongyang will receive the equivalent of an additional 950,000 tons of heavy fuel oil. In a side agreement between Hill and Kim, the United States pledged to resolve the Banco Delta Asia "sanctions" issue within thirty days.

As soon as information concerning the agreement was made public, many of the hard-liners who had supported Bush over the past six years complained bitterly that it was a bad deal that resembled Clinton's 1994 Agreed Framework. In an effort to shape the public debate as quickly as possible, the administration began a series of "background" conference calls with many Korea experts (including me) who might be speaking or writing about the February agreement. When information is provided on background, the recipient can use the information but cannot identify the source. Key elements of the message that I received were that President Bush seriously began this most recent push for a diplomatic solution when Hu Jintao, China's president, visited Washington on April 20, 2006. According to the information that I was given, Bush told Hu that Washington was ready to resolve the issue and Hu needed to make Pyongyang show up at the talks. In response, President Hu dispatched state counselor Tang directly from Washington to Pyongyang to meet with Kim Jong-il. Kim, according to my source, resented China's strong-arm tactics and that, in part, led to North Korea's nuclear test in October.

I have serious doubts as to whether President Bush committed to a negotiated settlement on April 20, 2006, just days after Chris Hill was prohibited from meeting with his North Korean counterpart in Tokyo, an action that Kim Jong-il later complained about to Chinese officials. If the February agreement is viewed as a stand-alone achievement, it clearly favors the North Koreans. But if it is, as the administration hopes it will be, the start of a process, it is a necessary and correct first step in the right direction. Unfortunately—for the United States, the region, and the administration—it is six years too late in coming.

While additional rounds of talks are to take place, the likelihood of significant progress that will lead to actual denuclearization is remote. Pyongyang's continued participation in the talks appears to be based on its desire to maintain a calculated quality in its relationship with Beijing. That is not to say that some concessions might not be agreed to in subsequent rounds of talks, but it is unlikely that Pyongyang will agree to disarm its nuclear weapons during the remainder of the Bush presidency.

The nuclear test conducted on October 9, 2006, has emboldened Pyongyang. North Korea now has two distinct negotiating strategies. It is willing to negotiate with the United States and others in the six-party process regarding its nuclear weapons program, but it has removed the products of that program—plutonium and any nuclear weapons that it may have manufactured—from any future negotiations with the Bush administration. By indicating its willingness to negotiate over its nuclear weapons program (reactor and related facilities), Pyongyang can be seen as fully engaged in the six-party process and committed to denuclearization. But even under the best of circumstances, it would take a significant amount of time to work out the terms for dismantling the reactor and related facilities and then to verify compliance. A discussion of the elimination of nuclear weapons is not likely.

Score Card Totals

By any objective evaluation, the Bush administration's stated goal of halting North Korea's nuclear weapons program has not been achieved. U.S. policy toward North Korea has been a failure. North Korea has succeeded in restarting its nuclear facilities, extracted significant amounts of plutonium, openly declared that it possesses nuclear weapons, by some accounts outmaneuvered the United States diplomatically, advanced its missile program, and exploited the differences in policy approach between the United States and South Korea. The inexperience of most administration officials in dealing with North Korea and the discrepancy between the administration's stated goal of negotiating a peaceful resolution and its desire to see the regime collapse have been significant contributors to policy failure. Worst of all, North Korea, in defiance of a united international community—whose unanimity is the goal of the multilateral six-party approach—conducted a nuclear test. As a result, the United States is less safe now than it was at the beginning of 2001 and the alliance with South Korea is in worse shape. The task of putting the genie back in the bottle has become exceedingly difficult. A few years ago I was somewhat optimistic that a negotiated resolution was possible; however, I am no longer confident that it is possible to walk back the North Korea nuclear program so that it is contained as completely as it was at the end of 2000.

Theoretically, the six-party talks are a framework for resolving the nuclear crisis that has the advantage of including the regional players in the effort to achieve a consensus resolution, but it has never been used to its fullest potential. That potential—the flexibility for serious, sustained bilateral talks between the United States and North Korea—has been specifically rejected by the Bush administration. Chapter 11 explains in detail the reasons why it is necessary to have a serious, sustained dialogue with Pyongyang and describes the poor results of engaging North Korea in a multilateral environment. By refusing to talk with North Korea, the Bush administration has failed to exercise the leadership and control that could have prevented North Korea from becoming a declared and demonstrated nuclear weapons state. The short bilateral session that Hill conducted with Kim Gye-gwan in Berlin should serve as the example and not the exception in making progress with North Korea.

A series of key missteps, beginning with the U.S. unilateral statement following the joint statement issued at the conclusion of the fourth round of six-party talks on September 19, 2005, wasted precious time and may have doomed the prospects of a negotiated settlement and, from North Korea's point of view, led to Pyongyang's decision to conduct a nuclear test. One of the more significant examples of failed diplomacy was the refusal, on instructions from Washington, of the U.S. chief negotiator to meet with his North Korean counterpart when all heads of delegation converged on Tokyo on the very thin pretext of attending the track-two Northeast Asia Cooperation Dialogue meeting in April 2006 (see chapter 9). Undoubtedly, the North Korean Foreign Ministry lost all credibility within Pyongyang's decisionmaking circles, leading the military to ask a rhetorical question: "If the United States will not even meet with us and continues to seek our demise, why should we delay completion of our nuclear deterrent any longer?" Kim Jong-il complained to Chinese state counselor Tang Jiaxuan that he had sent his negotiator to Tokyo in good faith but the United States had refused to meet—even in a six-party setting. In July 2006, Pyongyang launched a series of missiles and on October 9 tested a nuclear device. My skepticism about the continued utility of the six-party talks without a sustained bilateral component is based on the administration's solid record of failing at every opportunity over more than four years to prevent North Korea from becoming a nuclear state.

Unless the president of the United States makes a clear, strategic decision to accept the current North Korean regime as it is rather than wish for its demise; decides how to proceed; communicates his vision of what the relationship between the United States and North Korea would look like to Pyongyang following a negotiated nuclear settlement; and then instills the discipline in his staff to work toward that goal, with one voice, it is unlikely that a satisfactory resolution will be achieved during the remainder of the the current administration. If President Bush backtracks from the negotiating flexibility that he appears once again to have given to Chris Hill, he risks creating such a bleak scenario that it may well be too late for the next administration, Democratic or Republican, to undo the damage that his failed diplomacy has done. On inauguration day in January 2009, the next president may be faced with a permanent nuclear weapons state in North Korea.

Bilateral Engagement with Pyongyang: The Record

> Any country that truly wants a stable situation of the Korean Peninsula should clearly know that the nuclear issue on the peninsula is not a matter of international character described by the U.S. but an issue that should be settled between the DPRK and the U.S. and play a positive role to force the U.S. to come out to the dialogue with the DPRK without precondition.
>
> —*Pak Ui Chun, DPRK ambassador to Russia, at a press conference on December 31, 2003*

Since 1991, there have been several instances of crisis and confrontation on the Korean Peninsula. So far, only bilateral negotiations between the Democratic People's Republic of Korea and either the Republic of Korea or the United States have resulted in a satisfactory resolution of those crises. Multilateral talks, in contrast, have had a notable lack of success. Of course, critics of bilateral engagement with the DPRK are quick to point out that ultimately Pyongyang has failed to implement or uphold its obligations under the terms of bilaterally negotiated settlements and that therefore those talks should not be described as successful. That was the rationale used by the Bush administration during the president's first term in refusing to negotiate directly with Pyongyang to resolve the current nuclear crisis.[1] Nonetheless, examination of the changes in the format of the six-party talks beginning with the fourth round of talks in July 2005 shows that the predominant focus of the talks has been bilateral, within a multilateral context. The talks in Berlin in January 2007 make the point perfectly.

Bilateral Talks

One of the most noteworthy instances of bilateral negotiations between North and South Korea took place at the end of 1991 and resulted in the Agreement on Reconciliation, Nonagression, and Exchanges and Cooperation between the South and the North. The accord, while never implemented, was an impressive achievement. Among other things, it called for economic, cultural, and scientific exchanges; free correspondence between divided families; and the reopening of roads and railroads that had been severed at the line dividing North and South Korea.[2] That agreement was followed shortly afterward, on January 20, 1992, by the Joint Declaration of the Denuclearization of the Korean Peninsula, which was designed "to eliminate the danger of nuclear war through denuclearization of the Korean peninsula, and thus to create an environment and conditions favorable for peace and peaceful unification of our country and contribute to peace and security in Asia and the world."[3] That agreement likewise was never implemented.

The one bilateral agreement that was implemented—resulting in tangible, although temporary, nonproliferation effects—was the 1994 U.S.-DPRK Agreed Framework, which froze Pyongyang's known nuclear weapons program and placed key facilities and spent fuel rods under International Atomic Energy Agency (IAEA) monitoring until December 2002. Following a confrontation in October 2002 between the United States and North Korea over suspected North Korean uranium enrichment—a violation of the spirit and letter of the framework agreement—Pyongyang ejected IAEA inspectors, pulled out of the Nuclear Non-Proliferation Treaty, and restarted its five-megawatt nuclear reactor. It later announced that it had reprocessed all of the previously safeguarded spent fuel rods at Yongbyon, extracting enough plutonium to build perhaps six nuclear weapons. That confrontation led to the current nuclear crisis on the Korean Peninsula and the resulting six-party talks.

The Agreed Framework negotiations, along with others such as the June 2000 summit talks between ROK president Kim Dae-jung and DPRK leader Kim Jong-il, are aptly described in strategic terms. Other bilateral negotiations between North and South Korea resulting from the 2000 summit and specific instances of U.S.-DPRK negotiations have been more limited and "tactical" in nature. However, it is important in discussing the efficacy of talks on the peninsula to mention a few of the bilateral successes.

Three U.S.-DPRK tactical negotiations are worth reviewing. The first occurred in September 1996, a result of a bloody North Korean submarine incursion into South Korean territory that threatened to lead to even greater military tension on the peninsula. With the ROK's concurrence, the United States initiated talks with North Korea designed to end the potential escalation of tension and provide an opportunity to realize a joint U.S.-ROK call for strategic multilateral talks with North Korea. Over a period of three months following the submarine incident, the United States and North Korea engaged in serious and prolonged talks that ultimately ended in a North Korean public apology to the ROK. Throughout the talks, Washington was in continuous consultation with Seoul to make sure that the result of the negotiations would be satisfactory to South Korea.

Following two events in August 1998, the United States again entered into bilateral negotiations with North Korea that resulted in specific agreements that avoided the potential for more serious confrontation. The first incident was the allegation in the U.S. media that, in violation of the terms of the 1994 Agreed Framework, North Korea was recreating its plutonium-based nuclear weapons program at a secret underground facility at Kumchang-ri. The United States had been following intelligence developments regarding that possibility but was forced by the news leak to confront Pyongyang prematurely. However, the talks ultimately produced an agreement that allowed the United States to send multiple inspection teams (on what were referred to as "visits") to the suspected site to satisfy its concerns. Those inspections took place in May 1999 and again in May 2000 and, undermining the credibility of U.S. intelligence, revealed that Pyongyang was not involved in the re-creation of its plutonium program as feared.

The second incident occurred when, during the initial round of the Kumchang-ri talks, Pyongyang, without appropriate international warning, test fired a multistage Taepodong missile, claiming that it was done to place a small satellite into orbit for scientific purposes. The missile crossed over northern Japan, outraging the Japanese and others. Japan was an essential partner and financer in the Korean Peninsula Energy Development Organization (KEDO), which was charged with building two light-water reactors and providing heavy fuel oil under the terms of the Agreed Framework, and the missile launch threatened to derail implementation of the framework. Once again, the United States entered into bilateral negotiations with North Korea, producing an agreement in September 1999 by North Korea to end its long-range missile tests.

Multilateral Talks

In April 1996, President Bill Clinton and President Kim Young-sam of South Korea jointly called for four-nation peace talks involving the United States, South Korea, North Korea, and China to move beyond the armistice that ended active hostilities on the Korean Peninsula following the Korean War (which technically has never ended) and establish a more permanent peace mechanism. Following the resolution of the submarine incident, Pyongyang agreed to listen to a joint U.S.-ROK briefing on the four-party peace talks concept.

That briefing, which occurred in April 1997, was followed by three preliminary rounds of talks involving the four nations. While the preliminary talks did not achieve their goal of finding consensus for an agenda for the talks as a whole or establish the precise tasks of two subcommittees that were formed—one to replace the armistice and the other to reduce tension—it did offer an opportunity for each of the parties to meet collectively and in smaller groups to discuss other issues of importance. The United States took the leadership role, obtaining an early consensus that the parties could meet bilaterally or in any combination that all agreed on between or during full meetings of the four nations. Following that approach, at a time when North Korea would not meet bilaterally with South Korea, the United States organized a three-party meeting involving the United States, the ROK, and the DPRK. After establishing the precedent and after all three were comfortable with the arrangements, the United States abruptly withdrew from one of the three-party meetings while it was in progress—leaving the North and South Korean delegations to continue meeting bilaterally for the first time in a long time.

Formal four-party talks began in earnest in December 1997 in Geneva. While the four-party process eventually failed, it was intensive and far more frequent than the current six-party process. Three preliminary sessions of four-party talks took place at Columbia University and six formal plenary sessions in Geneva over twenty-one months; in contrast, only three sessions of six-party talks took place over the same length of time. The two subcommittees that were formed met as part of the overarching plenary meetings; deputies chaired the subcommittees and reported back to the delegation chairmen during plenary sessions. The four parties continued the precedent established during the preliminary sessions by meeting bilaterally and in other groupings before and during the week-long Geneva sessions. The robust bilateral element to the multilateral process led to a series of other bilateral successes, such as the June 2000 ROK-DPRK summit and the exchange of visits by DPRK vice marshal Jo Myong-nok and Secretary of State Madeleine Albright in October 2000.

In the end, Pyongyang failed to see much benefit in the multilateral process and simply refused to continue to participate. From the U.S. perspective, Pyongyang entered the four-party process reluctantly, with the primary objective of satisfying the request of and improving ties with the United States. Pyongyang maintained open dialogue with the United States in the months that followed the demise of the four-party process, agreeing to a missile moratorium, allowing inspections of Kumchang-ri, and engaging in the "Perry Process," the Clinton administration's second-term North Korea policy review process, led by former secretary of defense William Perry.

What Works and What Does Not

The fourth round of six-party talks is a perfect example of having the best of both worlds when it comes to negotiating with North Korea. The Bush administration was able to claim that the multilateral process was the overarching format and that any resolution arrived at would come because of the regional nature of the talks, not because the United States was repeating the failures of the Clinton administration by engaging Pyongyang bilaterally. However, the reality of the situation was clear to all participants: Washington and Pyongyang were engaged in serious bilateral negotiations. And all of the remaining parties to the talks (China, Russia, Japan, and South Korea) made it abundantly clear to the United States that they approved and supported direct dialogue between Washington and Pyongyang.

The U.S. delegation literally lost count of the number of bilateral sessions that it had with the North Koreans during the fourth round of talks. What placed an enormous burden on the U.S. delegation was the need to have separate reporting sessions with the Japanese and South Korean delegations. The political problems between Japan and its neighbors, China and South Korea (caused in part by Prime Minister Junichiro Koizumi's visit to Yasukuni Shrine), concerns about the historical accuracy of Japanese text books, and comments swirling about the sovereignty of Tokdo/Takeshima Island—as well as concerns over natural gas, exclusive economic zones (EEZs), and the Senkakus—spilled over into the six-party process.[4] Gone was the trilateral cohesiveness established with the TCOG (Trilateral Coordination and Oversight Group) process to develop a common approach to a North Korea policy for Japan, the United States, and South Korea. Instead of being able to exploit the possible synergistic effects of a trilateral U.S.-Japan-South Korea session, the United States had to shuffle between its allies and make choices about which advice it would or would not incorporate in its next bilateral session with North Korea. That undoubtedly contributed to exhausting the U.S. delegation, which was ready for the fourth round to come to a close.

The return to the multilateral forum during the short fifth round of talks in November 2005 provided another example of why sensitive issues primarily between North Korea and the United States cannot reasonably be resolved in an open setting involving several players. Pyongyang's initial reaction to U.S. application of section 311 of the Patriot Act (which covers special measures for jurisdictions, financial institutions, or international transactions that are of primary money-laundering concern) against Banco Delta Asia (BDA) of Macau was to call for a senior-level bilateral meeting between Vice Minister

Kim Gye-gwan and assistant secretary Chris Hill in Washington. However, the Bush administration was intent on preserving the fig leaf of separation between the six-party process and actions that it was taking with regard to North Korea's illegal nuclear activities. A meeting between Kim and Hill would look like the normalization negotiations envisioned as part of the final results of the six-party process, so the administration denied Kim a visa to travel to the United States. It did, however, keep open an invitation to provide a technical briefing to an appropriate level of North Korean specialists. That technical briefing was finally held in early March 2006, four months after the idea was first broached following the fifth round of six-party talks in November 2005.

During the meeting, Li Gun, the director general of American affairs and the senior member of the North Korean delegation, made four proposals to address the counterfeiting charges brought under the Patriot Act. The North Korean proposals, if accepted, would allow Pyongyang to return to six-party talks after having refused to return until the BDA "sanctions" were lifted. Reportedly, Li Gun asked that a nonpermanent bilateral committee be set up to discuss the counterfeiting concerns. He also demanded that the United States remove its financial sanctions, provide North Korea access to the U.S. banking system, and assist Pyongyang in detecting counterfeit bills.[5] The United States rejected Pyongyang's demands, saying that regulations to protect the U.S. financial system were not negotiable.[6]

Li also was quoted as saying, "We cannot go into the six-party talks with this hat over our head."[7] His dramatic insistence that Pyongyang could not return to six-party talks with the "hat of counterfeiting" over it is all too reminiscent of the North Korean delay in reciprocating a visit to Pyongyang by Bill Perry in his capacity as special adviser to President Clinton. Vice Minister Kim Gye-gwan, Li Gun's boss, told us in 1999 and throughout most of 2000 that a senior envoy representing Kim Jong-il could not come to Washington "with the hat of terrorism" over Pyongyang's head. North Korea was trying to use the U.S. desire for a reciprocal visit as leverage to get the administration to remove it from the list of state sponsors of terrorism. We did not. When it was in North Korea's interest to send an envoy to Washington, Pyongyang had no trouble doing so; there was no mention of the "hat of terrorism" getting in the way. Likewise, the "hat of counterfeiting" did not present a real obstacle to returning to six-party talks once Pyongyang decided that it was in North Korea's interest to do so. Pyongyang simply does not like being forced to wear what is, in symbolic terms, a sort of specialized dunce cap.

12

Establishing a
Permanent Security Forum

President Roh and President Bush . . . noted that the participants in the
Six-Party Talks agreed through the Joint Statement to look for ways and
means to promote security cooperation in Northeast Asia and that there
was a common understanding among the participants that the Six-Party
Talks could develop into . . . a regional multilateral security consultative
mechanism once the North Korean nuclear issue is resolved.

—*Joint Declaration on the ROK-U.S. Alliance and*
Peace on the Korean Peninsula, November 17, 2005

Conventional wisdom has consistently argued against the establishment of any type of unifying security mechanism in Northeast Asia, insisting
that the differences separating the major players in the region are simply too
extensive and difficult to overcome. The quote below is representative of that
line of thinking.

The chances for successful security cooperation are better when states
with similar characteristics and interests band together; hence, membership is selective in such organizations as NATO and the European
Union (EU). When states with diverse characteristics try to cooperate,
the prognosis for successful multilateral cooperation is often poor. This
is the case in Northeast Asia. Multilateral security cooperation in Northeast Asia will be possible only when participants can agree on which
threats they seek security from, how to address those threats, and what
their ultimate security goals are. Such a consensus is currently lacking."[1]

Opponents of an eventual multilateral security forum in Northeast Asia would
emphasize the final point made in the excerpt above by citing the following
events, which took place in 2005, as recent proof of the inability of the major
players in the region to get along:

—On February 23, 2005, the local assembly of Shimane Prefecture, a small
district located on the Sea of Japan, established February 22 as Takeshima Day.
Takeshima is the Japanese name for two islands claimed by South Korea that

are known in Korean as Tokdo. Japan incorporated the small islands in 1905 in the run-up to its occupation of Korea from 1910 until 1945. The situation was further exacerbated when the Japanese ambassador to Seoul followed the Shimane assembly's action by declaring that the islands were part of Japanese territory.[2] Because South Korea physically controls the islands today, the action by Japan resulted in an emotional outcry in South Korea.

—In early April 2005, protests erupted in China and South Korea following the adoption of new Japanese textbooks that many viewed as whitewashing Japan's actions and diluting its responsibility for atrocities it committed when it occupied Korea and China before and during World War II.

—In May 2005, Japan's vice foreign minister told a visiting delegation of members of South Korea's National Assembly that the United States and Japan were sharing critical intelligence but keeping it from South Korea because Seoul could not be trusted.

—To top things off—in what was supposed to be the Year of Friendship, marking forty years of normalized relations between Japan and South Korea—Beijing and Seoul strongly criticized Prime Minister Koizumi's visit in mid-October to Yasukuni Shrine, where, along with more than 2 million primarily military personnel who died in various wars, fourteen Class A war criminals from World War II are honored. Consequently, South Korean president Roh Moo-hyun dropped his plans to visit Japan, and the "Plus 3" meeting of the ASEAN Plus 3 scheduled for December 2005 was cancelled.

Those events tend to support conventional wisdom, which for years has suggested that because the nations in Asia in general and Northeast Asia in particular have such different and unique histories and relationships they would never agree to the establishment of a unifying organization to tackle security issues. In a speech given at the Institute for Corean-American Studies (ICAS) in Washington on October 11, 2005, the South Korean embassy's minister for political affairs gave a historical context for the divisions in Northeast Asia that is worth repeating:

> If I might sum up the last two centuries of the region, I would highlight three major waves in Northeast Asia: The first would be colonialism, the second communism, and the third market economy and pluralism. These were the major trends that swept into the region. They all contained a shared aspect: they were alien concepts not existing in the region until they were imported from outside. Colonialism reached our shores from Europe by way of Japan, communism entered via the former Soviet Union, and the doors to market economy and pluralism were opened by the United States.

The impacts of these mega trends were felt not only by their arrival in the region, but also by the response they provoked. In the case of colonialism a strong sense of nationalism rose to counter it and served as a force of anti-colonialism. In turn, anti-colonialism opened a window for communism to introduce itself to the region. The combination and timing of these ideologies explains why Asian communism took the traits of nationalistic anti-colonialism. Once communism found some toeholds in Northeast Asia, the United States tried to contain its spread by supporting anti-communism in South Korea and other strategic locations around Asia. The battle of communism/anti-communism became a mantra of the 20th century in the region. The final trend, the introduction of the market economy and pluralism, did not face the same direct opposition that colonialism and communism experienced, but was nevertheless forced to take root in a field already sown with the seeds of conflicting political ideologies from the previous period, leaving behind a strong influence of left-over ideologies. These three sets of divergent ebbs and flows were the zeitgeist that have defined Northeast Asia for nearly the last 200 years.

The three trends had other lasting effects as well, most notably keeping Northeast Asia divided along fault lines. During the colonial period, Japan faced off against most other countries in the region. Throughout the struggle between communism and anti-communism, Korea and Japan were pitted against the Soviet Union, China, and North Korea. As a result, Northeast Asia was divided for almost two centuries.[3]

Others have argued against conventional wisdom, calling for the establishment of various forms of permanent security dialogue in Northeast Asia. Recent documents made public in Seoul indicate that former South Korean president Park Chung-hee was looking at a possible security alignment of Japan, South Korea, and Taiwan against what he saw as the threat of communist China. Northeast Asian security forums were proposed by Soviet president Mikhail Gorbachev in 1986 and 1988, by Soviet foreign minister Eduard Shevardnadze in 1990, and again by South Korea's president Roh Tae-woo at the United Nations in 1990 and 1992. Other ventures—such as the Northeast Asia Cooperation Dialogue (NEACD), a nongovernment/academic "track-two" conference, and South Korea's proposed Northeast Asia Security Dialogue (NEASED)—were never fully accepted and failed to develop into talks at the official level.[4]

When distinctions between Europe and Asia are drawn, NATO is presented as a prime example of what is possible in one region but utterly impossible in the other. Yet there exist the beginnings of an organization in Asia that some would say may eventually become a NATO-like entity. The Shanghai Cooperation Organization, composed of Russia, China, Kazakhstan, Kyrgyzstan, Uzbekistan, and Tajikistan, first met in 2001 with the limited goal of promoting cooperation in former Soviet Central Asia. There is speculation that the organization may eventually add India, Pakistan, and Iran and evolve to become an alternative to U.S. influence in Eurasia.[5]

In a more compelling challenge to the conventional wisdom that "Asia is not Europe," Dorian Prince, the European Commission's ambassador to Seoul, reviewed the enormous historical, cultural, and ethnic barriers that confronted the architects of the European Union and the expansion of NATO, among other examples. In a presentation to the Third Jeju Peace Forum in June 2005, Prince cited deep-seated mistrust and enmity of several hundred years' duration as a real obstacle that nonetheless eventually was overcome.[6] Specifically, he cited the significant differences in the political and economic systems of the United States and Russia when the Commission on Security and Cooperation in Europe (CSCE) and the Helsinki Final Act were negotiated. Commenting on the dispute over textbooks in Asia, Prince quipped that the founding fathers of the European Union would not have gotten very far if they had insisted on adoption of a common history textbook by France, Germany, and Britain. In response to the claim that the cultural differences in Asia were too great, Prince asked whether the cultural commonalities of China, Korea, and Japan were not far stronger than those of Finland and Portugal. His presentation was almost a challenge to the countries of Asia to come up with a better rationale for why a Northeast Asia security mechanism could not be established, considering the real obstacles overcome by the Europeans in crafting their unifying organizations.

However, rather than attempt to force pre–cold war foes and historic competitors to find common ground by creating an overarching mechanism for security dialogue, the United States opted for a series of bilateral relationships with key allies. But the dynamics are changing.

Changing Environment

The increase in China's importance in both Southeast and Northeast Asia relative to that of the United States is one of the biggest changes to occur in the region over the last several years, and it has influenced political relationships among all the nations involved. The change can be seen in the evolution of the Association of Southeast Asian Nations (ASEAN) and in the changes in the bilateral relationships between the United States and Japan and between the

United States and South Korea. Highlighting Washington's interest in China and the shifting environment in general, a survey of country-specific public policy and informational programs for 2005 found that there had been 175 programs on China compared with 148 on Japan and 69 on Korea.[7]

SOUTHEAST ASIA

The Association of Southeast Asian Nations (ASEAN) was established in Bangkok on August 8, 1967, by Indonesia, Malaysia, the Philippines, Singapore, and Thailand, in part as a reaction against communist expansion in Vietnam and internal insurgency. There was an understanding that the moment for regional cooperation had come and that if the moment was not seized, the future of the region would remain uncertain. Brunei Darussalam joined on January 8, 1984; Vietnam on July 28, 1995; Laos and Myanmar on July 23, 1997; and Cambodia on April 30, 1999.[8] One of the more interesting developments to occur since December 1997 has been ASEAN's evolution from an anemic organization made up of ten "lightweight" Southeast Asian nations into a carefully crafted and inspired organization responsible for the creation of a viable ASEAN Plus 3 (China, South Korea, and Japan) summit. From the initial success of the Plus 3 addition, the East Asia Vision Group (EAVG) was established to identify goals for East Asia. In 2001 the group recommended moving toward establishment of an East Asia Community.[9]

The deliberate steps taken by ASEAN Plus 3 from the initial suggestion by ROK president Kim Dae-jung in 1998 to establish the EAVG to its evolution into the East Asia Study Group suggested that ASEAN was taking a measured approach toward eventually holding an East Asia summit. Through it all, ASEAN managed to retain a long-range goal of creating an institutionalized forum in East Asia, within its member nations' respective political comfort zones.[10]

According to reports on the first East Asia summit meeting, held December 14, 2005, in Kuala Lumpur, the future of the process is not at all clear. Even though the summit leaders pledged to make the summit an annual event, there appears to be a degree of caution over the role that China may play in the organization. The *Washington Post* reported that "a senior Chinese official said one goal was to begin a gradual realignment between Asian nations, particularly China, and the overwhelming military and political role played by the United States in Asia since World War II. While China has no desire to contest the strong U.S. presence in Asia, he said, the time has come to consider a greater role for Asia's own governments, and China in particular."[11] The United States was not invited to join, nor did it send an observer to the inaugural summit.

However cautious the summit leaders may have been at the first East Asia summit, the very existence of such an organizational meeting and their commitment to continue the meetings signifies a dramatic change in Asia—the development of a multilateral forum that has as one of its objectives a discussion of security issues.

NORTHEAST ASIA

It is, however, the combination of the shift in the regional security architecture designed by the United States after the end of World War II and the Korean War and the formation of the six-party process to deal with the current nuclear crisis on the Korean Peninsula that has given rise to the possibility that a more formal organizational framework for multilateral cooperation in Northeast Asia may be established. The "hub and spoke" arrangement favored by the United States is giving way to more independent attitudes among the anchors of U.S. security policy in Asia—Japan and South Korea.

The views of Japan and Korea regarding their place in a future security mechanism in Northeast Asia are colored by their complex reactions to U.S. initiatives to redefine the U.S. military presence and strategy in Asia as well as the maturing of their own philosophies regarding foreign policy and national security.

At the end of the cold war, in an effort to get out in front of the inevitable calls for a peace dividend (expenditures on security) following the collapse of the Soviet Union, the Department of Defense issued a report entitled *The East Asia Strategy Initiative* (EASI report) that justified and pegged U.S. force levels in Asia at 100,000, matching the downsizing that was going on in Europe. It was essentially an arbitrary number designed to protect force levels in Asia from being reduced.

While the United States was able to deflect serious challenges to its cold war structure in Asia—the large, forward deployed forces developed to confront or contain the Soviet Union—Japan and Korea were not immune to discussing the lingering effects of that structure, which did not match the new reality that followed the collapse of the Soviet Union and its attendant threat in Northeast Asia. Compounding the general desire for a peace dividend were several unfortunate incidents involving U.S. forces that reinforced the local perception that the U.S. military presence in Japan had become an increasingly unnecessary burden. In June 1995, the rape of a twelve-year-old Okinawa girl by three American servicemen—the worst and most unfortunate event to take place—galvanized public sentiment against the presence of U.S. forces in Japan. In an effort to defuse mounting negative public opinion, the Special

Action Committee on Okinawa (SACO) was established in November 1995. The rationale for the establishment of SACO was to "reduce the burden on the people of Okinawa and thereby strengthen the U.S.-Japan alliance."[12] One of the centerpieces of the SACO process was to be the relocation of the U.S. Marine Corps Air Station (MCAS) at Futenma, Okinawa. By 1995, the local population had encroached on the Futenma MCAS to the point of building elementary schools and houses next to the fence and immediately under the flight path of military aircraft, thereby creating a potentially dangerous situation. Those working on the SACO process promised a speedy remedy: development of a plan of action to include relocation of the Futenma military facilities within seven years.

Ten years later, the Joint U.S.-Japan Security Consultative Committee (SCC)—the same body that approved the 1996 final SACO report—was still dealing with the same unsolved problem. It approved new findings and recommendations on roles, missions, and capabilities as well as recommendations for realignments. Measures were designed to "enhance the alliance's capability to meet new threats and diverse contingencies," and they were expected, as a whole, to "reduce burdens on local communities, thereby strengthening security and ensuring the alliance remains the anchor of regional stability."[13] The language describing the purpose of the report was similar to that of the SACO final report, but it was distinguished by the addition of "and the alliance remains the anchor of regional stability."

The problems that prevented the implementation of the SACO final report also threaten to thwart the 2005 SCC report as it pertains to relocation of U.S. forces throughout Japan. "Not in my backyard" is a universal response, but it is especially strong in Japan when it comes to the relocation of U.S. military units. Provincial governors in areas that would be affected by the SCC report's realignment and relocation plan openly expressed their displeasure in a November 11, 2005, meeting, "saying they had not been given any briefing by the central government or opportunity to express their opinions during the negotiation process to draw up the report."[14]

Some problems are more intractable than others. In 1983, as a staff member of U.S. Forces Japan, I presented a briefing to senior Japanese civilian and military officers of the Japan Defense Agency describing how the United States had lost patience over the preceding years waiting for Japan to mollify local political leaders and identify a permanent field-carrier landing practice (FCLP) facility, which was needed to enable U.S. pilots assigned to the aircraft carrier home-ported in Yokosuka, Japan, to maintain their carrier landing proficiency at a land-based airstrip while the carrier was in port. Several years later, Tokyo came up with a temporary solution that required the pilots to fly several hundred miles to practice at a desolate strip at Iwo Jima. The October 29, 2005, SCC report has the following requirement regarding FCLP: "Identification of a permanent field-carrier landing practice (FCLP) facility. In the interim, the U.S. will continue to conduct FCLPs at Iwo Jima in accordance with existing temporary arrangements. The Government of Japan reiterates its commitment to provide an acceptable permanent FCLP facility for U.S. naval aviation forces."[15] Twenty-two years after I delivered the "This is the last straw" presentation on FCLP, the issue remained unresolved.

The best example of changes in South Korean attitudes is Seoul's desire to have wartime operational control returned to South Korea by the United States. Following the Korean War, the United States retained operational control of South Korean forces during both peace and wartime. In practical terms, that meant that a U.S. general officer commanded both U.S. and South Korean military forces. In 1994 the United States relinquished operational control of South Korean forces during peacetime. ROK president Roh Moo-hyun noted in his 2003 National Liberation Day speech that the Korean "military is still not completely equipped with its own independent capability and authority to implement combat operations," which translated into his request for the return of wartime control to South Korea.[16]

During the 2006 Security Consultative Meeting between the U.S. secretary of defense and the South Korean minister of defense, a timetable was agreed upon that would allow the return of operational control to Seoul between October 2009 and November 2012. Shortly after Secretary of Defense Donald Rumsfeld resigned, the United States acquiesced to South Korea's favored date, in 2012. Ultimately, the transfer of operational control will change the command structure from a combined command involving both nations operating under a single commander during wartime to one in which operations are conducted in parallel without a unifying single commander. While the desire to have operational control returned is natural, the end result will be a change in the security relationship.

Beyond Six-Party Talks:
A Permanent Northeast Asia Security Organization

The plenary sessions and ineffective, sporadic working-level meetings that characterized the six-party process from April 2003 until the start of the fourth round of talks in July 2005 would not seem to be a catalyst for serious discussions about a permanent security organization in Northeast Asia, but the near-continuous consultations among the participants that have resulted from the process suggest that regional cooperation on security issues is a real possibility. In testimony before the Senate Foreign Relations Committee on March 2, 2004, assistant secretary of state James A. Kelly indicated that the six-party process was going well and that he could envision an expansion of the talks to include other issues besides the current nuclear problem. He was referring specifically to the inclusion of the issues of conventional forces, missiles, and humanitarian concerns in North Korea—issues that were identified as concerns when the results of the first Bush administration North Korea policy review were announced on June 6, 2001. However, there is a danger that creating a permanent "trial" atmosphere in which a multilateral "jury" sits in judgment on the DPRK may cause the six-party process to collapse, much as the previous four-party process collapsed in late 1998. Expanding the current six-party process by simply adding other issues that the United States and others may wish to address with the DPRK misses the larger opportunity to maximize the benefits of the multilateral consultations created by the process in order to forge a new organizational mechanism to deal with broader regional security issues. That aside, it is highly improbable that Pyongyang would welcome or participate in an expanded six-party process whose goal was to examine and correct its shortcomings.

In the fall of 2003, James Laney, a former U.S. ambassador to the Republic of Korea, called for a permanent forum in Northeast Asia to address security and other concerns. At the time it appeared premature to conclude that the six-party talks had the potential to evolve into a track 1 (government-level) Northeast Asia security dialogue. Others, such as former ambassador James E. Goodby, had called for such a mechanism years earlier, but it is the unforeseen, unplanned, spontaneous development of consultations among the six parties on the margins of actual six-party sessions and during the critical intervening periods that have given rise to the possibility of establishing a more formal organization in Northeast Asia. Francis Fukuyama, in an article in *Foreign Affairs*, articulated the need for the United States to devise a new security architecture for eastern Asia, emphasizing that "a forward-looking foreign policy does not simply manage crises; it shapes the context for future policy choices through the creation of international institutions."[17]

One of the legitimate criticisms of the six-party process is that the initial phase, from April 2003 until July 2005, focused almost exclusively on form, not substance. But it is the nature of the development of the current six-party talks rather than any particular achievement (or failure) in the talks themselves that has given rise to the prospect that a security forum could develop as a result of the talks. Clearly the best chance that a permanent organization will follow the six-party process rests on the successful outcome of the current negotiations. However, it is unlikely that the current negotiations will succeed or that they will result in a timely resolution of the nuclear crisis that is free of the missteps and misunderstandings that always seem to accompany negotiated compromises.

Some might suggest that if the talks fail, increasing the potential for the current nuclear crisis to slip toward a nonpeaceful resolution, the prospects for a Northeast Asia security organization would likewise come to an end. However, it is the robust, if somewhat mechanical, consultations that have taken place between the six-party meetings that are the promise of a more permanent dialogue mechanism in Northeast Asia. The intense shuttle diplomacy begun by Beijing in March 2003 to ensure acceptance of the initial three-party talks and the equally intense shuttle diplomacy, again by Beijing, prior to each of the rounds of talks to date have set in motion an almost continuous dialogue involving all parties to the talks. An example is the regional consultations that have taken place at the foreign minister level. Those consultations started with the Chinese foreign minister's first trip to Pyongyang in five years, which took place March 23–25, 2004, and were continued by visits to Beijing by the foreign ministers of South Korea and Japan—all designed to keep the dialogue on six-party talks alive and to take advantage of whatever momentum was achieved during the second round of six-party talks in February 2004. The actions by each of the senior diplomats represented an attempt to secure a diplomatic solution to the North Korean crisis—a common goal that bound them together.

One organizational success story is the Trilateral Coordination and Oversight Group (TCOG), a subregional mechanism born of the desire to coordinate a common policy approach toward North Korea. The inaugural meeting was held in Honolulu, Hawaii, in April 1999. Originally designed to be a quarterly gathering of senior officials from Japan, South Korea, and the United States, it has evolved away from the formality that marked its origins to become an informal, but more frequent, consultative mechanism focused on the six-party talks. It has served the United States, Japan, and the Republic of Korea well over the last several years, but its success was not a foregone conclusion. As a participant in the inaugural meeting, I expected a series of U.S.-Japan and U.S.-ROK bilateral meetings, loosely tied together by a plenary session characterized by accommodation rather than genuine cooperation. Fortunately, I was wrong. In hindsight, the composition of the heads of delegation overcame any institutional reluctance by Japan and Korea to confide in one another and plan policy options for a common approach toward North Korea. The United States delegation was led by former secretary of defense William Perry in his capacity as the Clinton administration's Korea policy coordinator. The Japanese delegation was led by Ryozo Kato, most recently ambassador to the United States, while the Republic of Korea's delegation was headed by Lim Dong-won, at the time senior secretary to the president for foreign policy and national security. There could not have been three better people to initiate the process, which has served the three countries so well for so long.

Unfortunately, the formal structure of TCOG has suffered recently, much as ASEAN Plus 3 has, because of diplomatic rancor between Japan and China and South Korea. The unease between Japan and China and Korea, caused in part by Japanese prime minister Koizumi's official visits to Yasukuni Shrine, resulted in cancellation of the meeting between the "Plus 3" heads of state at the ASEAN Plus 3 meeting and postponement of South Korean president Roh Moo-hyun's visit to Japan in 2005. While Koizumi held fast to his right to visit Yasukuni and to his rationale for doing so, signs began emerging in December 2005 that Japan understood that it alone had the ability to reverse the death spiral its diplomacy in Northeast Asia was suffering. In short order, Foreign Minister Taro Aso, followed by Oshima Shotaro, the Japanese ambassador to Seoul, said that Japan must express "deep remorse" and "reflect deeply and with a spirit of humility" on all of the suffering that Japanese militarism had inflicted, specifically in China and Korea. Oshima stressed regional cooperation based on the shared values of democracy, freedom, and human rights.[18] Unfortunately, the early movement to ease the irritation among neighbors has not resulted in anything tangible.

I initially believed that it was best for a prospective Northeast Asia security organization to be based on the successful resolution of the six-party process. While in theory that would be desirable, I no longer believe it is essential. Events of 2006 suggested that the six-party process could have been headed in the wrong direction. What could be helpful with regard to the six-party process and the eventual establishment of a security mechanism in Northeast Asia would be to create a secretariat based in Beijing to formalize and record the proceedings as the six-party process plays out. But more important, the secretariat would be the dispute resolution mechanism should implementation of any final resolution occur. One of the flaws of the 1994 Agreed Framework was the lack of an arbitration mechanism. Because there was nothing in place to ensure a mutually satisfactory resolution when the parties interpreted their obligations differently and disputes arose, the United States and the DPRK entered into a series of new negotiations to deal with what each believed to be the other's failure to abide by the spirit or the letter of the agreement.

Pyongyang believed that the Agreed Framework was clear with regard to Washington lifting all economic sanctions. For its part, Washington eased restrictions in three specific areas but did not provide blanket relief from the sanctions because it believed that Pyongyang had not met its obligation to improve its relations with South Korea, among other reasons. North Korea demanded lifting of the sanctions as compensation for agreeing in separate negotiations in Berlin to a long-range missile moratorium in September 1999.

The prospect of establishing a framework for multilateral cooperation in Northeast Asia is enticing. In the post-9/11 environment—with its threats of terrorism, potential for the proliferation of weapons of mass destruction, and transnational health concerns such as SARS and avian flu—the prospect of a serious forum among nations where no forum has previously existed holds the promise of a degree of cooperation and stability thought impossible before. And in an opinion piece in the *International Herald Tribune* of December 29, 2005, the president of the Eurasia Group, along with former foreign ministers of Japan and South Korea, called for the establishment of a Northeast Asia regional forum.[19]

The reasons for establishing a framework for multilateral cooperation in Northeast Asia still hold true today, in an environment that has changed from optimism following the 2000 Korean summit to one of concern regarding the current nuclear crisis. With the exception of North Korea, each of the other participants in the six-party process has equally compelling reasons to participate in a Northeast Asia security framework. Just as the TCOG did not diminish the separate bilateral relationships between the United States, Japan, and the ROK, a Northeast Asia security organization would not eliminate the desire to maintain traditional alliances and ties. The time is right to begin thinking seriously about establishing a framework for multilateral cooperation. One of the most important first steps in any attempt to organize such a framework is to learn the primary lesson of the TCOG inaugural meeting: choose the right people to lead the effort.

The challenges, however, are formidable. The prospects for actually realizing a security organization rest on finding a leader among the major players in Northeast Asia who will step forward and lay out a plan of action. If the future of a permanent forum for security dialogue rests solely on the successful outcome (or, at a minimum, on the lack of failure) of the six-party process, inertia and lack of vision will overcome the promise of stability and transparency in Northeast Asia for years to come. The antidote to inertia is strong U.S. leadership.

Purpose

When trying to identify exactly what a Northeast Asia security organization would look like or how it would function, a "NATO of Asia" comes to mind. But in truth, a Northeast Asia organization would have very little in common with NATO. For example, NATO's purpose is to safeguard the freedom and security of its member nations by political and military means. It safeguards the common values of democracy, the rule of law, individual liberty, and the peaceful resolution of disputes and promotes those values throughout the Euro-Atlantic area. It provides a forum in which member nations can consult on security issues of common concern and take joint action to address them. It is committed to the principle that an attack against one or several members would be an attack against all members. All NATO decisions are taken jointly on the basis of consensus.[20] Clearly, the idea of a permanent organization that provides a forum in which member nations can consult one another, promote common values, and reach joint agreement on how best to implement actions that they have reached by consensus would apply equally in Northeast Asia. However, a NATO-like commitment to mutual defense is unlikely to be part of a Northeast Asia organization in the near term, and it probably never will be.

A number of specific objectives for a Northeast Asia security organization should be acceptable to all prospective members. Primary among these would be to

—encourage transparency and early notification of military or security-related actions among members

—resolve misunderstandings and prevent miscalculations concerning the intentions of others

—promote the peaceful resolution of disputes

—create the capacity for a coordinated, regionwide disaster relief effort

—undertake a common approach to energy security

—promote common research and response guidelines to SARS, bird flu, and other potential pandemics

—establish a regional agreement regarding incidents at sea.[21]

The list could be expanded by agreement of the members.

Membership

Membership in a Northeast Asia security forum initially would be open to China, Japan, South Korea, Russia, and the United States. ASEAN, Australia, Canada, the European Union, India, Mongolia, and North Korea should be invited to attend as nonvoting observers.[22] Eventually Taiwan should be added to the list of nonvoting observers. Actions by the forum would be by consensus; reports and studies would be initiated by a majority. The practical aspect of such an arrangement is that it allows a majority to call for any information that it believes the organization needs while preserving the right of individual members to prevent the forum from taking any action without their approval. The result would be a forum that could discuss sensitive issues that otherwise would be stricken from the agenda during the early life of the organization. As the organization matured, some sensitive subjects would become much easier to broach. The organization should create its own multilateral think tank, composed of a minimum of two scholars from each member nation working at the direction of the secretariat. This internal think tank could be supplemented by studies commissioned separately by member nations using their own nation's assets.

The most likely candidate for the site of the secretariat is Beijing, a P-5 nation with experience in organizing the six-party process. If Japan were to resolve its historical problems with its neighbors permanently, Tokyo would be an alternative location. Seoul would be another consideration.

CHALLENGES

The single biggest obstacle to creating a permanent security organization in Northeast Asia is the inevitable set-asides that member nations would insist upon. Beijing would not be likely to allow Taiwan to become an agenda item, claiming that anything related to Taiwan is a domestic issue; similarly, Seoul would have been unlikely to allow open discussion of its revelation of its laser experiments. But in truth, the ROK's experiments with laser enrichment of uranium in 2000 and its plutonium experiments of 1982 are perfect examples of security-related issues that could be on the agenda if there were a Northeast Asia security mechanism. While the laser experiments were a matter to be dealt with primarily under the terms of the Nuclear Non-Proliferation Treaty, an informal meeting would be ideal for clarifying the facts of such an issue in a nonconfrontational manner to the satisfaction of the nations in the region, even as the IAEA conducted its formal investigation and delivered its report. Such a process would be evidence of the sincerity of member nations' efforts to achieve transparency, which would be one of the objectives of a security organization. Although Japan would be likely to want to set aside the visits of its prime minister to Yasukuni Shrine, that too is an example of an issue that would benefit from a closed-door discussion among the regional players.

Although there will be certain sensitive issues that an embryonic security organization will not be able to place on the agenda, the benefits of regular and relatively transparent dialogue on ways to reduce tension and cooperate to maximize the region's potential far outweigh academic criticisms of any such organization's shortcomings. At this point, the question is not whether there will be a multilateral security forum in East Asia but whether the United States has been too slow in assuming a leadership role in the development of an organization that will meet its needs as well as the needs of the major players in Northeast Asia. Or has the East Asia summit begun to fill that niche at the expense of the United States?

During the inaugural meeting of the East Asia summit, Chinese premier Wen Jiabao commented that "the United States, the European Union and other countries and organizations *outside* the region are also welcome to develop relations with the East Asia cooperation mechanism." He also pledged that China would support the East Asia cooperation mechanism in coordinating with entities such as the Shanghai Cooperation Organization, the ASEAN Regional Forum, the Asia Cooperation Dialogue, and Asia-Pacific Economic Cooperation.[23]

Part of the joint statement issued after the fourth round of six-party talks notes that "the six parties agreed to explore ways and means for promoting security cooperation in northeast Asia."[24] Moreover, at their summit meeting before the 2005 APEC meeting in Korea, President Bush and President Roh issued a joint statement acknowledging the importance of establishing a security forum in Northeast Asia:

> President Roh and President Bush agreed to make common efforts to develop a regional multilateral security dialogue and a cooperation mechanism, so as to jointly respond to regional security issues. In this regard, both leaders noted that the participants in the Six-Party Talks agreed through the Joint Statement to look for ways and means to promote security cooperation in Northeast Asia and that there was a common understanding among the participants that the Six-Party Talks could develop into such a regional multilateral security consultative mechanism once the North Korean nuclear issue is resolved.[25]

The challenge for the United States is to look beyond the narrow confines of the six-party talks and to avoid basing the future security of Northeast Asia on the vicissitudes of North Korea's cooperation in resolving the current nuclear crisis. The United States opted out of a leadership role in the development and management of the six-party talks in favor of China; it cannot afford to repeat the same mistake when it comes to establishing a multilateral security mechanism in Northeast Asia.[26] Washington should act now, using the diplomatic coordination born of the six-party talks to call for a Northeast Asia vision group. Such a group could look at the success of the six-party consultations and establish a working summit of interested heads of state with the express purpose of creating a Northeast Asia security organization whose immediate task would be to agree on broad objectives, membership, governing rules, and establishment of a permanent secretariat.

The Consequences of Inertia

Failure to act in the near future could well mean that long-term U.S. influence in Northeast Asia will erode—politically, economically, and militarily—in comparison with the legitimate rise of China, the maturing of South Korea's foreign policy, and the inevitable increase in Japanese nationalism. Trying to create ad hoc security meetings among Northeast Asian nations on a case-by-case basis is an inefficient way to address serious concerns that offers no prospect for generating the appropriate level of attention. On a practical note, it dooms diplomats to expend vast amounts of time and energy devising potential trade-offs in order to get the right nations together whenever a particular issue rises to the top. If the issue in question is important enough or at all time sensitive, there is no guarantee that an ad hoc meeting could be pulled together quickly enough to prevent the issue from worsening.

On the other hand, expending the time and effort now to create a permanent security forum would permit the forum's permanent staff and research component to immediately address concerns at an early stage. Communications among the secretariat staff would constitute the first level of dispute resolution, framing the discussion for a meeting of more senior staff as expeditiously as possible. Impromptu gatherings such as that of six-party heads of delegation in Tokyo on the margins of the Northeast Asia Cooperation Dialogue in April 2006 would be the rule rather the exception.[27]

The benefits associated with the creation of a permanent security forum far outweigh any potential argument against it. Ultimately, it is the failure of the six-party talks that argues most forcefully for the creation of a security mechanism. Absent such a mechanism, there are no institutions to deal with the complex issues that will continue to face Northeast Asian countries or to prevent or deal with the next crisis. But there is a danger that this window of opportunity could be closed; if it is, the region could then fall back into an ad hoc process marked by the weaknesses that arise from distrust. The time is right to harness the spirit of consultation to create a permanent security forum in Northeast Asia. The conditions are favorable; the only real obstacle is inertia.

Epilogue

If at any time during the first six years of the Bush administration anyone had proposed providing a six-man North Korean delegation visiting the United States with fifteen security personnel and four limousines, the individual would have been laughed out of the room. However, that is exactly the treatment Vice Minister Kim Gye-gwan received when he visited New York City to participate in the normalization working group established under the February 13, 2007, agreement between the United States and the DPRK. Adding insult to injury for the hard-line element that had for so long dominated North Korea policy, the working group met in what had been the official residence at the Waldorf Hotel of John Bolton, the former U.S. ambassador to the UN.

The February 13 agreement envisions a process that is rather open ended. The first phase will be complete in sixty days. The second, more difficult phase—in which North Korea is to provide a list of all its nuclear programs and disable its nuclear facilities in exchange for 950,000 tons of heavy fuel oil or their equivalent—does not have a specified completion date. Dismantlement has not been negotiated, and nuclear weapons have not been discussed. Compare that with the U.S. proposal during the third round of six-party talks to have North Korea provide a complete list of all its nuclear activities and cease all nuclear operations; permit the securing of all fissile material and the monitoring of all fuel rods; and publicly disclose all nuclear weapons, weapon components, and key centrifuge parts and permit observation of their disablement—all within three months.

While the U.S. position has been inconsistent and unrealistic, the North Korean position has been consistently unrealistic. On September 20, 2005, Pyongyang issued a unilateral statement, following the joint statement of the day before, in which it declared that dismantlement of its nuclear facilities at Yongbyon would not occur before the DPRK was provided a light-water reactor. On March 4, 2007, I had a private dinner with Vice Minister Kim and members of his delegation. He repeated to me (and again at another meeting later in the week) that North Korea must be guaranteed a light-water reactor before dismantlement would begin. In chapter 8, I said that the Bush administration had, by agreeing to the inclusion of an LWR in the September 19, 2005, joint statement, given North Korea a false promise and provided Pyongyang with negotiating ammunition to use throughout the six-party talks. I was correct. The North Koreans have successfully moved discussion of the LWR from "an appropriate time" (meaning after total denuclearization) to early in the nuclear facilities dismantlement phase. It is unlikely that a serious discussion on the provision of a light-water reactor will take place before an agreement is reached on disposition of the actual nuclear weapons. But Pyongyang has introduced another obstacle that will have to be dealt with later on.

At the end of the fifth round of talks in November 2005, Vice Minister Kim proposed a five-point roadmap by which the DPRK would suspend nuclear tests, ban proliferation, ban further nuclear production, verifiably stop nuclear activities and dismantle facilities, and return to the NPT, allowing IAEA inspections, in exchange for aid and normalization of relations—which sounds eerily familiar to the agreement that was eventually worked out in Berlin in January 2007 and announced on February 13. Secretary Rice, who characterized the November 2005 offer as not helpful, embraced the February 13 deal fifteen months later—after North Korea's October 9, 2006, nuclear test.

As the first meeting of the U.S.-DPRK normalization working group concluded on March 6, 2007, it appeared that both the United States and North Korea were prepared to move beyond the first phase of the February 13 agreement without too much difficulty. The next phase, in which North Korea is required to list all its nuclear programs (both plutonium and enriched uranium) and disable its nuclear facilities, will be the first test for the Bush's administration new policy approach toward the DPRK. After six years of failed diplomacy, the administration needs some good news.

Letter from Charles L. Pritchard
to Kim Gye-gwan

June 13, 2001

Dear Minister Kim:

I am writing to you in my new capacity as Special Envoy. As you know, I have been appointed to replace Ambassador Kartman, who retired from the Foreign Service. Having served as Ambassador Kartman's deputy in negotiations with you over the past several years, I am pleased with the opportunity to continue this important work.

For the past several months, I have been fully engaged in the review of policy toward the DPRK. Such a review is normal at the beginning of every administration. The President announced on June 6 that the review was finished and the United States is prepared to undertake serious discussions with the DPRK. As Secretary of State Powell said publicly, we attach no preconditions to these discussions.

To begin this process, I propose that you and I meet at the end of this month or in early July, outside of capitals, at a place of your choosing.

I look forward to your positive reply and to renewing our acquaintance at the earliest time.

Sincerely,
/s/
Charles L. (Jack) Pritchard

Memo Outlining the Objectives, Themes, and Goals of Upcoming Trilateral Talks, April 2003

Trilateral U.S.-PRC-DPRK Talks

OBJECTIVES

—Long-term: Lay the groundwork for expanded multilateral talks for the resolution of the nuclear problem.

—Near-term: Halt the additional activities (reprocessing) at Yongbyon; solidify alliance support for the long-term resolution of the nuclear problem; and transition from the trilateral talks to five-six party talks involving the ROK, Japan, and perhaps Russia.

THEMES AND GOALS

Initial session: Establish conditions for successful initial meeting (including full PRC participation) and prospects for continued contact that supports short and long-term goals.

—Repeat, on the record, for the benefit of Japan, the ROK and the PRC:

U.S. seeks peaceful diplomatic solution.

North Korea is different from Iraq.

—Distinguish between U.S. concerns over DPRK nuclear/military issues and U.S. concerns for welfare of DPRK citizens.

—Seek freeze of additional activities at Yongbyon during talks.

—Seek PRC confirmation of common objectives of nuclear-free Korean Peninsula.

—Agree to open-ended agenda; confirm that DPRK can raise any issue.

—Explain why resolution can only occur in a truly multilateral setting. Review necessity and value of ROK and Japan participation.

U.S. aim to end DPRK nuclear threat verifiably and irreversibly but willing to listen to others' concerns; prepare as appropriate to address DPRK expressions of concern about security; after nuclear program ended, U.S. could discuss other issues of concern, would aim toward a situation providing mutual benefits for all sides if DPRK addresses our concerns.

Follow-on sessions: Put HEU in perspective.

—Review purpose and history of Agreed Framework. Emphasize that Framework was intended to be a permanent solution, but had turned out to be temporary. Any resolution had to be permanent and irreversible.

—Refer to what could have been: the Bold Approach, with intent of giving the DPRK a glimpse of what resolution of the nuclear issue could lead to. Explain sequence of what is required: renunciation of nuclear weapons program, verifiable and irreversible dismantling of the HEU and plutonium program.

—Be prepared to review status of KEDO and the LWR project; introduce possibility of energy assistance (conventional) via revamped KEDO *vice* LWRs *once* nuclear issue resolved.

—Propose continuation of talks in expanded five-six party format. Alternatively, if that is not initially acceptable, propose a step forward by including the ROK in a four-party format.

—Obtain agreement that DPRK discontinue/freeze further activity at the reprocessing facility, return to NPT, and allow IAEA monitors to return and reseal spent fuel storage facility and the reprocessing facility while expanded talks continue.

THINGS TO LOOK OUT FOR/AVOID

Be prepared for DPRK laundry list of U.S. provocations/hostile acts:
—U.S. unproven accusations about HEU
—U.S. led decision to cut off HFO
—Boarded the Sosan
—Axis of evil
—Preemptive strike list
—Additional forces to Peninsula (regardless of exercise justification)
—Movement of Carl Vinson into AO (regardless of backfill status of Kitty Hawk)

—Announcement of bomber package to Guam (support package)
—SECDEF reference to DPRK as terrorist regime
—Referral by IAEA to UNSC of DPRK NPT withdrawal
—Blocking of travel permits to National Prayer Breakfast.

Understand that DPRK will not resolve our concerns in one session.

DPRK will be playing to its home audience; will need to show it can stand up to the U.S.; avoid rising to the bait to respond to its rhetoric.

DPRK will want reciprocal actions, i.e., U.S. turn on the HFO in return for actions at Yongbyon.

DPRK will want security guarantee; President and Secretary have already given elements of political guarantees, but Pyongyang will seek more.

Statement of Assistant Secretary of State Christopher R. Hill

New York City, NY
September 19, 2005
North Korea—U.S. Statement

The following statement by the head of the U.S. delegation to the Six-Party Talks,
Christopher R. Hill, was released in Beijing on September 19, 2005

Assistant Secretary of State Christopher R. Hill's Statement at the
Closing Plenary of the Fourth Round of the Six-Party Talks
September 19, 2005

I would like to join with my colleagues from the ROK and Russian delegations in expressing my deep appreciation for China's leadership in chairing and hosting this fourth round of the Six-Party Talks. The United States is able to join in supporting the Joint Statement on the basis of the following understandings:

Let me start by noting that the goal of the Six-Party Talks is the prompt and verifiable denuclearization of the Korean Peninsula. When this goal is achieved, it will open up a new chapter for all Korean people. We know that the document includes undertakings for all the parties; my government is prepared to fulfill all our undertakings.

All elements of the DPRK's past and present nuclear programs—plutonium and uranium—and all nuclear weapons will be comprehensively declared and completely, verifiably and irreversibly eliminated, and will not be reconstituted in the future. According to these principles, the DPRK will return, at an early date, to the NPT and come into full compliance with IAEA safeguards, including by taking all steps that may be deemed necessary to verify the correctness and completeness of the DPRK's declarations of nuclear materials and activities.

But in addition to these obligations, there are also benefits that the DPRK will accrue. But these benefits will only accrue in the context of the denuclearization of the Korean Peninsula. In the statement of principles, there is a reference to the "appropriate time" to discuss the subject of the DPRK's use of nuclear energy for peaceful purposes, such as the subject of the provision of a light water reactor, but that "appropriate time" will only come when the DPRK has:

—Promptly eliminated all nuclear weapons and all nuclear programs, and this has been verified to the satisfaction of all parties by credible international means, including the IAEA; and,

—When the DPRK has come into full compliance with the NPT and IAEA safeguards, *and* has demonstrated a sustained commitment to cooperation and transparency and has ceased proliferating nuclear technology.

When these conditions have been met, I want to be very clear—we will *support* such a discussion.

The United States notes that the NPT recognizes the right of parties to the Treaty to pursue peaceful uses of nuclear energy in the context of compliance with Articles I and II of the Treaty. Foremost among the Treaty's obligations is the commitment not to possess or pursue nuclear weapons. The Treaty also calls for its parties to adhere to safeguards agreements with the IAEA. Thus, the DPRK's statement concerning its "right" to the peaceful uses of nuclear energy should be premised upon the completion of verification of the DPRK's elimination of all nuclear weapons and existing nuclear programs and full compliance with the NPT and IAEA safeguards.

I would like to note also that the United States supports a decision to terminate KEDO by the end of the year.

We should also note for the record that the United States will take concrete actions necessary to protect ourselves and our allies against any illicit and proliferation activities on the part of the DPRK.

The United States desires to completely normalize relations with the DPRK, but as a necessary part of discussions, we look forward to sitting down with the DPRK to address other important issues. These outstanding issues include human rights abuses, biological and chemical weapons programs, ballistic missile programs and proliferation, terrorism, and illicit activities.

The Joint Statement accurately notes the willingness of the United States to respect the DPRK's sovereignty and to exist with the DPRK peacefully together. Of course, in that context the United States continues to have serious concerns about the treatment of people and behavior in areas such as human rights in the DPRK. The U.S. acceptance of the Joint Statement should in no way be interpreted as meaning we accept all aspects of the DPRK's system, human rights situation or treatment of its people. We intend to sit down and make sure that our concerns in these areas are addressed.

The Joint Statement sets out a visionary view of the *end-point* of the process of the denuclearization of the Korean Peninsula. It is a very important first step to get us to the critical and urgent next phase—implementation of DPRK commitments outlined above and the measures the United States and other parties would provide in return, including security assurances, economic and energy cooperation, and taking steps toward normalized relations.

The United States believes that it is imperative to move rapidly on an agreement to implement the goals outlined in the Joint Statement. We look forward to working with all the other parties, including the DPRK, to do so.

Report on North Korean Nuclear Program

On Oct. 31 to Nov. 4, 2006, a delegation led by Prof. John W. Lewis, Stanford University, accompanied by Siegfried S. Hecker and Robert L. Carlin of Stanford University and Charles L. (Jack) Pritchard of the Korean Economic Institute, visited Pyongyang, Democratic People's Republic of Korea (DPRK). This report summarizes the findings regarding the DPRK nuclear program based on our discussions with officials from the Ministry of Foreign Affairs, the Korean People's Army, the Supreme People's Assembly, and the Yongbyon Nuclear Scientific Research Center. Three members of our delegation made similar visits to the DPRK in January 2004 and August 2005. Before and after the current trip to the DPRK, Lewis and Hecker also had extensive discussions about the DPRK nuclear program with Chinese officials from the Ministry of Foreign Affairs, the military, the Central Party School, the China Reform Forum, the China National Nuclear Corporation, and the Institute of Applied Physics and Computational Mathematics.

Summary Observations

This trip provided a status report of the DPRK nuclear program and yielded new, valuable insights related to the nuclear test, the plutonium production capacity, and the status of the nuclear weapons program.

This report was written by Siegfried S. Hecker, Center for International Security and Cooperation, Stanford University, November, 15, 2006.

Nuclear test. We were not able to meet with technical specialists responsible for the nuclear test or its design. DPRK political and military officials told us the test was fully successful and achieved its goal. We can still only speculate whether the DPRK nuclear device was designed to produce a relatively low yield with a large, simple Nagasaki-like device or if it was a sophisticated, missile-capable design with smaller dimensions. Although we cannot rule out the more sophisticated design, the more likely option is one proposed by Chinese nuclear specialists; that is, the DPRK tested a simple device of relatively low yield to make absolutely certain that they could contain the nuclear explosion in their underground test tunnel. The Chinese nuclear specialists concluded, "If the DPRK aimed for 4 kilotons and got 1 kiloton, that is not bad for a first test. We call it successful, but not perfect."

Plutonium production. Yongbyon nuclear center Director Ri Hong Sop appeared confident and satisfied with the operations of the 5 MWe reactor (which is accumulating approximately one bomb's worth of plutonium per year), and he is in no hurry to unload the fuel rods currently in the reactor. However, it appears that technical difficulties associated with fuel cladding integrity and refurbishment of the fuel fabrication facility may impact the political decision as to when to unload the reactor and process more plutonium. For technical reasons, the DPRK will be able to produce at most one bomb's worth of plutonium per year for the next few years. In addition, technical difficulties are slowing down the resumption of full-scale construction of the 50 MWe reactor, which would increase plutonium production ten-fold. Although a political decision on a full construction restart apparently has not yet been made, these difficulties will put the completion of the reactor and a significant scale-up of plutonium production at least several years into the future. On the other hand, the Yongbyon nuclear center appears to have fully mastered plutonium metal production and casting, including having prepared the plutonium for the DPRK nuclear test. My best estimate is that before the test, the DPRK had separated between 40 and 50 kg of plutonium, sufficient for roughly six to eight bombs. They most likely used approximately 6 kg for their first test.

Nuclear weapons. We know very little about the DPRK nuclear stockpile and the nation's nuclear strategy. DPRK officials stated the role of their nuclear weapons is to deter the United States and defend the sovereignty of their state. The officials we met appeared to have little appreciation for the new challenges they faced for nuclear weapons safety and security that results from the possession of nuclear weapons. They stated that DPRK's commitment to denuclearize remains unchanged in spite of their nuclear test, but it will require the

United States to stop threatening the DPRK state. They also pledged not to transfer nuclear weapons to other states or terrorists. Yet, my general impression is that the hurdles to convincing the DPRK to give up its nuclear weapons have increased substantially with its Feb.10, 2005, announcement of having manufactured nuclear weapons and its Oct. 9, 2006, nuclear test. It is essential for the United States to demonstrably address DPRK's security before there is any hope of denuclearization.

Nuclear test

On Oct. 9, 2006, the DPRK conducted a nuclear test in the northeastern part of the DPRK. On Oct. 16, the U.S. Office of Nuclear Intelligence issued the statement: "Analysis of air samples collected Oct. 11, 2006, detected radioactive debris which confirms that North Korea conducted an underground nuclear explosion in the vicinity of P'unggye on Oct. 9, 2006. The explosion yield was less than 1 kiloton." Reports of seismic signals from around the world ranged from a magnitude of 3.5 to 4.2 on the Richter scale. There is uncertainty in translating these measurements to explosion yield because of lack of knowledge of the exact geology at the test site. Most of the yield estimates reported to date range from 0.2 to 1.0 kiloton.[1,2] Subsequent press reports suggested that there was evidence that the test was of a plutonium bomb.[3] However, such information would be difficult to obtain and has never been officially confirmed.

The director of the Yongbyon nuclear center did not discuss the test results beyond the fact that his facility produced the plutonium metal for the test device. He told us that plutonium metal was used and it was of the type that they allowed me to hold (in a sealed glass jar) during my January 2004 visit to Yongbyon.[4,5,6] He indicated that his responsibilities end with plutonium metal production. The technical specialists associated with nuclear weapons design and testing were not made available for discussion during our visit. So, our questions regarding technical details of the test—such as the type of device, the yield, test diagnostics, and post-explosion diagnostics—remained unanswered.

The diplomatic officials and military officials were not reluctant to discuss the nuclear test. They declared the nuclear test "powerful and fully successful." Their comments included "the test has given us hope for the future; we are confident and full of pride." When we inquired about press reports that the nuclear test may have been a failure or only partially successful, they indicated that they are aware of the criticism but "the criticism does not conform to reality." They reiterated, "The test was successful. We don't care what others say. We are confident the test achieved our goals." All of our DPRK hosts projected an attitude of pride and confidence during this visit.

When asked about why the DPRK decided to test and why now, they responded that the test was "a result of U.S. political pressure. The test is an active self-defense measure." They also indicated that the nuclear test was legal because the United States withdrew from the Agreed Framework and the DPRK withdrew from the Nuclear Nonproliferation Treaty (NPT). "Without this pressure there would have been no test." They also indicated that it is quite natural for a nuclear weapons state to test. The United States should not have been surprised. None of the officials we met gave us the impression that they are planning a second nuclear test. We told our hosts that they are the first country to announce its first nuclear test. Moreover, the apparent DPRK explosion yield is much lower than those of the first tests conducted by other countries. Why did they announce their test? The military official answered, "We could either not announce, or announce and make certain that the test is carried out safe and secure. Which is more beneficial and reasonable?" To summarize the DPRK nuclear testing discussions, their officials declared it a successful test of a plutonium nuclear device.

We were told that the DPRK gave both the Chinese and Russian embassies two hours advance notice of the test. We received no definitive response to our question of whether or not this notice included an estimate of the expected explosion yield of the test. We were subsequently told in China by officials from the Ministry of Foreign Affairs and other organizations that China was given the following advance notice about the test: time, location, and an estimated explosion yield of approximately 4 kilotons.

Based on independent seismic measurements around the world, the test had an explosion yield between 0.2 and 1 kiloton. It was confirmed to be a nuclear test based on radioactive air sampling results reported by the United States. A plutonium device is consistent with the DPRK plutonium production program. That is all we know for certain at this time. The explosion yields of the first nuclear test conducted by the seven declared nuclear weapons states range from approximately 10 to 60 kilotons. The Nagasaki bomb yielded approximately 21 kilotons. So, by comparison, the DPRK explosion yield was low.

We can only speculate whether the DPRK nuclear device was designed to produce a relatively low yield with a large, simple device along the lines of a Nagasaki design or if it was a sophisticated design with smaller dimensions and mass so as to fit onto a Nodong medium-range missile. A test of a sophisticated device could readily explain the low yield since it is very difficult to get all technical parameters correct the first time. Opting for testing a sophisticated device would represent a big step for a first test. I should add that given the low yield results and without further tests, it is highly unlikely that they have gained sufficient confidence to field such a device on a missile. Although we cannot rule out their willingness to take such a step, I find it more likely that they opted for the more conservative approach of a simple design. Our discussions with Chinese nuclear specialists provided some interesting insight. First, they told us that the Chinese seismic stations close to the DPRK test location recorded a magnitude of 4.1 to 4.2, from which they estimate an explosion yield close to 1 kiloton. They believe that the DPRK opted for a simple design at 4 kilotons to make absolutely certain that they contain the nuclear explosion in their underground test tunnel without massive radioactive leakage.[7] We were told, "If the DPRK aimed for 4 kilotons and got 1 kiloton, that is not bad for a first test. We call it successful, but not perfect." This appeared to be a technical judgment, not one related to the utility of a nuclear weapon of similar design. In my opinion, that is a reasonable assessment based on the facts we have at this time. The availability of plutonium may also affect test decisions in the DPRK. As noted below, the DPRK's weapons-usable plutonium inventory is limited to 40 to 50 kg. Therefore, they will keep the number of tests to a minimum. However, for the first test, I do not believe the amount of available plutonium influenced the decision to test a simple vs. a sophisticated design.

Plutonium production

The director of the Yongbyon nuclear center, Dr. Ri Hong Sop, met us in Pyongyang to present a status update of Yongbyon nuclear activities. During our January 2004 visit to Yongbyon, he took us to the 5 MWe reactor, the spent-fuel storage pool, and the plutonium reprocessing facility (called the Radiochemical Laboratory). We also drove by the construction site for the 50 MWe reactor and discussed its status. In August 2005, the director provided us a status report on all of these facilities in a meeting in Pyongyang.

The 5 MWe reactor.[8] Director Ri informed us that the reactor was operating but with some restrictions. Although the reactor is operating at its full 25 MWt (thermal power), the output temperature has been reduced to 300°C from 350°C. He indicated that the lower temperature produces higher weapons-quality plutonium, but it reduces the efficiency of the electrical power output. However, the principal reason for lowering the temperature was to avoid fuel cladding failures.[9] "The reactor operators decide the operating temperature based on what is best for the safety of the fuel rods.

Replacing fuel rods is time consuming, so running at a lower temperature is more advantageous."

We asked if they had many on-off cycles in reactor operations in the current campaign.[10] He claimed not. They have removed damaged fuel rods a couple of times. They inspect the fuel rods carefully before loading, and they examine them periodically while in the reactor. This is the only time they have lowered the power. He stated, "There have been no big fluctuations in power over the past year. We only did this during planned inspections." He said that in 2005 they were concerned about the fuel rods, but that reprocessing campaign demonstrated that the fuel rods and cladding were generally in good shape. The fuel rods for the third campaign were also all fabricated before the 1994 shutdown prompted by the Agreed Framework. He was not particularly concerned about the current load of fuel rods because these were inspected before loading. Only a small number of rods had corroded. They found replacements for these rods. His overall assessment of reactor operations was that he is happy with reactor operations during the past year. They had to lower the temperature and do some minor maintenance and fuel rod replacements.

We asked about plans to unload the reactor, which has been operating with the current fuel load since June 2005. Director Ri said that from a technical standpoint they would do so sometime next year. However, there are other factors that he does not decide. "The political situation may change. So, sometimes we unload the reactor earlier even though it is less favorable for us technically." When asked about the availability of another reactor core load of fuel rods, he said that at this point they still have a number of fuel rods from the pre-1994 inventory that was inspected by the International Atomic Energy Agency (IAEA). There were insufficient fuel rods for a full reactor core load of 8,000 fuel rods.

Fuel fabrication facility. We inquired about the status of the fuel fabrication facility.[11] He stated, "We are finalizing facility preparations now." He indicated that although parts of the original line had collapsed, they were in the final stages of refurbishment now. They expect to begin new fuel fabrication in 2007. It will take them approximately one year to fabricate an entire reactor core of fresh fuel rods. Since they still have spare fuel rods from the previous inventory, they can replace fuel rods as necessary. So, when they shut down the reactor, they plan to have a fresh charge ready to go. If it is decided to shut down the reactor earlier, they will consider doing a partial unloading, replacing the rods in the center of the reactor core first. They would use the remaining spare rods and whatever fresh rods they had fabricated by then. In response to our question of whether or not they had all the materials they needed for the refurbishment, including stainless steel, indigenously, he replied, "Yes, we do."

Reprocessing facility and plutonium metal production.[12] Director Ri told us that when they conducted the second reprocessing campaign in 2005, they decided to postpone the waste treatment activity to 2006. That is what they are doing now at Yongbyon, and because of the resulting high radiation levels during this operation, they do not allow outsiders to visit. He confirmed that the 30 percent improvement in throughput in plutonium reprocessing that he mentioned in August 2005 was obtained by replacing some of the mixer-settlers with pulsed columns. He indicated that they made this change only for the uranium–plutonium co-extraction line, not for the entire line because of the complexity of changing an operating line. If they could do it all over again, they would use pulsed columns instead of mixer-settlers in the entire line. When we expressed surprise they were able to make this change at all noting how difficult it is to do in our facilities, he said, "Well, we did it. Maybe it shows our technicians are more advanced than yours." Our rejoinder was that, nevertheless, it is a big deal to make these kinds of changes in an operating facility.[13] To this he answered, "Yes, but because of the nuclear threat (meaning the threat from the United States), we had to do this in spite of the risk." We asked again if they had all the necessary equipment indigenously, and the reply was yes. He said they can produce corrosion-resistant steels in the DPRK and all the chemicals are produced domestically, including the tributyl phosphate used in the separations process.

Director Ri also stated with pride that they have mastered the entire plutonium production cycle. They initially designed the Radiochemical Laboratory for a commercial nuclear fuel cycle, that is, "We make plutonium oxalate and plutonium oxide. However, following the U.S. cutoff of heavy fuel oil in Nov. 2002, we decided to resume reactor operation and changed the design of the Radiochemical Laboratory to go from plutonium oxalate, to plutonium oxide, to plutonium tetrafluoride, to plutonium metal, which is then electrorefined, alloyed, and cast." The electrorefining step is to purify the plutonium metal. He stated: "Because we completed the (entire) process, we announced in Feb. 2005 that we produced nuclear weapons."

We inquired about the nature of the plutonium metal and shape used for the nuclear test and if it was manufactured at Yongbyon. Director Ri indicated that the metal is of the nature I touched in Jan. 2004. He can't tell me anything about the shape. They cast the gross plutonium shapes at Yongbyon; the device is fabricated elsewhere beyond his jurisdiction. He also indicated that most of their plutonium research is focused on ensuring a sound cast product. They do extensive examination of the purity, density, and uniformity of the plutonium castings. They do little plutonium properties research because most properties of plutonium are well known.

50 MWe and 200 MWe reactors.[14] In Jan. 2004, we drove by the 50 MWe reactor in Yongbyon. The outside of the reactor building looked in bad repair. Apparently, nothing had been done to the site during the Agreed Framework freeze. In August 2005, Director Ri told us that they had completed a design study that concluded that construction of the reactor could continue on its original site with much of its original equipment. He said that the core of the reactor and other components were not at the Yongbyon site. He said their workers are ready to go back to reactor construction, although he did not give us an expected completion date.

During this visit, we were told that virtually nothing had been done at the 50 MWe reactor site and that they have run into some difficulties. Director Ri stated, "We are now in a partial preparation, not in full swing." The current effort is directed at "recovering the original state of the equipment; for example, removing rust from the steel." He said, "The main problem is the preparation by other industries, recovery in other factories, not on site at Yongbyon. This is not a simple job, nor a small job. The problem is in outside industrial facilities." Responding to our question about having all materials for this construction job available within the DPRK, he answered, "It is difficult to import, so we must do everything ourselves. It will take longer." When asked about the timing of resuming full operations, he said, "I have sent a schedule to the higher level, but have not yet received instructions. I expect to get instructions soon."

The 200 MWe construction site is at Taechon, about 20 km from Yongbyon. Nothing has been done at the site since the Agreed Framework freeze was instituted in 1994. Director Ri told us last year that they are still studying what to do with the reactor. He said it is most likely less expensive to start over than to continue on the current site. During this visit, he told us that there is nothing new on this reactor. He said: "We will sequence the decision. First, we will do the 50 MWe reactor, then we'll address the 200 MWe reactor."

When considering plutonium production, the status of the 5 MWe reactor is important. DPRK plans to unload the current reactor core of fuel rods and reprocess them. Future plans for reloading are difficult to assess. Some of the key decisions are clearly high-level political decisions. And, although the Yongbyon leadership appears confident, it appears that technical difficulties associated with fuel cladding integrity and refurbishment of the fuel fabrication facility may impact the political decision. For technical reasons, the DPRK will be able to produce at most one bomb's worth of plutonium per year for the next few years. It also appears that technical difficulties are slowing down the resumption of full-scale construction of the 50 MWe reactor. Although a political decision on a full restart apparently has not yet been made, these difficulties will put the completion of the reactor and a significant scale-up of plutonium production at least several years into the future. On the other hand, the Yongbyon nuclear center appears to have fully mastered plutonium metal production and casting, including having prepared the plutonium for the DPRK nuclear test.

Uranium enrichment

We held no discussions during this visit related to potential DPRK enrichment efforts. During our previous visits, the DPRK Ministry of Foreign Affairs officials denied having any part of an enrichment program. We concluded, however, that in light of the suspected DPRK procurement activities in the 1990s, confessions of A.Q. Khan and recent statements by Pakistani President Pervez Musharraf, it is very likely that the DPRK has at least a research-scale uranium enrichment effort. We should note that four years after U.S. Assistant Secretary of State James Kelly first accused the DPRK of having a covert enrichment program, we have no additional information about these activities.

Nuclear weapons

We know even less about DPRK's nuclear weapons than about their nuclear test. DPRK officials told us that they have demonstrated their deterrent. They emphasized, "DPRK needs the deterrent; otherwise it can't defend its sovereignty." We probed their view of nuclear weapons as a deterrent and what they considered their new responsibility now that they have demonstrated a nuclear capability. Specifically, we asked what they are doing to ensure nuclear weapons safety and security. We expressed concern that if they have their weapons ready to use in order to deter, they may be particularly vulnerable to safety and security problems. It would be catastrophic for everyone if one of their weapons detonated accidentally on their own soil. They reiterated that, "The DPRK will not use nuclear weapons first, nor give them to terrorists like al Qaeda. We make these expensive weapons to defend our right to survive." However, in discussions during all three of our visits, we found little appreciation for the serious risks entailed by a weaponized nuclear deterrent and found little thought given to nuclear strategy.

What about denuclearization in light of what they called their successful nuclear test? We were told, "Our commitment to denuclearization and the Sept. 19, 2005, agreement remains unchanged, but we will make tougher demands that the United States remain faithful to its own (Sept. 19, 2005) commitments." The military official agreed, "If the DPRK feels that it could trust the United States, then there is no need even for a single nuclear weapon and we will dismantle them." The Ministry of Foreign Affairs officials also offered some hope by stating, "To achieve the Sept. 19 agreement, we must have both short-term and long-term objectives in the talk. We must suspend our nuclear activities. Without this, the nuclear weapons will increase. What others should do during the period between suspension and dismantlement is to build trust and confidence. The DPRK should stop production, testing, and transferring weapons. This should be done in a verifiable way. The United States should take actions in a verifiable way also."

Yet, my general impression is that the Oct. 9, 2006, nuclear test, which followed DPRK's Feb. 10, 2005, announcement of having manufactured nuclear weapons, will make it much more difficult to convince the DPRK to give up its nuclear weapons. The officials with whom we met presented the united front of pride and confidence instilled by what they called a "fully successful" nuclear test. It is also important to note that historically South Africa is the only nation to voluntarily give up nuclear weapons that it produced itself. However, the political and security circumstances were very different. The prevalent view we found in China, with which I concur, is that the United States must demonstrably address DPRK's security before there is any hope of denuclearization.

Summary Estimate of DPRK Nuclear Weapons Program

PLUTONIUM INVENTORIES

- < 1994 (IRT reactor & 5 MWe reactor) ~ 8.4 kg[15,16] (1+ weapons worth)
- 2003 (5 MWe reactor) ~ 25 kg (4-6 weapons worth)
- 2005 (5 MWe reactor) ~10-14 kg (~ 2 weapons worth)
- As of Nov. 2006 ~ 4-8 kg in reactor now (not separated)
- As of Nov. 2006, DPRK is highly likely to have 40 to 50 kg of separate plutonium (sufficient for six to eight nuclear weapons).

PLUTONIUM PRODUCTION CAPACITY

- 5 MWe reactor capacity ~ 6 kg/yr (1 weapon worth/yr)
- Future 50 MWe reactor ~ 60 kg/yr (~ 10 weapons worth/yr)

(Status: Recovery of components in progress. No visible construction on site. Decision on full restart expected soon from high level. Technical issues slowing progress.)
- Future of 200 MWe reactor ~ 200 kg/yr
  (Status: Decision postponed. Most likely costs more to continue than to start over.)

Nuclear weapons

- We still know very little. After 2004 visit, we concluded that given demonstrated technical capabilities, we must assume DPRK has produced at least a few simple, primitive nuclear devices.
- No information on whether or not devices are missile capable.
- U.S. report on Oct. 9, 2006, test: It was a nuclear test. DPRK confirmed it was a plutonium device. The explosion yield was estimated at ~ 4kt, but resulted in a yield < 1 kiloton.
- DPRK Nov. 2006 statement: It was fully successful. No more tests needed.
- China analysis: DPRK predicted 4 kt, achieved 1kt: "Successful, but not perfect."
- Even with test, still a long way to go to get missile-capable device.

Uranium enrichment

- We know even less. Continued denial by Ministry of Foreign Affairs against evidence that they have had some level of effort in this area.

We acknowledge with thanks support for this visit from the John D. and Catherine T. MacArthur Foundation, the Ploughshares Fund, Dr. Marjorie Kiewit, the Nuclear Threat Initiative, the Korea Economic Institute of America, and Stanford University's Center for International Security and Cooperation.

Notes

Chapter 1

1. Unpublished paper by Li Gun, December 2003 (copy in author's files).
2. Condoleezza Rice, "Campaign 2000: Promoting the National Interest," *Foreign Affairs* (January-February 2000).
3. "Clinton Won't Visit North Korea," Associated Press, December 28, 2000.
4. Jane Perlez, "U.S. Will Restart Wide Negotiations with North Korea," *New York Times*, June 7, 2001, p. A-1.
5. National Security Council, "Press Backgrounder Points," June 6, 2001.
6. Letter to DPRK Vice Minister Kim Gye-gwan (see appendix A).
7. KCNA, June 18, 2001.
8. U.S.-DPRK Joint Communiqué, Washington, D.C., October 12, 2000.
9. Glenn Kessler, "Three Little Words Matter to N. Korea," *Washington Post*, February 22, 2005, p. 10.
10. Testimony of Charles L. Pritchard before the House Committee on International Relations, Subcommittee on East Asia and the Pacific, 107 Cong., 1 sess., July 26, 2001.
11. Ibid.
12. KCNA, January 25, 2001: "The spokesman of the Foreign Ministry of the Democratic People's Republic of Korea gave today the following answer to the question put by KCNA as regards the recent provocative remark made by U.S. Secretary of State Powell against our supreme leadership. At a U.S. Senate confirmation hearing held on January 18, he dared make such reckless remark going against the elementary common sense as slandering our supreme leadership as 'dictator of north Korea.' . . .

The DPRK cannot but interpret what he said as a statement reflecting the sinister intention of big war industrial monopolies and other conservative hardliners in the U.S. to keep the U.S.-DPRK relations in the hostile and belligerent relationship forever and thus fish in troubled waters."

13. Republic of Korea, Office of the President, "South–North Joint Declaration," press release, June 15, 2000. President Bush is referring to a pledge by Kim Jong-il to reciprocate a visit by South Korea's president, Kim Dae-jung, to Pyongyang in June 2000.

14. White House, "Remarks by the President in Roundtable Interview with Asian Editors," internal transcript, October 16, 2001 (copy in author's files).

15. "Spokesman for DPRK Foreign Ministry Slams Bush's Remark," KCNA, October 23, 2001.

16. *Minju Chosun,* commentary, October 29, 2001. The North Korean reference to adopting at least the same stand as the preceding administration is meant more as a comment on the tone of the dialogue and the fact that there were a series of high-level exchanges of officials that came close to producing a summit meeting between President Clinton and Kim Jong-il.

17. "Bush's Remark Assailed," *Rodong Shinmun,* October 29, 2001.

18. White House, press conference, April 28, 2005 (www.whitehouse.gov/news/releases/2005/04/05).

19. "North Korea Hurls Taunts at Bush," *International Herald Tribune,* May 11, 2005 (quoting from *Rodong Shinmun,* April 29, 2005).

20. KCNA, May 14, 2005.

21. White House, State of the Union Address, January 29, 2002 (www.whitehouse.gov/news/releases/2002/01/29).

22. KCNA, February 2, 2002.

23. White House, "Remarks by President Bush during Press Availability with ROK President Kim Dae-jung, Seoul, Korea, February 20, 2002," press release (www.whitehouse.gov/news/releases/2002/02/20).

24. *Rodong Shinmun,* commentary, February 22, 2002.

Chapter 2

1. Enriching uranium requires linking together several thousands of centrifuges in what is referred to as a cascade. Uranium hexafloride (UF6) is introduced at the beginning of the cascade, and fissionable material is then separated from unneeded material; this process is repeated continuously until the uranium is enriched (concentrated) to the point that it is of weapons-grade quality.

2. Mitchell B. Reiss and Robert Gallucci, "Red-Handed," *Foreign Affairs* (March/April 2005).

3. KCNA, June 30, 2002 (www.kcna.co.jp).

4. There is more to the story of my own involvement in the process that led to the DPRK "regret" statement that will have to wait for another occasion to be told.

5. Jeff Baron, who worked in the Agreed Framework unit of the Korean affairs desk, drafted the initial speech, which I then reworked with an eye toward satisfying even the hard-line element of the administration.

6. "USG Remarks for KEDO Concrete Pouring Ceremony," delivered August 7, 2002, by the author.

7. General Hayden was promoted to lieutenant general and went on to be chief of Air Force Intelligence, director of the National Security Agency, first deputy director at the Director National Intelligence, and director of the Central Intelligence Agency.

8. It is important to note that the Pyongyang officials had no inkling that the United States would confront them over HEU; they fully expected the meeting to be a presentation of the Bold Approach. This may help explain the reaction by First Vice Minister Kang Sok-ju when he learned that we were there to confront them about HEU.

9. In August 1998, the U.S. intelligence community was following developments at Kumchang-ri, concerned that North Korea might have been trying to replicate underground its nuclear reactor and reprocessing facility at Yongbyon, which had been frozen by the 1994 Agreed Framework. The information was prematurely leaked, requiring the United States to confront North Korea and enter into eight months of negotiations that ultimately led to the United States sending an inspection team to Kumchang-ri on two occasions over a year. The inspection team concluded that there was no nuclear activity at Kumchang-ri.

10. Assistant secretary Christopher Hill before the House International Relations Committee, *The Six-Party Talks and the North Korean Nuclear Issue: Old Wine in New Bottles?* 109 Cong.,1 sess., October 6, 2005.

11. Unpublished paper by Li Gun, DPRK director general for American Affairs, December 2003 (copy in author's files). The preemption policy was first articulated in "The National Security Strategy of the United States," issued September 20, 2002. The following is the section of concern to Pyongyang: "The United States has long maintained the option of preemptive actions to counter a sufficient threat to our national security. The greater the threat, the greater is the risk of inaction—and the more compelling the case for taking anticipatory action to defend ourselves, even if uncertainty remains as to the time and place of an enemy's attack. To forestall or prevent such hostile acts by our adversaries, the United States will, if necessary, act preemptively."

12. See KEDO's website: www.kedo.org.

13. KEDO executive board statement, November 14, 2002 (www.kedo.org, archived news).

14. White House, Office of the Press Secretary, "Statement by the President," November 15, 2002 (www.whitehouse.gov/news/releases/2002/11/15).

15. Commentary in *Rodong Shinmun*, carried by KCNA, November 25, 2002 (www.kcna.co.jp).

16. December 12, 2002, letter from Ambassador Pak Gil Yon to Ambassador Jack Pritchard.

Chapter 3

1. NSPD 1 replaced both the Presidential Decision Directives and the Presidential Review Directives of the previous administration. NSPD 1, dated February 13, 2001, was formally approved for release by the National Security Council staff on March 13, 2001.

2. As reported to the author by a senior State Department official involved in the first meeting.

3. Lawrence Wilkerson, "Weighing the Uniqueness of the Bush Administration's National Security Policy: Boon or Danger to American Democracy?" presentation at the New America Foundation, Washington, October 19, 2005.

4. Bob Woodward, *Bush at War* (New York: Simon and Schuster, 2002), pp. 339–40.

5. "DPRK Stance toward Terrorist Attacks on U.S.," KCNA, September 12, 2001 (www.kcna.co.jp).

6. "Mr. Bush's Nuclear Legacy," *New York Times*, September 2, 2006.

Chapter 4

Portions of this chapter were first published in Charles "Jack" Pritchard, "The Korean Nuclear Crisis and Beyond," in *Brookings Northeast Asia Survey 2003–2004*, edited by Richard C. Bush, Sharon Yanagi, and Kevin Scott (Brookings); portions were further modified and published as "The Korean Peninsula and Role of Multilateral Talks," *Disarmament Forum*, vol. 2 (Geneva: UN Institute for Disarmament Research, 2005). For this book, I have added a significant amount of new material at the beginning of the chapter.

1. State of the Union Address, January 28, 2003.

2. "The United States Must Come Forth to DPRK-U.S. Direct Talks," commentary, *Rodong Shinmun*, March 11, 2003.

3. Trilateral U.S.-PRC-DPRK Talks. See appendix B.

4. In addition to the letter of resignation, I sent a detailed e-mail to Powell's chief of staff, Larry Wilkerson, providing more information on my decision to resign. When Secretary Powell received my resignation, he called me to his office and said that he understood and could not argue against my rationale. He then told me that he wanted to keep me at the State Department and asked me to give him a little time to figure out how he could best use me. He asked me not to tell anyone that I had resigned and to continue to work in the interim to realize the six-party talks. Out of respect for Powell, I honored his request until we had arranged for the first six-party talks in late August 2003. I then resubmitted my resignation and left government service.

Chapter 5

1. Condoleezza Rice, "Campaign 2000: Promoting the National Interest," *Foreign Affairs* (January-February 2000).

2. Norwegian Nobel Committee, press release, October 13, 2000,Oslo.

3. Office of the Press Secretary, February 15, 2001(www.whitehouse.gov/news/releases/2001/02/15).

4. Office of the Press Secretary, "Joint Statement between the United States of America and the Republic of Korea," March 7, 2001 (www.whitehouse.gov/news/releases/2001/03/07).

5. Opening statement by Secretary-designate Colin L. Powell, Washington, January 17, 2001.

6. Secretary of State Colin Powell, at a March 6, 2001, joint press conference with Swedish foreign minister Anna Lindh.

7. "U.S. Quits ABM Treaty," CNN.com/Inside Politics, December 14, 2001.

8. Brad Knickerbocker, "Allies Keep Balking at U.S. Missile Defense," *Christian Science Monitor,* March 9, 2001.

9. Speech to the Los Angeles World Affairs Council, November 12, 2004.

10. "Roh Shows Firm Belief in Peaceful End of Nuclear Row," *Korea Times,* December 5, 2004.

11. The veteran Korea hand insists on anonymity but graciously allowed me to use his views without attribution.

12. "Ban Credited with Improved Seoul-Washington Ties," *Yonhap,* January 2, 2006.

13. "Alliance Adjusts to Equal Footing: Ban," *Korea Times,* August 24, 2006.

Chapter 6

1. "Japan to Demand Kidnappers," *Japan Times,* January 10, 2006.

2. UN Security Council, Department of Public Information, 5551st Meeting of the Security Council, "Security Council Condemns Nuclear Test by Democratic People's Republic of Korea, Unanimously Adopting Resolution 1718" (2006).

3. Kang Chan-ho, "Analyst says U.S.-Korea Ties Troubling," *JoongAng Daily,* March 1, 2006.

4. "DPRK Entitled to Develop Peaceful Nuclear Program," *Xinhua,* August 16, 2005.

5. Murray Hiebert, "As U.S. Tries to Prod Pyongyang, Some Ask If Russia Can Do More," *Wall Street Journal,* June 28, 2005.

6. The Treasury Department, concerned that North Korea was conducting money laundering and counterfeiting activities at Banco Delta Asia, issued an advisory to U.S. banks warning them against doing business with the bank. Consequently, North Korean accounts were frozen pending the results of the U.S. investigation and the bank almost failed.

Chapter 7

1. "Spokesman for DPRK Foreign Ministry on Recent DPRK–U.S. Contact," KCNA, August 1, 2003 (www.kcna.co.jp).

2. "Vice Foreign Minister Wang Yi, Head of Chinese Delegation to the Six-Party

Talks, Gives a Press Conference," press briefing following the conclusion of the first round of six-party talks, Beijing, August 29, 2003 (www.fmprc.gov.cn).

3. *Chinese Commercial News*, Manila, September 2, 2003.

4. Report of a KCNA broadcast of October 21, 2003, *Yonhap News*, October 22, 2003 (http://english.yna.co.kr).

5. "Spokesman for DPRK Foreign Ministry on Proposed Written Assurances of Non-Aggression," KCNA, October 25, 2003 (www.kcna.co.jp).

6. Knight Ridder Newspapers, December 20, 2003.

7. Xinhua News Agency, Beijing, February 28, 2004 (www.xinhua.org/eng).

8. ITAR-TASS, Moscow, February 29, 2004 (www.ITAR-TASS.com/eng).

9. Xinhua News Agency, Beijing, March 5, 2004 (www.china.org.cn/english/international/89318.htm).

10. Testimony of assistant secretary of state James Kelly before the Senate Committee on Foreign Relations, *Report on the Latest Round of Six-Way Talks Regarding Nuclear Weapons in North Korea*, 108 Cong., 2 sess., July 15, 2004.

11. DPRK news conference at the six-way talks in Beijing, June 25, 2004 (www.xignite.com/xWorldNews.aspx?count=100&category=Korean%20&criteria=5&articleid=KPP20040625000125).

Chapter 8

1. Department of State biography, April 13, 2005 (www.state.gov/r/pa/ei/biog/44553.htm).

2. *The NewsHour with Jim Lehrer*, July 28, 2005.

3. Daily press briefing conducted by Sean McCormack, spokesman, Washington, June 29, 2005 (www.state.gov/r/pa/prs/dpb/2005/48767.htm).

4. "Bush Election 'Stopped Kim Jong-il Visiting Seoul,'" *Chosun Ilbo*, July 31, 2006, quoting from Jiang Zemin, "For a Better World: Jiang Zemin's Overseas Visits," World Affairs Press of China, Beijing, July 2006.

5. "China Rejects U.S. Suggestion to Cut Off Oil to Pressure North Korea," *Washington Post*, May 7, 2005.

6. "Kim Jong-Il Says N. Korea to Attend Nuclear Talks," Agence France-Presse, October 28, 2005.

7. "China's Exports of Crude Oil, Cereals to DPRK up in First Half of 2005," Xinhua News Agency, Shenyang, October 12, 2005.

8. "NK Diplomat Denies HEU, Rejects Seoul's Electricity Offer," *Yonhap*, October 28, 2005.

9. Charles L. Pritchard, "What I Saw in North Korea," *New York Times*, January 21, 2004.

10. Powell was interviewed by Nicholas Kralev and quoted in Kralev, "Diplomats Fight Their Stuffed-White-Shirt Image," *Washington Times*, March 8, 2004 (www.nicholaskralev.com/WT-FS-2.html):

Secretary of State Colin L. Powell said most Foreign Service officers feel the way

Mr. Boucher does, but there are a few who are not as "dedicated as I would like" them to be. He said that Jack Pritchard, the State Department's former special envoy for talks with North Korea who resigned in the summer over the administration's refusal to talk directly to the North, "is an example in point." "Jack was here for a couple of years," Mr. Powell said in an interview. "He was an expert in these matters, and he thought we ought to be moving in another direction, and I said, No, the president wants us to do it this way. And he left, and now he's writing long, tortured articles about how we are doing it wrong. Fine—you do it on the outside. But if you are in here, do it our way."

That prompted me to send the following e-mail message to Powell's chief of staff:

I am sorry facts and truth have been lost in only six short months. Perhaps the Secretary should reread my letter of resignation and the separate e-mail I sent you.

As for facts, perhaps the Secretary should reread the memo I sent to him on my recommendations on how to proceed, which he was in agreement with and forwarded to the President. We never had a conversation in which the Secretary told me "No, the president wants . . ." I value loyalty and have been both accurate and supportive of the Secretary while in government service and since my departure. I found it hard to believe that the Secretary actually implied that I had not "done it our way" while in the administration. The logic here is equally bizarre. I faithfully carried out the Secretary's instructions, defended the administration publicly, provided my advice in private and when I was left out of the equation in April (without a simple courtesy call to discuss the decision), I resigned. I refused to speak to the press the week after I left government while the August 2003 initial round of talks in Beijing was taking place. Once clear of the August talks I "did it on the outside" (as the Secretary suggests is proper). If the Secretary bothered to read my "long and tortured" articles, he would find I have never openly criticized the President or him. Revisionism does not suit the Secretary. I am very disappointed."

11. Conversation between Kim Gye-gwan and the author in Pyongyang on August 26, 2005.

12. Pritchard e-mail of August 8, 2005.

13. Assistant secretary of state Hill in an informal question-and-answer session with the press, September 11, 2005 (http://usinfo.state.gov/eap/Archive/2005/Sep/12-218864.html).

14. Kim Kwang-tae, "U.S. Rejects N. Korea's Demand for Light-Water Reactor," *Yonhap*, September 14, 2005.

15. Edward Cody, "Talks Deadlock Over N. Korea's Demand for Reactor; U.S. Could Seek Sanctions at U.N.," *Washington Post,* September 16, 2005.

16. "China Sets Saturday Deadline for Joint N. Korea Document," Agence France-Presse, September 16, 2005.

17. Ibid.

18. Ibid.

19. Joseph Kahn and David Sanger, "U.S.-Korean Deal on Arms Leaves Key Points Open," *New York Times* (Beijing), September 20, 2005.

20. Ibid.

21. "Spokesman for DPRK Foreign Ministry on Six-Party Talks," KCNA , September 20, 2005 (www.kcna.co.jp).

22. Sonni Efron, "A Tilt toward N. Korea," *Los Angeles Times*, September 21, 2005.

23. North Korea–U.S. statement at the closing plenary session of the fourth round of the six-party talks, September 19, 2005 (see appendix C).

24. Japanese statement at the conclusion of the fourth round of the six-party talks, September 19, 2005 (www.mofa.go.jp/region/asia-paci/n_korea/6party/remark0509.html).

25. North Korea–U.S. statement at the closing plenary session of the fourth round of the six-party talks.

26. Testimony by assistant secretary Christopher Hill before the House International Relations Committee, *The Six-Party Talks and the North Korean Nuclear Issue: Old Wine in New Bottles?*, 109 Cong.,1 sess., October 6, 2005.

27. Qin Gang, Foreign Ministry spokesman, press conference, September 20, 2005 (www.fmprc.gov.cn/chn/xwfw/fyrth/t212974.htm).

28. Unofficial translation of remarks by Alexander Alexeyev, Russian deputy minister of foreign affairs, at the final plenary session of the fourth round of the six-party talks, September 19, 2005 (www.mid.ru/brp_4.nsf/e78a48070f128a7b43256 999005bcbb3/8ae23e97b0361654c3257084002ea09b?OpenDocument).

29. North Korea–U.S. statement at the closing plenary session of the fourth round of the six-party talks.

30. "N. Korea, U.S. to Meet Bilaterally During Recess" *Yonhap*, November 11, 2005.

31. "DPRK's Stand on Six-Party Talks Reclarified," KCNA, June 1, 2006 (www.kcna.co.jp).

32. Bill Gertz, "U.S. Accuses North Korea of $100 Bill Counterfeiting," *Washington Times*, October 12, 2005.

33. David Sanger, "U.S. Widens Campaign on North Korea," *New York Times*, October 24, 2005.

34. "Treasury Targets N. Korean Entities for Supporting WMD Proliferation," *US Fed News*, October 21, 2005.

35. Sanger, "U.S. Widens Campaign on North Korea."

36. "N. Korea Tops Agenda of Bush's Asia Trip," *Chosun Ilbo*, November 15, 2005.

37. "Pyongyang Unveils Five-Step Road Map for Nuke Disposal," *Yonhap*, November 14, 2005.

38. "Rice Slams N. Korea's Roadmap to Denuclearization," *Chosun Ilbo*, November 16, 2005.

39. *Xinhuanet*, Beijing, November 11, 2005 (www.xinhuanet.com).

40. Glenn Kessler, "Semantic Dispute Cancels N. Korea, Treasury Meeting," *Washington Post*, December 1, 2005.

Chapter 9

1. CBS News interviewed Kim Gye-gwan in Pyongyang in December 2005. The *60 Minutes* episode was telecast on January 15, 2006.

2. National Security Strategy, section V.C.I., March 2006 (www.whitehouse.gov/nsc/nss/2006/).

3. "Founded in 1993, NEACD is a multilateral 'track two' forum involving foreign ministry officials, defense ministry officials, military officers, and academics from China, Russia, North and South Korea, Japan, and the United States. NEACD keeps vital lines of communication open in Northeast Asia by providing regularly scheduled meetings in an informal setting, allowing participants to candidly discuss issues of regional security and cooperation" (www.wiredforpeace.org [January 17, 2007]).

4. Lee Chi-dong, "Hill Says Contact with N.K. Impossible Unless It Returns to Six-Way Talks," *Yonhap*, April 10, 2006.

5. The reference to Chris Hill completing the metamorphosis into former assistant secretary James A. Kelly is not meant in any pejorative way, but rather to draw attention to the fact that the diplomatic freedom of movement that Hill enjoyed in the beginning of his tenure had been completely withdrawn by the administration and that Hill now operated under the same onerous restrictions that Jim Kelly faced throughout his tenure as head of delegation to the six-party talks. To what degree Hill embraced as his own the views that he conveyed in Tokyo and to what degree the frustration evident in his public sparring with North Korea contributed to what I describe as his metamorphosis is known only to Hill himself.

6. "Hill Snubs N. Korea's Chief Nuclear Negotiator," April 12, 2006 (http://english.chosun.com/w21data/html/news/20060412).

7. National Security Strategy, section V.C.I., March 2006.

8. Letter to the President, dated October 20, 2006, from Senators Harry Reid (D-Nev.), Carl Levin (D-Mich.), and Joseph Biden (D-Del.).

9. I continue to believe that the United States made a strategic error in agreeing to language in the joint statement that included the United States in a discussion about a light-water reactor for North Korea. However, having signed the statement, the United States must find a way of honoring the spirit of the agreement without being seen as reneging on its pledge.

10. Treasury Department, "North Korea: What You Need to Know about Sanctions" (www.treas.gov/offices/enforecment/ofac/programs/nkorea/nkorea.pdf).

11. Henry A. Kissinger, "The Next Steps with Iran; Negotiations Must Go beyond the Nuclear Threat to Broader Issues," *Washington Post*, July 31, 2006, p. A15.

Chapter 10

1. This section on the July 4, 2006, DPRK missile launch and the section following, "Missile Moratorium Primer," were adapted from an article that I wrote for the Korea Economic Institute's July 2006 edition of *Insight*.

2. UN Security Council, Department of Public Information, "Security Council Condemns Democratic People's Republic of Korea's Missile Launches, Unanimously Adopting Resolution 1695 (2006), July 15, 2006."

3. Japanese Ministry of Foreign Affairs, "Japan-DPRK Pyongyang Declaration" (www.mofa.go.jp/region/asia-paci/n_kora/pmv0209/pyongyang.html).

4. "DPRK Foreign Ministry Clarifies Stand on New Measure to Bolster War Deterrent," KCNA, October 3, 2006 (www.kcna.co.jp).

5. UN Security Council, Department of Public Information, "Security Council Condemns Nuclear Test by Democratic People's Republic of Korea, Unanimously Adopting Resolution 1718 (2006)."

6. "U.S. Negotiator Urges North Korea to End Standoff on Financial Curbs," Associated Press, Beijing, December 22, 2006.

Chapter 11

1. It was U.S. policy under the Bush administration to seek serious (bilateral) talks with the DPRK from June 2001, when its North Korea policy review was announced, until the confrontation over highly enriched uranium in October 2002.

2. Don Oberdorfer, *The Two Koreas: A Contemporary History* (New York: Basic Books, 2001), p. 262.

3. *Joint Declaration of the Denuclearization of the Korean Peninsula*, January 20, 1992 (www.ceip.org/files/projects/npp/resources/koreadenuclearization.htm [January 8, 2007]).

4. Japan incorporated the two small islands that it refers to as Takeshima into its territory in January 1905. Korea contends that that was Japan's first step toward its colonization of Korea from 1910 to 1945. Since the end of World War II and Japan's occupation of Korea, Korea has taken political and military control of the islands, which it calls Tokdo.

5. Glenn Kessler, "N. Korea Sets Terms for Return to Nuclear Talks," *Washington Post*, March 9, 2006.

6. George Gedda, "U.S. Rejects Financial Talks With N. Korea," Associated Press, March 10, 2006.

7. Kessler, "N. Korea Sets Terms for Return to Nuclear Talks."

Chapter 12

1. Ralph Hassig and Kongdan Oh, "The Dilemma of Security Cooperation in Northeast Asia," in *The Newly Emerging Asian Order and the Korean Peninsula* (Washington: Korea Economic Institute, 2005), p.158

2. Takahashi Kosuke, "Japan-South Korea Ties on the Rocks," *Asia Times Online*, March 23, 2005.

3. Wi Sung-lac, ICAS presentation, October 11, 2005 (www.icasinc.org).

4. Chung Ok-Nim, "Solving the Security Puzzle in Northeast Asia: A Multilateral Security Regime," Working Paper, Center for Northeast Asian Policy Studies, Brookings, September 1, 2000.

5. Fred Wier, "Russia, China Looking to Form 'NATO of the East'?" *Christian Science Monitor*, October 26, 2005.

6. Ambassador Dorian Prince, in comments delivered at the Third Jeju Peace Forum, Jeju, Korea, June 9–11, 2005. Recorded in *Building a Northeast Asian Community*, vol. 2 (Yonsei University Press, 2006).

7. Results of a Korea Foundation survey presented to potential grant seekers at an August 29, 2006, briefing held at the Korea Economic Institute, Washington. A copy of the survey results is in the author's files.

8. "About ASEAN" (www.ASEANSEC.org).

9. Ron Huisken, "What to Expect at the First East Asia Summit," PacNet 54A, December 12, 2005.

10. Ibid.

11. Edward Cody, "East Asian Summit Marked by Discord: New Group's Role Remains Uncertain," *Washington Post*, December 14, 2005.

12. SACO Interim Report, April 15, 1996 (www.niraikanai.wwma.net/pages/archive/15496.html).

13. Security Consultative Committee, "U.S.-Japan Alliance: Transformation and Realignment for the Future," October 29, 2005 (www.state.gov/documents/organization/55886.pdf).

14. "Government Must Heed Locals on Bases," *Yomiuri Shimbun*, November 22, 2005.

15. Security Consultative Committee, "U.S.-Japan Alliance."

16. Address by President Roh Moo-hyun on the 58th Anniversary of National Liberation, August 15, 2003 (www.korea.net/korea/boardDetailView.asp?board_no=74&code=B0203&lang_no=).

17. Francis Fukuyama, "Re-Envisioning Asia," *Foreign Affairs* (January-February 2005), pp. 75–87.

18. Chris Nelson, "Japan Reaches Out to ROK; US?" *Nelson Report*, December 12, 2005.

19. Ian Bremmer, Choi Sung-Hong, and Yoriko Kawaguchi, "Northeast Asia: Defusing a Dangerous Region," *International Herald Tribune*, December 29, 2005.

20. "What Is NATO?" (www.nato.int).

21. The first three objectives are taken in substantial form from a paper by Ambassador James Goodby entitled "The Six-Party Talks: Opportunity or Obstacle?" written in June 2005 while he was a public policy scholar at the Woodrow Wilson International Center for Scholars in Washington and later presented at the Third Jeju Peace Forum, Jeju, Korea, June 9–11, 2005. Recorded in *Building a Northeast Asian Community*, vol. I (Yonsei University Press, 2006).

22. Since the proposed forum is not meant to be a substitute for the six-party process, excluding North Korea becomes a prudent choice. As seen all too often, when

North Korea is involved as a consensus stakeholder, it withholds its basic agreement to meet unless certain preconditions are met. A recent example of the negative influence Pyongyang can have on an organization was seen at the July 2006 ASEAN Regional Forum meeting, where there was a strong consensus to issue a statement condemning North Korea for its July 4 missile launches. Pyongyang's foreign minister, Pak Nam-sun, threatened to "reconsider" its future attendance at forum meetings if such a strong statement were adopted. Despite the fact that North Korea was not a member, the language was subsequently softened in an effort to maintain Pyongyang's participation in future meetings.

23. "China Urges Transparency of E. Asia Cooperation," *Xinhuanet* (Kuala Lumpur), December 14, 2005 (www.chinaview.cn).

24. Joint Statement of Agreed Principles, Beijing, September 19, 2005 (www.state.gov/r/pa/prs/ps/2005/53490.htm).

25. White House press release, "Joint Declaration on the ROK-U.S. Alliance and Peace on the Korean Peninsula," November 17, 2005 (www.whitehouse.gov/news/releases/2005/11/20051117-6.html).

26. This view was confirmed on March 8, 2006, at an oversight hearing of the Subcommittee on Asia and the Pacific of the House International Relations Committee, "East Asia in Transition: Opportunities and Challenges for the United States," by chairman Jim Leach: "'The six-party process is beginning to appear moribund. It's time for the United States to lead,' he said, rather than 'indebting us to the diplomacy of countries that may have different interests.'" Glenn Kessler, "N. Korea Sets Terms for Return to Nuclear Talks," *Washington Post*, March 9, 2006.

27. Even though the initial intent for an informal meeting of six-party heads of delegation was not realized, subsets of the six parties did meet.

Appendix D

1. R. L. Garwin and F. N. von Hippel, *Arms Control Today*, vol. 36, no. 9. November 2006.

2. Jungmin Kang and Peter Hayes, "Technical Analysis of the DPRK Nuclear Test," Nautilus Institute Policy Forum Online 06-89A: Oct. 20th, 2006 (www.nautilus.org/fora/security/0689HayesKang.html).

3. Thom Shanker and David Sanger, "North Korean Fuel Identified as Plutonium," *The New York Times*, October 17, 2006.

4. Siegfried S. Hecker, Senate Committee on Foreign Relations Hearing, "Visit to the Yongbyon Nuclear Scientific Research Center in North Korea," Jan. 21, 2004.

5. Siegfried S. Hecker, "The Nuclear Crisis in North Korea," *The Bridge*, National Academy of Engineering, 17-23, Summer 2004.

6. During the Jan. 2004 visit, Yongbyon nuclear center officials showed me a thin-walled conical-shaped piece of plutonium that they said was a scrap piece cut off from one of their castings. They told me that the piece weighed 200 grams, had a density between 15 and 16 grams per cubic centimeter, and was alloyed. Alloying plutonium

with a few atomic percent gallium or aluminum is a metallurgical technique used to make it easier to produce sound plutonium castings because in the unalloyed state plutonium is notoriously difficult to manufacture. This technique was used in the United States during the Manhattan Project to manufacture the plutonium components for the Trinity test and the Nagasaki bomb.

7. Containing a 20-kiloton explosion in a horizontal tunnel with sufficient depth and overburden is technically quite feasible. Although there is ample information in the open literature on how to accomplish this, it is not clear how confident the DPRK technical specialists were given the disastrous political consequences of a significant radiation leakage. It is also known that sealing an underground explosion cavity completely is actually easier to do with a 20-kiloton explosion than an explosion of one to four kilotons. However, the DPRK technical specialists may have been mostly concerned with a major breach of the tunnel and, therefore, opted to be conservative.

8. The 5 MWe reactor is an indigenously built graphite-moderated, gas-cooled reactor that was shut down during the Agreed Framework freeze (with only routine maintenance allowed) and restarted in February 2003 (see note 3 for more detail). Its plutonium production capacity is approximately 6 kg (or roughly one weapon's worth) per year.

9. The uranium-aluminum alloy fuel is clad with a magnesium alloy that can degrade at elevated temperature. This reactor experienced considerable fuel cladding problems during the early operating experience before the 1994 shutdown.

10. We refer to three reactor campaigns. The first resulted in the 8,000 spent fuel rods that were stored in the spent fuel pool during the Agreed Framework freeze from 1994 to 2003. The second campaign refers to the fuel rods loaded in 2003 when the reactor was restarted, and according to the director's claims in August 2005, were reprocessed in 2005. The third campaign refers to the fuel rods loaded in June 2005. These fuel rods are still in the reactor as of Nov. 3, 2006.

11. In August 2005, Director Ri told us that parts of the fuel fabrication facility had corroded so badly that they collapsed during the Agreed Framework freeze. However, they were in the process of refurbishing the facility and expected to fabricate new fuel rods in 2006.

12. In August 2005, Director Ri told us that they were close to finishing the reprocessing of all the fuel rods from the second campaign, which was in the reactor from Feb. 2003 through March 2005. He also indicated that they had made some equipment improvements that allowed them to increase the throughput by 30 percent.

13. One of the greatest difficulties is having to work inside a heavily shielded, highly radioactive environment in which normal operations are done remotely with manipulators.

14. These reactors are described in references 3 and 4. In brief, the 50 MWe reactor was claimed to be within a year of completion and the 200 MWe reactor within a few years of completion when the Agreed Framework was adopted in 1994. The plutonium production potential of the 50 MWe reactor is roughly 60 kg of plutonium per year (roughly ten times that of the 5 MWe reactor). The production potential of the 200 MWe reactor is roughly forty times that of the 5 MWe reactor.

15. David Albright, Kevin O'Neill, editors. *"Solving the North Korean Nuclear Puzzle,"* ISIS Reports, The Institute for Science and International Security, Washington, D.C., 2000.

16. A recent report by the Institute for Science and International Security reports somewhat larger ranges of potential plutonium inventories. David Albright and Paul Brennan, "The North Korean Plutonium Stock Mid-2006" (www.isis-online.org/publications/dprk/dprkplutonium.pdf).

Index